REF

PR
1903
.D5

Dillon, Bert.

A Chaucer dictionary

DATE			

A CHAUCER DICTIONARY
Proper Names and Allusions

Excluding Place Names

Bert Dillon

G. K. HALL & CO., 70 LINCOLN STREET, BOSTON, MASS. 1974

Library of Congress Cataloging in Publication Data

Dillon, Bert.
    A Chaucer dictionary.

    Bibliography: p.
    1. Chaucer, Geoffrey, d. 1400--Dictionaries.
I. Title.
PR1903.D5   821'.1   74-2442
ISBN 0-8161-1112-X

REF
PR
1903
.D5
cp.1

Contents

Introduction

This book is "A" *Chaucer Dictionary*, not "The" *Chaucer Dictionary*. We like to talk about the universality of great literature, about its ability to touch man through the ages. But any complex body of literature based on concepts unfamiliar to the modern reader and couched in language alien to him requires interpretation before it can be understood well enough to have impact. For Chaucer's writings it seems that the most pressing need is for a guide to names, allusions, and borrowings which a contemporary reader would recognize immediately while a modern reader must consider them a puzzle. The definitive Chaucer dictionary would contain more than that, of course, but its core would be this kind of a key to the poet's use of proper nouns and sources, acknowledged by him or implicit in his writing. However, although the need for definitive treatment of that area is clear and even urgent, the best that can be done now is to establish a foundation for work that must continue to evolve. I wish more could be done now, but I think not. The problem is something like the chicken and egg dilemma: a dictionary presents in convenient form scholarship in a well-defined area; but scholarship tends towards diffusion until it is focused on an area by such a work as a dictionary. Progress towards a completely satisfactory dictionary, then, must proceed by stages in which available information is consolidated so that it can be outstripped by independent investigators troubled by its weaknesses. This book is such a stage. Some day in the future, when Chaucer scholarship has produced the essential information and defended it all convincingly, there will be time for "The" Chaucer dictionary. Now, however, one can only create a model for that eventual work in the hope that it will be a useful tool for today while it serves to stimulate scholarship that will make its revision necessary tomorrow. This, therefore, is A *Chaucer Dictionary;* and so far as I know it is the first.

Of course there have been earlier attempts at some of what I have done: partial lists of proper nouns in the Chaucer canon, occasionally locating their appearances in the writings, sometimes with explanations of their functions and derivations. Four of the most significant of those early attempts come to mind immediately because they are valuable in other connections and provide a starting point in this one. Seminal are Hiram Corson's *Index of Proper Names and Subjects to Chaucer's Canterbury Tales,* and those parts of Skeat's edition entitled "Index of Proper Names" and "Index of Authors Quoted or Referred To."[1] Somewhat less stimulating in this area is similar apparatus in Robinson's edition: "Proper Names" rarely locates the names in the writings, and "Explanatory Notes" is inadequately cross-referenced.[2] For present purposes, The Tatlock-Kennedy *Concordance* is minimally functional: like any concordance, it is useful for isolating

---

[1] Corson, *Index of Proper Names and Subjects to Chaucer's Canterbury Tales* (London and Oxford, 1911)—Chaucer Society Publications, 1st Series, No. 72. W. W. Skeat, ed., *The Complete Works of Geoffrey Chaucer,* 2nd ed. (Oxford, 1894–1900), VI, 359–80, 381–89.
[2] F. N. Robinson, ed., *The Works of Geoffrey Chaucer,* 2nd ed. (Boston, 1957), pp. 993–1002, 649–882.

specific locations of proper nouns that explicity appear in the writings; but, like any concordance, it is of little help in tracking implicit references and allusions; and, still like any concordance, it is absolutely useless when one seeks an explanation of anything.[3]

None of what I have said so far should be taken as disparagement of my predecessors, for I honor them at least implicity on every page that follows. What I have done is to describe briefly an historical situation I have had to confront in order that my successors might more easily cope with what I have done. I have used these great books; they might not have to use them. If my successors do use those books, they should recognize the need to lean on them only gently. My predecessors have not troubled to include allusions and borrowings in these works; they have used as references various editions of Chaucer's writings; and—of course—they have been unable to embrace the findings of subsequent scholarship. I have had the temporary advantage of time, which has allowed me to benefit from work they could not have known. More to the point, I have tried to do directly something that was only a side issue for them. And I have had the advantage of being able to use their work.

What I have tried to do is to provide scholars with the essential reference work for proper names—exclusive of place names, for reasons I will give shortly—that they need in order to guide their studies more clearly; and I also have tried to give all but the most casual reader of Chaucer a handy companion through encounters that now should make his reading both more profitable and more enjoyable. This book systematizes and records names and sources in a way that indicates Chaucer's intellectual and poetic concerns: borrowing; developing or recurring interest in certain authors, books, characters, and figures; conflation of sources; and treatment of historical and mythological names. Among its uses, therefore, is not only the obvious service as a quick guide through specific problems, but also the more leisurely possibility for access to Chaucer's literary melieu.

All that is potential unless the user of this dictionary is aware of its scope and method. Again, it presents proper nouns, allusions, and borrowings in Chaucer's writings. It does not include place names because Magoun recently has done so in such complete fashion that to treat them again here and now would be supererogatory.[4] Among non-Chaucerian reference works I have drawn largely from Harvey's *Oxford Companion to Classical Literature*. Its strength reveals the weakness of scholarship in medieval literature: some entries in this present dictionary emphasize classical rather than medieval referents simply because the earlier period is well-defined, while the later is imperfectly understood and its contexts are hotly disputed.

But I have not automatically accepted and transmitted any information. Although the occasion has made it improper for me to argue for acceptance or rejection of any point, I have been careful in each entry to see—to the limits of my own knowledge and mental equipment—that nothing arbitrary has been passed along and, of course, that nothing pertinent has been omitted. These are evanescent goals, certainly, but even though one must fail to attain them, work that gives up the striving must be worthless. In most cases it has been possible to check traditional ascriptions (preserved primarily in Skeat and Robinson) against primary scholarship recorded in dissertations as well as in more available publications. I have also consulted editions and primary works in most areas, and found it necessary to reject some ascriptions traditional in Chaucer studies. All such testing was

---

[3] John S. P. Tatlock and Arthur G. Kennedy, *A Concordance to the Complete Works of Geoffrey Chaucer* (Washington, D. C. 1927; reprinted, Gloucester, Mass., 1963).
[4] F. P. Magoun, Jr., *A Chaucer Gazetteer* (Chicago, 1961).

necessary in order to avoid taking coincidental verbal similarities between Chaucer and other writers as evidence of a source relationship or tradition. Certain enumerations have been omitted when Chaucer followed a source seriatim or verbatim in one work only.[5] There are other omissions too. When it is possible for a user who wishes to pursue a point in detail to discover all relevant work on the point in a particular piece of scholaship, I have simply cited that piece of scholarship and not attempted to give a complete checklist again here. (When there is no reference to scholarship in a particular entry, the reader should understand that everything known about the point can be found in the works I have discussed in this introduction—and, therefore, that there is a need for intensive studies on the point.)

It has been difficult to be steadfastly consistent in matters of style and content; however, as Samuel Johnson remarks in the preface to his *Dictionary,* "uniformity must be preserved in systematical works, though sometimes at the expense of propriety." For that reason I have had to normalize the spelling and forms of names, but I have recorded the most important variants of them parenthetically. It seemed wise, too, to exclude certain classes of proper nouns arbitrarily: nationalities, languages, and cultures are excluded because they are given excellent treatment by Magoun; "Heaven," "Hell," and "Paradise" because references are ambiguous; seasons because they represent changes in climate rather than chronology. I may be wrong on that last point because astrology and other occult sciences in Chaucer's day are imperfectly understood.

I have tried to use simple, easily-remembered conventions in the plan of this dictionary, and to keep them minimal. First, when it is clear that Chaucer was using a classical divinity in the sense of a diety, I have given a mythological explanation of that god; but when it is equally clear that he had in mind the planet associated with that divinity, my explanation is astrological. Second, I have cross-referenced whenever possible and appropriate such general allusions as "olde bokes," "myn auctour," "clerkes," and "the philosophre." Third, I have converted to general divisions source works found in particular editions so that one need not have the *Patrologia Latina,* for example, to consult the works of Alanus de Insulis. Fourth, when there is a possibility that reference to a prolific scholar in a descriptive note might be insufficent as a clue to the user of this dictionary who wants to pursue the point in the literature, I have given the reference a numeral which locates the work in the bibliography that concludes this book. Finally, I have adopted certain symbols and certain abbreviations. These are explained immediately preceding the dictionary proper.

Bert Dillon

The Center for Cultural Development
University of South Carolina

---

[5] For example, the following which are collected in W. F. Bryan and Germaine Dempster, eds., *Sources and Analogues of Chaucer's "Canterbury Tales"* (1941; reprinted, New York, 1958):
1) BN ms fr. 1165 and Petrarch and ClT (viz. *Decamerone* 10.10 as the source for Petrarch's *De Obedientia* and *Le Ménagier de Paris* [see Severs, S&A, 296ff. and *PMLA,* 47 (1932), 431–52]); 2) BN ms fr. 578 and Mel (see Severs, S&A, 560ff.); 3) Frere Lorens *Somme* and ParsT (see Dempster, S&A, 723ff.); 4) Deguileville and ABC (see *Skeat,* 1.58–61, 261–71).

Abbreviations of Chaucer's Works

[according to the order of the major works established by Tatlock, and the Pratt order for the <u>Canterbury</u> <u>Tales</u>]

Rom	Romaunt of the Rose	PardT	Pardoner's Tale
BD	Book of the Duchess	SecNT	Second Nun's Tale
HF	House of Fame	CYT	Canon's Yeoman's Tale
A&A	Anelida and Arcíte[1]	MancT	Manciple's Tale
PF	Parliament of Foules	ParsT	Parson's Tale
Bo	Boethius (Boece)	Ret	Retraction[4]
T&C	Troilus and Criseyde[2]	ABC	An ABC[4]
LGW	Legend of Good Women	Pity	Complaint unto Pity
GP	General Prologue[3]	Lady	Complaint to his Lady
KnT	Knight's Tale	Mars	Complaint of Mars
MillT	Miller's Tale	Rose	To Rosemunde[4]
RvT	Reeve's Tale	WomNob	Womanly Noblesse
CkT	Cook's Tale	Adam	Adam Scriveyn
MLT	Man of Law's Tale	FormAge	Former Age
ShipT	Shipman's Tale	Fort	Fortune
PrT	Prioress's Tale	Truth	Truth[4]
Thop	Tale of Sir Thopas	Gent	Gentilesse
Mel	Tale of Melibee	Sted	Lak of Stedfastness
MkT	Monk's Tale	Ven	Complaint of Venus
NPT	Nun's Priest's Tale	Scog	Lenvoy a Scogan
WBT	Wife of Bath's Tale	Buk	Lenvoy a Bukton
FrT	Friar's Tale	Purse	Complaint to his Purse
SumT	Summoner's Tale	WomUnc	Woman Unconstant
ClT	Clerk's Tale	ComA	Complaynt d'Amours
MerchT	Merchant's Tale	MercB	Merciles Beaute
SqT	Squire's Tale	BalCompl	Balade of Complaint

ABBREVIATIONS OF CHAUCER'S WORKS

FranklT	Franklin's Tale	Prov	Proverbs
PhysT	Physician's Tale	Astr	Astrolabe[4]

[1]Robin Anel
[2]Robin Tr
[3]Robin Gen Prol
[4]Not listed in Robin

Abbreviations of Works Frequently Cited

[complete citations will be found in the Bibliography]

Adv. Jov.	Epistola adversus Jovinianum, St. Jerome
Aen.	Aeneidos, Virgil
ALMA	Arthurian Literature in the Middle Ages, ed. R. S. Loomis
Amores	Amores, Ovid
Argo.	Argonauticon, Valerius Flaccus
Ars Amat.	Ars Amatoria, Ovid
C&C	Chaucer and Chaucerians, ed. D. S. Brewer
CCS	Companion to Chaucer Studies, ed. Beryl Rowland
CMA	Chaucer's Mind and Art, ed. A. C. Cawley
De Casibus	De Casibus Virorum Illustrium, Boccaccio
De Civ. Dei	De Civitate Dei contra Paganos, St. Augustine
De Clar. Mulier.	De Claris Mulieribus, Boccaccio
De Gen. Deor.	De Genealogiis Deorum, Boccaccio
De Nat. Deor.	De Natura Deorum, Cicero
EB	Encyclopaedia Britannica
Ecl.	Eclogae, Virgil
Ecl. Theod.	Ecloga, Theodulus
EFA	English Friars and Antiquity, Beryl Smalley
Etym.	Etymologiarum sive Originum, Isidore of Seville
Ex Ponto	Epistolae ex Ponto, Ovid
Fasti	Fasti, Ovid
Filo.	Filostrato, Boccaccio
Georg.	Georgicon, Virgil
Gesta Rom.	Gesta Romanorum
Hamm	Eleanor P. Hammond, Chaucer, A Bibliographical Manual

Abbreviations of Works Frequently Cited

Hero.	Heroides, Ovid
Hist. Brit.	Historia Regum Britanniae, Geoffrey of Monmouth
Ibis	Ibis, Ovid
Inf.	Inferno, Divina Commedia, Dante
Leg. Aurea	Legenda Aurea, Jacobus Januensis (Jacobus de Voragine)
Louns	T. R. Lounsbury, Studies in Chaucer
Meta.	Metamorphoseon, Ovid
MGH	Monumenta Germaniae Historica
Miroir	Miroir de Mariage, Deschamps
Myth. I, II, III	Scriptores Rerum Mythicarum Latini Tres. ed. G. H. Bode
Parad.	Paradiso, Divina Commedia, Dante
PG	Patrologia Graeca, Migne
Phars.	Pharsalia, Lucan
PL	Patrologia Latina, Migne
Policraticus	Policratici sive De Nugis Curialium et Vestigiis Philosophorum, John of Salisbury
Purg.	Purgatorio, Divina Commedia, Dante
Rem. Am.	Remedia Amoris, Ovid
RR	Roman de la Rose, Jean de Meun and Guillaume de Lorris
Robin	F. N. Robinson, The Works of Geoffrey Chaucer, 2 edn.
Roman de Troie	Roman de Troie, Benoît de Ste. Maur
S&A	Sources and Analogues of Chaucer's Canterbury Tales, ed. W. F. Bryan and Germaine Dempster
SATF	Société des Anciens Textes Francais
Servius in Aen.	Maurus Honoratus Servius, Commentarius in Vergilii Aeneidos
Servius in Ecl.	Maurus Honoratus Servius, Commentarius in Vergilii Bucolica
Shannon	Edgar F. Shannon, Chaucer and the Roman Poets
Skeat	W. W. Skeat, ed., The Works of Geoffrey Chaucer, 2 ed.
Spec. Doct.	Speculum Doctrinale, Speculum Majus, Vincent of Beauvais

Spec. Hist.	Speculum Historiale, Speculum Majus, Vincent of Beauvais
Spec. Nat.	Speculum Naturale, Speculum Majus, Vincent of Beauvais
Tes.	Teseida, Boccaccio
Theb.	Thebaidos, Statius
Tusc.	Disputationes Tusculanae, Cicero
Valerii	Epistola Valerii ad Rufinum de Non Ducenda Uxore, De Nugis Curialium, Walter Map
Vulg.	Biblia Sacra juxta Vulgatam Clementinam

Symbols

( )   in CT: parenthetical line numbers indicate the traditional numbering of Group B^2 indicated in <u>Robin</u> by *

( )   in LGW: parenthetical line numbers indicate Text G

[ ]   square brackets indicate an indirect reference

< >   pointed brackets indicate unacknowledged references; i.e. ascriptions

+   indicates possible alternate source(s)

?   indicates doubtful ascription

_____   underscored line numbers indicate that the reference has not been traced

*   indicates that Chaucer's title is Englished

p   prologue

e   epilogue

i   introduction

Form of Entry

Entries are arranged alphabetically and information within entries is represented in the following sequence:

First, the name is listed in a normalized, modern spelling. Second, the most important variants in spelling are listed parenthetically. Third, the name is briefly identified with references to primary or secondary works from which Chaucer may have taken the name or details about the entry. The identification includes references to scholars whose works may be consulted for further suggestions about the importance of the name or work for Chaucer. Fourth, and most importantly, the occurrences of the name or allusions to the works given are listed according to the accepted chronological order for the major works (based on Tatlock) and the Pratt order for the <u>Canterbury Tales</u>.

The scheme may be represented:

NAME(variants), identification; references to other works or entries; references to scholars who discuss the entry.
List of occurrences.

The object in all of the listings is to determine, as nearly as possible, the associations in the poet's mind and his interest in his sources. Thus, for example, the Bible is arranged according to the order in the Vulgate in an attempt to see if there are any patterns in Chaucer's association of materials from the various adjacent books of the Bible.

A Chaucer Dictionary

A

ABIGAIL (Abigayl), the diplomatic wife of NABAL, who saved her rash
husband and later became the wife of DAVID; I Samuel 25.1-42.
Mel 1100(2290)
MerchT 1369

ABRAHAM, the patriarch, "father of a multitude," husband of SARAH
and father of ISAAC; Genesis 11.27ff., Adv. Jov. 1.5.
WBT p55

ABSALOM (Absolon),
(1) the handsome but rebellious son of DAVID; II Samuel 13-19.8.
LGW 249(203), 539
ParsT 639
(2) the love-sick admirer of Alysoun
MillT 3313, 3339, 3348, 3353, 3366, 3371, 3387,
3389, 3394, 3398, 3657, 3671, 3688, 3711,
3714, 3719, 3723, 3730, 3733, 3741, 3744,
3749, 3764, 3766, 3767, 3772, 3783, 3793,
3804, 3852
RvT p3856

ABSTINENCE, one of the hypocrites sent by the god of Love to rescue
Fair Welcome.
Rom 5848, 6056, 6341, 7323, 7354, 7364, 7398,
7428, 7435, 7481, 7503, 7671

ACADEMICIS (Achademycis), the Academics, followers of PLATO.
Bo 1.p1.67

ACHATES (Achate), the armor-bearer and trusted companion of AENEAS;
Aen. 1.120, 174.
HF 226
LGW 964, 976, 1023, 1129, 1136

ACHELOUS (Acheloys, Acheleous), the river-god defeated by HERCULES
for the hand of DEIANIRA; Meta. 9.1-97.
Bo 4.m7.43, 45
MkT 2106(3296)

ACHILLES (Achille), the chief hero of the Greeks in the Trojan war,
noted for his strength and petulance and cruelty in love and
war; HF 398 refers specifically to his treatment of BRISEIS and
the reference in SqT is to the spear which wounded TELEPHUS and
with which he was healed; Shannon 321. Achilles' death for the
love of POLYXENA (Achilles and ARCHILOCHUS were ambushed in the
temple of Apollo where Achilles met Polyxena to be married) is
told in DARES 34, JOSEPH OF EXETER 6.402ff., Roman de Troie
21838ff., and GUIDO 13ᵛ.
BD 329, 1066
HF 398, 1463
PF 290
T&C 2.416

1

T&C 3.374
T&C 5.1559, 1806
MLT 198
NPT 3148(4338)
SqT 239

ACHITOPHEL (Achitofel), the treacherous counselor of DAVID who
    deserted to ABSALOM; II Samuel 15.31ff.
        BD 1118
        ParsT 639

ACTAEON (Attheon), changed into a stag by DIANA (because he had
    seen her bathing) and torn to pieces by his own hounds; Meta
    3.138-252.
        KnT 2065, 2303

ADAM, the first man, whose sin resulted in the loss of Paradise and
    the consequent moral frailty of his descendants; Genesis 2-5.6.
        HF 970
        LGW 286(189)
        MkT 2007(3197), 2012(3202)
        NPT 3258(4448)
        WBT p696
        MerchT 1325
        PardT 505, 508
        ParsT 323, 325+EVE, 331, 332, 333, 516+EVE, 682,
            819+EVE, 926, 928
        ABC 182

ADAM, Scrivener, an unidentified scribe admonished by Chaucer.
        Adam 1

ADMETUS (Amete), king of Pherae, whose wife ALCESTIS was restored
    to him by HERCULES after she had consented to die for her
    husband; not in Filo.
        T&C 1.664

ADONIS (Adoon, Adon), incestuous son of Cinyras and Myrrha, beloved
    of VENUS, killed by a boar (sent by DIANA or MARS). Because he
    was claimed by both Venus and PERSEPHONE Jupiter decided that
    he should spend part of the year with each; Meta. 10.503ff.
        T&C 3.721
        KnT 2224

ADRASTUS, legendary king of Argos, leader of the seven against
    Thebes, father-in-law of POLYNICES and TYDEUS. When the
    expedition failed Adrastus escaped on his horse ARION; Aen.
    6.480, Ex Ponto 1.3.79, Fasti 6.433, Theb. 4.74, etc.
        A&A 61

ADRIANE see ARIADNE.

ADVENTURE (Aventure), wild speculation, the "mother of tidings."
    HF 1982

[AEACUS, the father of Telamon and Peleus, gave THESEUS a friendly
    welcome after his flight from Crete; Meta. 7.472-89, "CEFFI."
    Cf. Meech.
    LGW 2156]

AEETES (Oetes), king of Colchis, brother of CIRCE and father of
    MEDEA; Meta. 7, Hero. 6 and 12, GUIDO Book I, Argo., Theb. 5.
    See Shannon 208ff.
    LGW 1438, 1593

AEGEUS (Egeus), son of Pandion and father of THESEUS. Aegeus
    plunged into the sea after he saw the black sail (mistakenly
    hoisted) which was supposed to herald his son's death in Crete.
    The sentenious Aegeus of KnT is Chaucer's creation.
    LGW 1944, [2178]
    KnT 2838, 2905

ST. AEGIDIUS (Seint Gile, seynt Gyle), fl. sixth or seventh cent.,
    an Athenian who, at the death of his parents, distributed his
    possessions and went to Arles. He moved to a nearby desert
    where he was discovered by Flavius, king of the Goths, who
    built a monastery and made Giles the first abbot. St. Aegidius
    is the patron of lepers, beggars, and cripples.
    HF 1183
    CYT 1185

AEGYPTUS (Egiste), brother of DANAUS, allowed his 50 daughters to
    marry the sons of Danaus after they promised to murder their
    husbands on the wedding night; all did except HYPERMNESTRA who
    allowed LYNCEUS to live. See Hero. 14, De Gen. Deor. 11.25,
    and "CEFFI."
    LGW 2570, 2600, 2618, 2623

AENEAS (Eneas, Enee), son of ANCHISES, one of the heroes of the
    Trojan war, founder of Rome, and hero of VIRGIL's Aen.; cf.
    Hero. 7 and Roman d'Eneas.
    BD 733
    HF 165, 175, 217, 231, 240, 253, 286, 293, 320,
        356, 427, 434, 440, 452, 461, 1485
    T&C 2.1474
    LGW 927, 940, 976, 983, 1015, 1023, 1027, 1047,
        1057, 1062, 1097, 1103, 1108, 1124, 1128,
        1137, 1144, 1153, 1158, 1206, 1226, 1232
        1243, 1252, 1285
    MLT 164

AENEID (Eneidos, Eneydos), see VIRGIL.

AEOLUS (Eolus), god of the wind, depicted in Aen. 1.50-9; Meta.
    1.262-4, 14.223-6. Chaucer has, quite naturally, followed the
    tradition of the conflated Aeolus who enjoyed a medieval
    reputation as a trumpeter; see Shannon 92-3. Louns 2.382
    attributes the association of Aeolus and his two trumpets to
    ALBRICUS.
        HF 203, 1571, 1586, 1602, 1623, 1636, 1671,
            1719, 1764, 1789, 1800, 1861, 2120

AESCULAPIUS (Esculapius), Asclepius, son of APOLLO and god of
    medicine. His mother was Coronis who was killed by Apollo
    when he was told by the crow of her infidelity. Asclepius
    learned medicine from CHIRON and restored HIPPOLYTUS to life,
    for which he was killed by Jupiter. Apollo, in revenge, killed
    the Cyclopes who made the thunderbolt. In expiation Apollo
    served ADMETUS for a year.
        GP 429

AESON (Eson), brother of Pelias and father of JASON.
    LGW 1398, 1402

AESOP (Isope), the Greek fabulist who fl. in the middle of the
    sixth cent. B.C.
        Mel 1184(2374)

AFFRICAN see SCIPIO AFRICANUS MAJOR.

AGAMEMNON (Agamenon), son of Atreus, brother of MENELAUS, husband
    of CLYTEMNESTRA, king of Mycenae and leader of the Greek host
    in the Trojan war.
        Bo 4.m7.1, 6, 8, 14
        T&C 3.382

AGATHON (Agaton), a tragic poet and friend of PLATO. The
    Symposium (279-80b where the story of ALCESTIS is told) is a
    celebration of Agathon's victory in 416 B.C. Chaucer's direct
    source is unknown; see Skeat 3.xxxiii-iv.
        LGW 526(514)

OF AGE see CICERO, De Senectute.

AGENOR, king of Tyre, mentioned in connection with his daughter
    EUROPA.
        LGW 114

AGLAUROS (Aglawros), daughter of Cecrops, sister of HERSE and
    Pandrosos, who offended Pallas by betraying the secret of
    Erichthonius and who was turned to stone because she defied
    Mercury who gave her money to give him access to Herse: she
    was made envious by Pallas and therefore thwarted Mercury;
    Meta. 2.708-832.
        T&C 3.730

4

AHASUERUS (Assuerus, Assuere, Assuer), the king of the Persians
who, for love of Esther, favored the Jews against the treachery
of HAMAN. ESTHER was advised by her uncle MORDECAI; Esther
passim.
    Mel 1101(2291)
    MerchT 1374, 1745

ALANUS DE INSULIS (Aleyn), Alain de Lille, c. 1128-c. 1202, shared
the title Doctor universalis with Albertus Magnus. Alain
probably became a Cistercian about 1178 and served as a
professor at the University of Paris between 1179 and 1195,
when he retired to Citeaux. The Anticlaudianus dates c. 1183.
See Hamm 84, Louns 2.344-52, Skeat 1.74, Donovan.
    PF 316
  De planctu naturae

PF 316		
<ml.57-8	Rom 4768	(PL 210.432)
pl.1-43	PF 298	(435)
	342	(435-6)
	343	(436)
	T&C 3.1415	( )
	LGW 137	( )
p3	PF 380-1	(443)
m4	Rom 63	(447)
p4	HF 730	(453)
	PF 379	( )
	PhysT 20	( )
m5	Rom 4685ff.	(455-6)
p8	PF 379	(476)
p9	"	(479)
	Rom 4768	(482)>
<Anticlaudianus		
1.1	Frankl T 829-34	(PL 210.487-8)
	Scog 38-9	( )
1.3.20-2	PF 204-7	(490)
3.3	Frankl T p721-5	(516)
4.5.4	HF 930ff.	(525)
4.6	965-8	(526)
5.7	930	(538)
5.9.1		( )
7-8	LGW 127	(557-8)
		+ MACHAUT + RR
8.9	Frankl T 1613-5	(571)>
<Parabolae		
1.31	PhysT 107	(PL 210.581)
.45-6	T&C 1.948-50	(582)
.61-2	RvT 3881-2	( )
.65	T&C 1.946-7	( )
.83	2.1335	(583)
.109	1.951	( )
.110	1.952	( )

    <Parabolae (cont.)

3.1–2	CYT 962ff.	(	585)
5.61	T&C 2.36–7	(	591)
6.18–9	3.1219–20	(	592)>

ALAN (Aleyn, Alayn), one of the Cambridge clerks who brought about
the miller's ruin.
      RvT 4013, 4016, 4018, 4022, 4024, 4031, 4040,
           4073, 4076, 4084, 4089, 4091, 4108, 4160,
           4168, 4188, 4192, 4198, 4234, 4249, 4273,
           4305, 4316

<ALBERTANUS BRIXIENSIS, Albertano of Brescia, an Italian judge who
died c. 1270 whose Liber Consolationis et Consilii has been
taken as the source for Mel. Albertano wrote a Latin morality
for each of his sons as he came of age: the Liber de Amore for
Vincenzio in 1238, the De Arte for Stephano in 1245, and the
Liber Consolationis for Giovanni in 1246; see Severs in S&A
560–1, Hamm 84–5, Louns 2.384, Skeat 3.426–7, 5.355, 358, 442–3.
For proof that Chaucer used the French translation of RENAUD DE
LOUENS, done in 1336, see S&A 560ff.
Liber de Amore Dei, c. 1238(Cuneo, 1507)

39v	MerchT 1323–5, 1384–8	
40r	1311, 1381–2, 1405–17	
40v	1537–42	
60v	T&C 1.964	

De Arte Loquendi et Tacendi, c. 1245(ed. Sundby, 1869)

xcvi	T&C 3.292–4	
	MancT 332–3	+RR
xcviii	325–8, 355–8	
cvi	357	
cviii	Mel 1330(2520)	
cx	MancT 329	+RR
cxv	335–8	

Liber Consolationis et Consilii, c. 1246(ed. Sundby, 1873)

c. 4(p. 14)	Mel 1071(2261)	
c. 5(pp. 16–20)	1076(2266)–79(69)	
( )	MerchT 2277–90	
(p. 17)	1356–80	
(p. 18)	1376>	

DON ALBON, the name which the Host applies to the MONK.

<ALBRICUS PHILOSOPHUS, also known as Albericus Londinensis and
Mythographus Tertius (Mai and Bode), the author of a 13th cent.
compilation of allegorized mythography in the tradition of
Fulgentius; it is more correctly the Liber Ymaginum Deorum.
Albricus is improperly identified with Alexander Neckam because
Neckam used an anonymous redaction of the Liber which then got
transferred to his name. This mistake was transmitted by Robert
Holkot in his Moralia super Ovidii Metamorphoses. See Seznec
170–2; cf. Hamm 85, Louns 2.381–2, Skeat 5.78, 82.

De Deorum Imaginibus in Mythographi Latini (ed. Munckerus,
Amsterdam, 1581)
   3(pp. 302-3) KnT 2041
   5(pp. 304-6)   1955
   12(pp. 315-6)LGW 530-1(518-9)
   13(pp. 316-7)HF 1571>

ALBYN see DECIUS ALBINUS.

ALCESTIS (Alceste), the wife of ADMETUS who, after the refusal of
his father and mother, consented to die for her husband.
Shortly thereafter, HERCULES, on the way to one of his labors,
visited Admetus' castle; Admetus, in obedience to the laws of
hospitality, concealed Alcestis' death and welcomed the hero.
Hercules discovered the truth, intercepted Thanatos, and
restored Alcestis to her husband. Alcestis is the simple,
unromantic epitome of wifely devotion.
   T&C 5.1527, 1778
   LGW (179), (209), (216), (223), (317), 432, (422),
     [456(446)], 511(499), 518(506), (530), (532)
   MLT 175
   FranklT 1442

ALCHABITIUS (Alcabucius), probably Abd-al-Aziz, a 10th century
astrologer. His Introductorium ad scientiam judicialem
astronomiae [i.e. the 13th cent. translation by Johannes
Hispalensis] is quoted in VINCENT OF BEAUVAIS' Speculum
Naturale 15.42. See Skeat 1.499-500.
   Astr 1.8.13
   [Introductorium
     Differentia 1   Astr 1.8.13]
     <Differentia 1   Mars 119>

ALCIBIADES (Alcebiades, Alcipyades), died 404 B.C., a handsome and
talented but arrogant and unscrupulous Athenian general. He
was a friend of Socrates, and figures in Plato's Alcibiades and
Symposium. BD and Bo refer to his beauty; FranklT to his love
for TIMANDRA.
   BD 1057
   Bo 3.p8.44
   FranklT 1439

ALCYONE, a daughter of Aeolus and wife of CEYX, son of the morning
star. She was changed into the halcyon to be reunited with
Ceyx after he drowned; Meta. 11.410ff.
   BD 65, 145, 196, [201], 220, 264, 1327
   MLT 157

ALCMENE (Alcmena), the daughter of Electryon and wife of AMPHITRYON.
Her husband on returning triumphantly from avenging Alcmene's
brothers on the Teleboans, was preceded by Jupiter who lay with
her one night which was three because Mercury, at Jupiter's

command, had ordered Helius to quench the solar fires, have the
Hours unyoke his team, and spend the following day at home.
Mercury also ordered the Moon to go slowly and Sleep to make
mankind so drowsy that no one would notice what was happening.
The result of the union was HERCULES. Theb. 6.288-9, 12.300ff.;
Roman de Thebes (SATF 2.88); De Gen. Deor. 13.1; Amores 1.13;
Tes. 4.14. The allusion, together with the aubade, is not in
the Filostrato.
    T&C 3.1428

ALDIRAN (Aldrian), a disputed astronomical reference; Robin 719.
    SqT 265

ALECTO (Alete) see FURIES.

ALEXANDER (Alisaunder, Alisander), Alexander the Great, Alexander
    III of Macedon (356-323), son of Philip II and Olympias; during
    the Middle Ages he was one of the Nine Worthies. For his
    reputation see Cary; cf. Bennett.
        Rom 1152
        BD 1060
        HF 914, 1413
        MkT 2631(3821), 2658(3848)
        MancT 226

<ALEXANDER NECKAM, 1157-1217, author of De Naturis Rerum (probably
    written c. 1180) which was one of the most important medieval
    compendia of "scientific" information; Manitius 3.784-94.
    De Naturis Rerum (Rolls Series No. 34)
        c.   T&C 1.1024   (p. 54)
       .173   " 3.931-8   (p. 295)>

ALGARSIF (Algarsyf), one of Cambuskin's sons. The name is
    unexplained.
    SqT 30, 663

ALGUS (Argus), Muhammad ibn-Mūsa al Khwārizmi, 780-c.850, the
    principal figure in the early history of Arabic mathematics,
    he influenced mathematical thought throughout the Middle Ages.
    His works are responsible for the introduction of Arabic
    numerals, called algorisms after him; his work on arithmetic
    was translated into Latin in the 12th century as De Numero
    Indorum, later entitled Liber Algorismi; Hitti 379-80. The
    form Argus is probably from RR 12994, 13731; Skeat 1.475.
        BD 435
    [augrims
        MillT 3210
        Astr 1.7.6;8.6]

ALISON (Alisoun, Alice), a common female name,
    (1) the carpenter's wife

MillT 3366, 3401, 3523, 3577, 3617, 3639, 3649,
       3653, 3678, 3698, 3790, 3824, 3832
(2) the WIFE OF BATH
    WBT p320, 804
(3) the gossip of the Wife of Bath
    WBT p530, 548

ALKABUCIUS see ALCHABITIUS.

ALKARON see KORAN.

ALLA, Aella, historically the first recorded king of Deira (d. 588);
    Chaucer uses the name but forsakes much of the pseudo-history
    of TRIVET's Chronique.
       MLT 578, 604, 610, 659, 688, 691, 725, 876, [883],
           893, 897, 984, 988, 996, 1003, 1006, 1014,
           1016, 1022, 1032, 1045, 1046, 1051, 1073,
           1088, 1097, 1100, 1128, 1141, 1144

ALMACHIUS (Almache), the Roman prefect responsible for the death
    of St. Cecilia.
       SecNT 362, 405, 410, 421, 431, 435, 458, 468, 487,
           524

ALMAGEST see PTOLEMY.

ALNATH, alpha-Arietis in the head of Aries, used to determine the
    true equinoctal point; Skeat 5.394-5.
       FranklT 1281

ALOCEN, Alhazen, Abū 'Alī al-Hasan ibn al-Hasan ibn al-Haytham,
    c. 965-1039, one of the principal Moslem physicists. His chief
    work, on optics, is lost but the translation made in the time
    of Gerard of Cremona survives. Almost all medieval writers on
    optics base their works on the Opticae Thesaurus, in which the
    theory of Euclid and Ptolemy (that the eye sends out visual
    rays to the object of vision) is opposed; Hitti 628.
       SqT 232

ST. AMBROSE, Aurelius Ambrosius, 340?-397, was educated in Rome and
    became prefect of Liguria in Milan. In 374 he became bishop
    of Milan and took up the controversy against the Arians in
    which he achieved complete victory in the synod in Aquileia
    in 381. St. Ambrose, who was a living example of his realiza-
    tion of the dignity of the priesthood and the episcopacy,
    inculcated the necessity for faith in the Christian life and
    the belief in divine grace for human sin. The reference in
    SecNT, as Robin notes, is to the Ambrosian liturgy, i.e. the
    Preface to the mass for St. Cecilia's Day; for PhysT see Young.
       SecNT 271
       ParsT 84
    [Sermo 25.1   ParsT 84   (PL 17.655)]

<Libri Tres de Virginibus (PL 16.187-232)
```
2.7         PhysT 43
 .9               118ff.
 .10              117ff.
 .14              118ff.
3.5               58-9
 .9               48
 .25              61ff.
 .31              72ff.>
```

AMETE see ADMETUS.

AMPHIARAUS (Amphiorax), an Argive hero and seer, who took part in
   the Caledonian boar hunt with MELEAGER and the expedition of
   the Argonauts. His wife, ERIPHYLE, bribed by POLYNICES with
   the necklace of Harmonia (the brooch of Thebes in Mars 245),
   persuaded him to take part in the expedition of the Seven
   against Thebes although he knew that all would perish except
   Adrastus. Amphiaraus was swallowed in the earth as he re-
   treated; Theb. 7. The reference in WBT is from Jerome, Adv.
   Jov. 1.48.
      A&A 57
      T&C 2.105
          5.1500
      WBT p741

AMPHION (Amphioun) and his twin brother Zethus were sons of Jupiter
   and Antiope. They ultimately became the rulers of Thebes and
   built its walls: Amphion harped with such skill that the stones
   fell into place. Meta. 6.177ff., 224ff., 271ff., 402ff.;
   15.427 and Theb. 1.9-10; 8.232; 10.873.
      KnT 1546
      MerchT 1716
      MancT 116

AMPHIORAX see AMPHIARAUS.

ANAXAGORAS (Anaxogore), the Greek philosopher, c. 500-428 B.C.,
   who had a great influence on Pericles. About 450 he was
   prosecuted on a charge of impiety (for holding the opinion that
   the sun was an incandescent stone) and forced to flee Athens.
      Bo 2.p6.52, 57

[ANAXARCHUS of Abdera, 323 B.C., oppressed by NICOCREON, king of
   Cyprus. See VALERIUS MAXIMUS 3.3: Skeat 2.433.
      Bo 2.p6.52, 57]

ANCHISES, a member of the royal house of Troy (he was Priam's
   cousin) who was the father, by Aphrodite, of AENEAS. He
   boasted of the goddess's favor and was struck blind or paralyzed
   by the thunder of Jupiter. Aeneas carried him out of burning

Troy on his shoulders. He died in Sicily and was buried on
Mt. Eryx.
>   HF 168, 171, 442
>   LGW 944, 1086, [1295]

<ANDREAS CAPELLANUS, Andrew the Chaplain, fl. 1182-6 at the court
of Marie de Champagne, for whom Andreas wrote De Amore, or
De Arte Honesti Amandi, a work which became the standard on
courtly love. It is believed to be a book intended to portray
conditions at the court of Eleanor of Aquitaine (Marie's mother).
The work, addressed to "Walter," is divided into three parts:
the first is an introduction to the nature of love, the second
teaches the reader how to retain love, and the third is a rejection of the other two parts. The De Amore survives in 12
nearly complete MSS; see Robertson 393-448 and Kreuzer.
De Amore
>   1.1 and 2   Rom 4809
>   2.8(Rule 17)   T&C 4.415>

ANDROGEUS, the son of MINOS and Pasiphaë. After winning every
contest in the Athenian games he left for funeral games in
Thebes but he was ambushed and killed at the instigation of
Aegeus. Traditionally, his murder was political: Aegeus was
afraid that Androgeus would persuade his father to support the
rebellion of the fifty sons of Pallas. According to Meech 186,
Chaucer probably got Androgeus's excellence in philosophy from
VINSAUF (Faral 269).
>   LGW 1896

ANDROMACHE (Andromacha), the wife of HECTOR and mother of Astyanax.
Astyanax was thrown from the walls of Troy; Andromache became
the prize of PYRRHUS (Neoptolemus) who gave her to Helenus.
For her dream see DARES 24; BENOÎT or Roman de Troie 15263ff.;
GUIDO i 4ᵛ.
>   NPT 3141(4331)

ANELIDA (Anelyda), the victim of Arcite's falsity. Her name is
unexplained.
>   A&A 11, 49, 71, 139, 147, 167, 198, 204, 349, 351

ANNE, Anna, the sister of Dido; see Aen. 4.
>   HF 367
>   LGW 1168, 1178, 1182, 1343

ST. ANNE, the wife of St. Joachim and mother of the Virgin Mary;
see the apocryphal Gospel of James and Gospel of the Nativity
of Mary as well as Leg. Aurea 222. Cf. Cline.
>   MLT 641
>   FrT 1613
>   SecNT p70
another seith,
>   Mel 1439(2629) see PUBLILIUS SYRUS.

11

ST. ANSELM, 1033–1109, became the archbishop of Canterbury in 1093.
His canonization was instituted by Becket in 1163. In the
13th cent. his devotional works in the form of prayers and
meditations began to exercise a profound influence; EB.
        ParsT 169
    [Meditatio Secunda (PL 158.724)
        ParsT 169]

ANTAEUS (Antheus), king of Libya, the giant son of Neptune and Ge
with whom HERCULES wrestled after one of his Labors. When
thrown Antaeus arose stronger because he came in contact with
his mother, Earth; Hercules lifted him in the air and crushed
him. The account in Bo is probably based on Phars. 4.590–660;
cf. Meta. 9.184, Hero. 9, and De Clar. Mulier. 22: Shannon
312ff.
        Bo 4.m7.51
        MkT 2108(3298)

ANTENOR (Antenore), one of the elders of Troy in favor of restoring
Helen since she had been taken by treachery. It was said that
the Greeks, recognizing his fairness, spared him and his
family; later legend made him a traitor; see Roman de Troie
24397ff.
        BD 1119
        T&C 2.1474
            4.50, 133, 137, 149, 177, 189, 196, 203, 209,
            212, 347, 378, 665, 792, 878, 1315
            5.71, 77, 905

ST. ANTHONY, the third or fourth cent. ascetic desert father whose
intercession cured erysipelas.
        ParsT 427

ANTICHRIST, during the Middle Ages, generally regarded as the
personification of iniquity. In Jewish tradition, the Antichrist was identified with Antiochus IV Epiphanes; in the early
Christian church, with 2 Tessalonians 2, Revelations, the
Apocalypse, and the Sibylline fragments. The medieval commentaries on these books transmitted the Antichrist into the
encyclopaedic tradition. In the Apocalyptic tradition signs
precede his advent; Joachim of Fiore predicted his advent and
a third age of the Holy Spirit by 1260. The Antichrist was
the subject of a number of tracts at the University of Paris,
particularly those of William of St. Amour.
        Rom 7009, 7155, 7191
        ParsT 788

ANTICLAUDIANUS (Anticlaudian) see ALANUS DE INSULIS.

ANTIGONE, Criseyde's niece. Although Antigone is associated with
the story of Thebes, the origin of the idea of the relationship with Criseyde is unknown.

    T&C 2.816, 824, 879, 887, 1563, 1716
        3.597

ANTILOGUS (Antylegyus) see ARCHILOCHUS.

ANTIOCHUS (Anthiocus), Antiochus IV Epiphanes, 176-164 B.C., the
    Seleucid king who defeated Egypt's attempt to recover Palestine
    and invaded and occupied Egypt until driven out by the Romans.
    He is also known for his attempt to suppress Judaism by force,
    the persecutions resulting in the Maccabean rebellion; see II
    Maccabees 9.
        MLT 182
        MkT 2575(3765)

ANTIPUS (Santippe) see XANTIPPUS.

ANTONIUS,
        Bo see ANTONINUS,
        LGW and KnT see MARCUS ANTONIUS.

ANTONINUS, Marcus Aurelius Antoninus, Caracalla, 186-217, the
    eldest son of Septimus Severus (d. 211) on whose death he
    murdered his brother Geta and his followers, among them
    PAPINIANUS the jurist.
        Bo 3.p5.49

ST. ANTONY see ST. ANTHONY.

ANTYLEGYUS see ARCHILOCHUS.

APELLES, the Jewish fabricator of Darius's tomb; see GUALTIER.
        WBT p499
        PhysT 16

APIUS, the Roman judge responsible for the martyrdom of Virginia;
    Livyking is given as Chaucer's source. See S&A 398ff.
        PhysT 154, [158], [161], [165], [171], [175], 178,
            [188], [196], 204, [206], 227, [256], [258],
            265, 267, 270

APOLLO (Appollo), the son of Jupiter and Leto and brother of
    Diana; the god of medicine, music, archery, and prophecy,
    also associated with flocks and herds. With the Romans and
    in medieval tradition he was especially the god of poetry and
    music. He is also known by his epithet Phoebus (Phebus), the
    bright.
    APOLLO
        HF [1091], 1092, 1232
        T&C 1.70, 72
            2.843
            3.541, 543, 546
            4.114, 1397

        5.207, 1853
    FranklT 1031
PHOEBUS
    T&C 1.70, 659
        3.726
        4.120
    LGW 986
    MkT 2745(3935)
    MancT 105, 125, 130, 139, 156, 196, 200, 203, 238, 242
            244, 249, 262
As the equivalent for the sun:
APOLLO
    SqT 671
PHOEBUS
    Rom 5342
    Bo 1.m3.15; m6.2, 3
        2.m3.1; m6.14; m8.4
        3.m2.36; m11.12
        4.m1.11; m5.27
    T&C 2.54
        3.1495, 1755
        4.31, [1591]
        5.8, 278, 1017, 1107
    LGW 773, 1206
    KnT 1493
    MLT 111
    MkT 2753(3943)
    MerchT 2220
    SqT 48, 263
    PhysT 37
    Mars 27, 81, 88, 105, 114, 140

APOLLONIUS OF TYRE (Tyro Appollonius), the hero of the medieval
    romance of the same name. He solved the riddle of Antiochus's
    incestuous relations with his daughter, returned to Tyre and
    from there embarked on a series of marvelous adventures.
        MLT 181
the apostle,
        WBTp see ST. MATTHEW
        Mel, WBT, SumT, PardT see ST. PAUL

APRIL (Aprille, Averill, Aperil), the fourth month of the modern
    calendar, was the second of the medieval calendar; it was the
    month of rejuvenation, which followed the aridity of March.
    The significance of the meeting of Troilus and Criseyde and
    of the Canterbury pilgrims is thus chronologically reinforced;
    Wood, pp. 161-72.
        Rom 3978
        A&A 309
        T&C 1.156
            3.360
            4.751

        GP 1
        MLT i6
        WBT p546
        Mars 139
        Astr 1.10.3, 13
              2.45.27

<LUCIUS APULEIUS, fl. c. 155, the author of Metamorphoses, who also
    wrote a treatise on the Platonic doctrine of God and the demons,
    De Deo Socratis, which was used by Alanus and St. Augustine;
    Anticlaudianus 4.6 and De Civ. Dei 8.16.
    De Deo Socratis
        passim   HF 925
        c.10   965-6>

AQUARIUS, the 11th sign of the zodiac, between Capricorn and Pisces,
    entered on 20 January. The sign is known as the Waterbearer or
    Cupbearer, thought by the ancients to have been Ganymede or
    Deucalion.
        Astr 1.8.4
              2.6.17; 28.38

AQUILON see BOREAS.

ARCHEMORUS see OPHELTES.

ARCHILOCHUS, confused as Antilochus and Antilegius, slain with
    Achilles from ambush in the temple of Apollo in revenge for
    the death of Hector and Troilus. See DARES 34; Roman de Troie
    21838ff.; JOSEPH OF EXETER 6.402ff.; GUIDO 1 3ᵛ.
        BD 1069

ARCITE (Arcita), the perfidious lover of Anelida in A&A; Palamon's
    rival in LGW and KnT. Philostrate is the name given to Arcite
    when he returns in disguise: in Tes. the name is Penteo which
    Boccaccio employed to mean "vanquished by love"; i.e. Chaucer
    preferred the title of the source of T&C.
        A&A 11, 49, 85[em], 92, 106, 109, 140, 141, 155,
            168, 175, 179, 198, 210, 264, 323, 349
        LGW 420
        KnT 1013, 1031, 1080, 1112, 1116, 1126, 1145,
            1152, 1202, 1210, 1211, 1219, 1276, 1281,
            1333, 1336, 1344, 1348, 1355, 1379, 1393,
            1449, 1488, 1497, 1519, 1525, 1528, 1540,
            1557, 1577, 1580, 1596, 1627, 1628, 1636,
            1657, 1698, 1724, 1791, 1871, 2094, 2155,
            2256, 2258, 2315, 2368, 2421, 2424, 2428,
            2436, 2582, 2628, 2633, 2639, 2658, 2673,
            2676, 2688, 2705, 2742, 2743, 2761, 2815,
            2855, 2858, 2873, 2891, 2939, 2957, 3059
        PHILOSTRATE
            KnT 1428, 1558, 1728

ARCTURUS, alpha-Bootis in Libra. The Great Bear is also known as
the Wain, in which case the constellation Arctophylas becomes
Bootes, the "waggoner." The morning rising of Arcturus, one
of the three brightest stars in the northern hemisphere, in
early September was regarded as the time of the vintage and
as the time when the cattle left the upland pastures; EB.
>   Bo 1.m5.27
>   4.m5.2

ARGONAUTICA (Argonauticon) see VALERIUS FLACCUS.

ARGUS,
>   (1) BD see ALGUS
>   (2) the craftsman who designed the "Argo"
>   LGW 1453
>   (3) the herdsman that Juno set to guard Io; he was called
>   Panoptes because he had eyes all over his body, i.e. he
>   never slept. When Mercury killed him, by Jupiter's order,
>   Juno placed his eyes in the peacock's tail; Meta. 1.713-49.
>   Mercury, in the guise of a herdsman, lulled Argus to sleep
>   with the pipes from the story of Syrinx and Pan.
>   T&C 4.1459
>   KnT 1390
>   WBT p358
>   MerchT 2111

ARGYVE, in T&C 4 the name given to Criseyde's mother; no source,
not in Filo. In T&C 5 the name is the equivalent of Argia,
Polynices' wife; Theb. 2.297.
>   T&C 4.762
>   5.1509

ARIADNE (Adriane), the daughter of MINOS and Pasiphaë and sister
of PHAEDRA and ANDROGEUS, who fell in love with THESEUS and
enabled him to escape the Labyrinth after he had slain the
Minotaur. Theseus carried her off, but according to late legend,
abandoned her at Naxos; Hero. 10. Her legend is told in LGW,
Theseus's perfidy is referred to in HF, and she is listed as
one of Chaucer's Saints of Cupid in MLT.
>   HF 407, 411
>   LGW 268(222), 1969, 1977, 2078, 2146, 2158,
>   2171, 2175, 2181, 2460, 2545
>   MLT 167

ARIES, the Ram, the first sign in the zodiac; cf. Wood.
>   T&C 4.1592
>   5.1190
>   GP 8
>   SqT 51, 386
>   FranklT 1282
>   Astr 1.8.3; 17.16, 23, 27; 21.73
>   2.1.4; 3.23; 6.14; 12.10; 17.25; 20.6;

16

22.2; 25.16, 31, 39, 46, 51; 28.13,
37; 31.5

ARION, a semi-mythical poet, fl. c. 625 B.C., who, returning from
Italy with great wealth, was thrown overboard after being
allowed to sing a parting song which so charmed a dolphin that
he carried Arion to land. Arion's lyre and the dolphin were
translated to the stars.
        HF 1005, 1205

ARISTOCLIDES, tyrant of Orchomenos, presumably in Arcadia, who
pursued STYMPHALIS to the temple of Diana and killed her at
the image. The Arcadians made war and avenged her; see Adv.
Jov. 1.41.
        FranklT 1387

ARISTOTLE, 384–322 B.C., the Greek philosopher, known to the
medieval West through Latin translations of Arabic commentaries.
Aristotle went to Athens in 367 and studied under Plato for
20 years; in 342 he was appointed tutor to Alexander the Great.
In 335, when Alexander started his expedition to Asia, Aristotle
returned to Athens and opened a school of philosophy. After
the death of Alexander (323), he was forced to leave Athens
and he died the following year at Chalcis. In Bo 3 Chaucer
duplicates the mistaken attribution to Aristophanes made by
Boethius and the French translation attributed to Jean de Meun;
the reference in SqT has not been located.
        HF 759
        Bo 3.p8.40
           5.pl.63; p6.30
        [LGW 381(365)]
        GP 295
        SqT 233
        [De Physica
           2.4-5   Bo 5.pl.63]
        [De Caelo
           esp. 1(279B ff.)   Bo 5.p6.30]
        <[De Metaphysica
           10.3(1054B)   T&C 3.404-6; probably from
                                    Aquinas or Scotus>

ARNALDUS DE VILLANOVA, c. 1235-c. 1314, a French physician,
theologian, astrologer, and alchemist; see Louns 2.393, Skeat
5.432.
        CYT 1428
        [De Lapide Philosophorum (Lyons, 1532)
           f.304ʳ   CYT 1428]
        <Expositiones Visionum
           1.4   WBT p581
           2.2   >

ARPIES see HARPIES.

17

ARRAY (Aray), one of the necessary companions of Cupid.
     PF 219

ARRIUS, a character in Walter MAP's Dissuasio Valerii in the De
     Nugis Curialium.
          WBT p758, 762

ARSEMIUS, Chaucer's "senatour," the husband of Helen who, according
     to Chaucer, is Constance's aunt.
          [MLT 961, 967, 976, 981, 998, 1002, 1010, 1016,
               1023, 1046]

ARSECHIELES see ARZACHEL.

ART, one of the characters seen just outside the temple of Venus;
     i.e. the artful request.
          PF 245

ARTEMISIA (Arthemesie), the sister and wife of Mausolus, king of
     Caria (one of the Persian satraps), she ruled solely 353-350
     B.C. She built for her husband, in Halicarnassus, the mag-
     nificent mausoleum which was one of the seven wonders of the
     world. She was also known as a botanist and medical researcher;
     see Adv. Jov. 1.44, and VALERIUS MAXIMUS 4.6.1.
          FranklT 1451

ARTHUR (Arthour), legendary king of Britain, one of the Nine
     Worthies.
          Rom 1199
          WBT 857, 882, 890, 1089

ARVERAGUS, the Breton knight whose wife, Dorigen, was compromised
     by his squire, Aurelius. The name is a Latinized Celtic name,
     spelled Arviragus in Hist. Brit. 4.12.
          FranklT 808, 814, 837, 969, 1087, 1351, 1424, 1460,
               1517, 1526, 1551, 1595

ARZACHEL, abu-Isḥāq Ibrāhūm ibn-Yahya al-Zarqāli, c. 1029-c. 1087,
     was a Toledan who was the chief contributor to the so-called
     Toledan tables. He was foremost as an astronomer; he devised
     an improved type of astrolabe and was the first to prove the
     motion of the solar apogee with reference to the stars. His
     works were translated by Gerard of Cremona; his findings were
     also used by Raymond of Marseilles; Hitti 571.
          Astr 2.45.2

ASCALAPHUS (Escaphilo), the son of Acheron, who revealed that
     Proserpina had eaten some pomegranate seeds while in the lower
     world. He was changed into an owl; see Meta. 5.539ff., 6.432,
     10.453, 15.791. He is not mentioned in Filo.; hence, the
     Italian form of the name is unusual.
          T&C 5.319

18

ASCANIUS, or Iulus, the son of Aeneas. There seems to be confusion
    in the reference in HF; but Skeat, 3.250, is probably correct
    in considering Iulus parenthetical.
        HF 177, 178
        LGW 941, 1138

ASSURANCE, Assured Manner, one of the companions of Pity who attends
    the hearse.
        Pity 40

ASSUERUS (Assuere, Assuer) see AHASUERUS.

ATALANTA (Athalante), a swift-footed huntress, she was the first
    to wound the Calydonian boar during the hunt held by MELEAGER.
    She refused to marry any man who could not defeat her in a
    foot-race; she was overcome by HIPPOMENES who was helped by
    Venus's gift of the apples of the Hesperides. Their son was
    PARTHENOPAEUS.
        PF 286
        KnT 2070

ATHALANTES see ATLAS.

ATHALUS see ATTALUS.

ATHAMAS, the son of Aeolus and king of Thebes who was driven mad
    because of Juno's hatred of his wife, Ino. Ino was Semele's
    sister; Semele was the mother of Dionysus by Jupiter; Meta.
    4.420ff. The oath, not in Filo., is probably due to Inf.
    30.1-11.
        T&C 4.1539

ATITERIS see CYTHERUS.

ATLAS (Athalantes), the son of Iapetus and Clymene and brother of
    Prometheus, was the father of the Pleiades, Hyades, and
    Hesperides; the daughters referred to here are the PLEIADES.
        HF 1007

ATRIDES see AGAMEMNON.

ATROPOS see FATES.

ATTALUS (Athalus), Attalus III Philometer, king of Pergamum who
    succeeded in 138 B.C. When he died in 133 he willed the throne
    to Rome. Robin. notes that in RR 6691-2 he is called the
    inventor of chess. Skeat, 1.480, notes that Jean de Meun is
    following Policraticus 1.5.
        BD 663

ATTHEON see ACTAEON.

ATTILA (Attilla), king of the Huns who succeeded in 433 and d. 453
   while celebrating his marriage to Ildico; see Jordanes 49.
      PardT 579

AUGUST (Augustus), the eighth month of the modern calendar.
      Astr 1.10.4, 12, 14, 19

ST. AUGUSTINE (Austin), 354-430, bishop of Hippo (396-430), one
   of the four great fathers of the Church. He was trained as a
   rhetorician, and while lecturing in Milan he fell under the
   spell of Ambrose and was baptised in 387. He was ordained in
   391. In addition to De Civitate Dei, begun in 413, he was the
   reputed author of a monastic rule (really Epistola 211 and
   Sermones 355, 356); see Kellogg.
      Rom 6583, 6613, 6691, 6700
      LGW 1690
      GP 187, 188
      ShipT 259(1449), 441(1631)
      Mel 1617(2807), 1643(2833)
      NPT 3241(4431)
      [PhysT 117]
      ParsT 97, 101, 150, 230, 269, 302, 368, 381, 383,
            484, 535, 630, 678, 694, 741, 754, 768, 831,
            845, 921, 958, 987, 1020, 1026
   [De Civitate Dei
      1.19   LGW 1690
      14.15   ParsT 535
      19.15   "   754]
   [De Corruptione et Gratia
      35   ParsT 694   (PL 44.266)]
   [De Opere Monachorum
      passim   Rom 6583   (PL 40.547ff.)
                        GP 187, 188   (   )]
   [De Vera et Falsa Poenitentia   (PL 40)
      10.25   ParsT 985
      24   "   302]
   [Enarrationes in Psalmi
      31   ParsT 741   (PL 36.260)
      104.25   PhysT 117   (PL 37.1399)   Chaucer's
                                                        addition
                        ParsT 484, 678   (   )]
   [Epistolae
      211   GP 187, 188   (PL 33.958ff.)
      265   ParsT 101   (" .1089)]
   [Sermones
      9.16   ParsT 150   (PL 38.87)
      20.3   694   (.140)
      181.4   1020   (.981)
      351.2   97   (39.1537)
      355   GP 187, 188   (.1568ff.)
                        Mel 1643(2833)   (   ) not in
                                                        source]

AUGUSTINIANS (Augustins), the Augustinian Hermits or Friars,
    sometimes called Black Friars, became powerful in the 13th
    cent.; they quickly abandoned the hermitage; see Knowles.
        Rom 7459
        [GP 210]

AUGUSTUS see CAESAR AUGUSTUS.

<AULUS GELLIUS, c. 130-180, Latin grammarian born in Rome where he
    studied rhetoric and grammar. In 143 he was in Athens studying
    philosophy. The Noctes Atticae is a compilation made for his
    children based on notes and stories acquired in Athens; see
    Young.
    Noctes Atticae
        preface   HF 647-57
                             PF 15-6, 22-5
                             LGW (17-26), (30-4)>

AURELIAN, Lucius Domitius Aurelianus, emperor 270-75, proclaimed
    at the death of Claudius II Gothicus. After turning back the
    Goths and other Germanic tribes, Aurelian undertook an expedi-
    tion to the east in 271 against ZENOBIA of Palmyra. At the
    same time he defeated and put to death Firmus, self-proclaimed
    emperor of Egypt, and then defeated Tetricus, emperor in the
    west, at Chalons. The restoration of the empire was assured;
    Aurelian's triumph in Rome in 274 was adorned with the persons
    of Zenobia and Tetricus. He was assassinated in the same year
    while on an expedition against the Persians.
        MkT 2351(3541), 2361(3551)

AURELIUS, the squire who, by releasing Dorigen from her pledge,
    demonstrated his nobility. The name is Roman in origin but
    was known and used among the Britons; see Hist. Brit. 6.5.
        FranklT 938, 965, 970, 979, 982, 989, 1006, 1007,
                1020, 1037, 1100, 1102, 1183, 1188, 1226, 1235,
                1241, 1256, 1297, 1303, 1499, 1514, 1557, 1592

AURORA, Eos, goddess of the dawn, the daughter of Hyperion and
    Theia. By Astraeus she was the mother of ZEPHYRUS, NOTUS,
    BOREAS, and HESPERUS and the stars. By Tithonus she was the
    mother of Memnon.
        [T&C 3.1466, 1469]
        LGW 774

AURORA in BD 1169 see PETRUS DE RIGA.

AUSTER, or NOTUS, the south wind.
        Bo 1.m7.3
            2.m3.11; m4.7; m6.25(Notus)
            3.m1.8(Notus)

author (auctor): my, our, etc.
    Rom 7   see MACROBIUS
    HF 314
    T&C 3.502, 575, 1196, 1325, 1817
        5.1088   see LOLLIUS
    LGW 470
        1139, 1228, 1352   see OVID
    NPT 2984(4174)   VALERIUS
                                  MAXIMUS
    ClT 1141   PETRARCH

AVARICE, one of the Seven Deadly Sins, depicted on the wall outside
    the Garden of Mirth in RR.
    Rom 209, 231, 239, 306, 1155
    T&C 3.1805

AVERROES (Averrois), abu-al-Walīd Muhammad ibn-Ahmad ibn-Rushd,
    1126-1198, was born in Cordova and spent most of his life there
    until called to Marrakesh in 1182 as court physician. His
    medical reputation was surpassed only by his reputation as a
    commentator on Aristotle; Hitti 582-4.
    GP 433

AVICENNA (Avycen), abu-'Ali al-Husayn ibn-Sīna (Heb. Aven Sina L.>
    Avicenna), 980-1037, the most illustrious Arabic physician
    after al-Razi. His al-Qānūn fi al-Ṭibb, the epitome of Greco-
    Arabic medicine, was translated by Gerard of Cremona. His
    kitāb al-Shifā' was a philosophical encyclopaedia; Hitti 367-8.
    GP 432
    PardT 889
  [al-Qānūn
    4.fen 6   PardT 890]

B

BACCHUS (Bacus, Bachus), the god of wine, the son of Jupiter and
    Semele. He was born on Nysa and was especially fond of Naxos
    where he married ARIADNE after her abandonment by THESEUS and
    of Cithaeron (in Boeotia near Thebes); Aen. 3.125, 4.300-3
    and Meta. 3.582-691.
    PF 275
    Bo 1.m6.16
       2.m5.7
    T&C 5.208
    LGW 2376
    MerchT 1722
    PhysT 58
    MancT p99

HARRY BAILLY see HOST.

BALTHASAR see BELSHAZZAR.

[BARCE, the nurse of SICHAEUS, the husband of DIDO, treacherously
    slain by his brother-in-law PYGMALION; Aen. 4.632.
        LGW 1346]

BARNABO VISCONTI see VISCONTI.

<BARTHOLOMAEUS ANGLICUS, an English Franciscan, lecturer at Paris
    c. 1220 and Magdeburg c. 1230. The De Prop. Rerum dates from
    c. 1250.
    De Proprietatibus Rerum
        6.24-7   HF 1ff.
        12.8   PF 361
         .9   363>

ST. BASIL (Basilie), Basil the Great, c. 330-379, bishop of
    Caesarea who succeeded Eusebius in 370. He helped stamp out
    Arianism; his improved liturgy is still used in the Eastern
    Church; he propagated a monastic life that substituted hard
    labor, works of charity and the common life, for the existing
    hermitical asceticism.
        ParsT 221
    [Homily on Psalm 28.7   (PG 29.298)
         s6   ParsT 221]

BASILIUS, the informer against Boethius.
        Bo 1.p4.112

BAUDERIE, bawdy, one of the personifications depicted on the walls
    of the temple of Venus; Tes. 7.56.
        KnT 1926

BAYARD, specifically the name of the horse given to Renaud (one
    of the four sons of Amyon) by Charlemagne; but generally applied
    to any horse.
        T&C 1.218
        RvT 4115
        CYT 1413

BEAR, the Great Bear, also known as the Wain, one of the brightest
    of the northern constellations; cr. ARCTURUS.
        HF 1004
        Bo 4.m6.8

BEAUTY (Beautee, Beaute), the personification of physical perfection.
        Rom 952, 1006
        PF 225
        KnT 1926
        Pity 39, 66, 70, 75
        ?Lady 25

BEGUIN (Bygynne), an association of lay religious women who led a
life of religion without taking religious vows; from Lambret le
Bègue (d.c. 1187). Apparently they were always suspect because
their associations were either subsumed by orders or served as
refuges for poor women.
>   Rom 6861, 7366

BEHEST (Beheste) see ART.

BELIAL, equated with the devil, the epitome of evil, mentioned
frequently in the Old Testament; the reference is probably to
I Samuel 2.12.
>   ParsT 897, 898

BELLONA, the Roman goddess of war; Theb. 2.704, 715ff. In Aen.
she is the sister of Mars; in De Gen. Deor. 5.48 she is the
sister and charioteer of Mars. The confusion with Pallas may
result from apposition; see Pratt.
>   A&A 5

BELSHAZZAR (Balthasar), a Babylonian general of the sixth cent.
B.C.; in Daniel he is son and heir of Nebuchadnezzar but he
was never king.
>   MkT 2183(3373), 2205(3395)

ST. BENEDICT (Beneit, Benedight), of Nursia, c. 480-c. 553, the
founder of western monasticism and associated with Monte Cassino.
His strict rule served as the basis for monastic organization and
ideals. Two of his best known disciples were Maurus and
Placidus.
>   GP 173
>   MillT 3483

BENEDICTINES (Benedictines), or Black Monks, were the major
missionaries in western Europe with their center at Subiaco.
The first establishment of a house outside Italy was in England.
>   Rom 6695

<BENOÎT DE STE. MAURE, the author of the Roman de Troie, c. 1160,
and perhaps the Chronique des ducs de Normandie, c. 1172. In
the Roman Benoît mentions Homer as his authority but he actually
uses DARES and DICTYS. The Roman marks the first appearance of
the Troilus and Briseida episode in the vernacular literature
of western Europe; see Root, Meech, Lumiansky.
>   Roman de Troie

?general reference	BD 326-31	
45-70	HF 1479-80	
91-2	T&C 1.146	
110-6	HF 1479-80	
555-8	T&C 5.1045	
805ff.	MkT 2117(3307)	= Trophee
2793-804	T&C 4.548	

2939	T&C 2.1398
3143–8	2.616–8
3147–8	2.611–44
3187ff.	4.548
3990–2	3.1774–5
3991–2	2.157–61
4059–68	4.548
5211–24	5.799–805
5275–88	5.806–26 + DARES
5393–446	5.827–40 + DARES
5439–46	2.157–61
5817ff.	1.68–70
5817–927	4.1411
6685–90	5.403
10201–18	2.611–44
10283ff.	2.611–44
11996–12006	4.38–42
12551–65	4.50–4
12822–13120	4.57–8
12965ff.	4.169–210
13079–120	4.137–8
13167ff.	5.176–92
13429–94	4.18–21
13469–77	4.1415–21
13495–7	4.1415–21
13511–15	5.109–12
13522–5	5.164–5
13526–9	5.155–61
13529–712	5.92–189
13529–84	5.92–175
13552–55	5.164–5
13555–60	5.132
13556–8	5.155–8
13561–6	5.155–61
13567–76	5.113–7
13576	5.138–9
13579–80	5.138–9
13591–6	5.155–8
13596–610	5.113–6
13617–8	5.176–89
13637–40	5.176–89
13655–8	5.166–8
13673–5	5.1002–14
13676ff.	5.176–92
13676–8	5.176–89
13677–9	5.1000–1
13690–9	5.143–7
13706–8	5.176–89
13709–11	5.1013
13713ff.	5.176–92
13768–73	4.1397–8, 1404–11
13771–3	5.1849–55

   Roman de Troie (cont.)

13803–9	T&C 4.1478–82
13859–66	4.18–21
14238–76	5.1037–9
14983–5	5.1002–14
15046–7	5.1037–9
15053–6	5.1010–1
15079–172	5.1037–9
15102–4	5.1042–3
15176–9	5.1042–3
15263ff.	NPT 3141(4331) + DARES + GUIDO
16007–316	T&C 5.1548–61
16166–77	5.1558–61
16185ff.	5.1558–61
16635–44	3.540
17552ff.	1.295–8
18443–59	1.232–52
19995–20156	5.1751–64
?20075	5.1705
20131–46	5.1044–50
20194–271	5.1044–85
20202–8	5.1044–50
20228–308	5.1044–85
20237–340	5.1051–85
20462–600	5.1751–64
20597ff.	2.611–44
20620ff.	2.611–44
20832–7	5.1751–64
21005–189	5.1751–64
21440–50	3.374–5
21679–83	5.1849–55
21698–706	5.1849–55
21838ff.	BD 1069 + DARES + JOSEPH + GUIDO
24397ff.	1117
25920–3	T&C 4.120–6
26113ff.	BD 1246ff.>

ST. BERNARD, c. 1090–1153, joined the Cistercians at Citeaux in
1098 and became abbot of Clairvaux at its foundation in 1115.
St. Bernard opposed Anacletus II, the antipope, and was ultimately successful against Abelard. He was a popular preacher
(he instigated the Second Crusade in 1146); in addition to his
sermons he wrote a great many letters, hymns, and treatises
on dogma, asceticism, monasticism, and ecclesiastical govern-
ment.
    LGW 16(16)
    SecNT p30
    ParsT 130, 166, 253, 256, 274, 690, 723
[Sermo ad Prelatos in Concilio
    §5   ParsT 166   (PL 184.1098)]

BERNARD GORDON see GORDON

<BERNARDUS SILVESTRIS, of Tours, a 12th cent. neo-Platonist who
    composed the De Mundi Universitate for Thierry of Chartres
    between 1145 and 1153. The first part, the Megacosmos, is an
    address of Nature to Intellect; the second part, the Microcosmos,
    is an address of Intellect to Nature. See Hamm 86, Louns 2.385,
    Skeat 5.147, Silverstein, Manitius 3.205-15.
    Megacosmos
        KnT 2031-4
        MLT 197ff.>

BEVES OF HAMPTON (Beves), the hero of an extremely popular and
    marvelous 14th cent. romance; the earliest ME version dates
    from c. 1330. See Wells [6].
        Thop 899(2089)

BIALACOIL, Bel Accuiel, the art of fair welcome, the son of
    Courtesy.
        Rom 2984, 2999, 3011, 3067, 3081, 3084, 3113,
            3139, 3151, 3167, 3357, 3563, 3568, 3573,
            3589, 3591, 3606, 3609, 3623, 3650, 3724,
            3755, 3806, 3817, 3824, 3853, 3874, 3883,
            3888, 3908, 3945, 3991, 3998, 4017, 4027,
            4052, 4108, 4280, 4295, 4302, 4347, 4367,
            4377, 4417, 4488, 4511, 4551, 4601, 4605,
            4612

BIBLE, the Holy Scriptures or sacred writings of the Roman Church.
    For specific treatments of Chaucer's use, see Evans and
    Thompson; cf. Grace W. Landrum's unpublished dissertation
    (1921) and the summary of her results in PMLA 39(1924) 75-100.
        BD 987
        GP 438
        WBT p650, 687
        SumT 1845
        PardT 575=Old Testament, 578, 586
    GENESIS
        [1.27   FranklT 880]
        [1.28   WBT p28
                                 ParsT 883]
        [2.18   MerchT 1328-9]
        [2.23-4   1335-6]
        [2.24   ParsT 842ff.
                                     918]
        [3.18   ABC 150]
        [4.10   PrT 578(1768)]
        [4.14   ParsT 1015]
        [4.21   BD 1162-6]
        [5.24   HF 588]
        9.18-27   ParsT 755

GENESIS (cont.)
   [9.19-23   BD 1162
                              A&A 150
                              WBT p54
                              SqT 551]
   [19.24-5   ParsT 839]
   [19.33   PardT 487]
   [22   ABC 169]   + Hebrews
   [27   Mel 1098(2288)ff.]
   [31   ParsT 443]
   [37   NPT 3130(4320)-5(5)]
   [39.8   ParsT 880]
   [40   NPT 3130(4320)-5(5)]
   [41   BD 282
                              NPT 3130(4320)-5(5)]
   [41.1-7   HF 516]
   [47.7   ParsT 443]
EXODUS
   [3.2   ABC 89]
   [14.21-31   MLT 488-90]
   20.3   ParsT 750
   [20.7   ParsT 588]
   [20.14   ParsT 837-8]
   [20.17   ParsT 842ff.]
   [34.28   SumT 1885]
LEVITICUS
   [10.9   SumT 1894]
   [19.20   ParsT 837ff.]
   [19.32   743]
   [20.10   837ff.]
   [21.9   ]
NUMBERS
   [6.3   PardT 555]
   [25.17   ParsT 574]
DEUTÉRONOMY
   [32.21   ParsT 837ff.]
   [32.24   195]
   [32.33   ]
JOSHUA
   ?<9.21   KnT 1422>
JUDGES
   general   MkT 2046(3236)
   [4.17-21   KnT 2007]
   [13.4-5   PardT 555]
   [13-16   MkT 2015(3205)ff.]
   [19.22   ParsT 897-8]
I SAMUEL = I KINGS (Vulg.)
   [2.12   ParsT 897-8]
   <2.13   900>
   [2.30   189]
   [11.3   WBT p35-43]

```
I SAMUEL = I KINGS (Vulg.) (cont.)
    [17.4              MLT 934]
    [18.19-20          SumT 2116]
    [25                Mel 1098(2288)]
    [28.7              FrT 1510-1]
II SAMUEL = II KINGS (Vulg.)
    [2.11              HF 588]
    [2.28              HF 1245
                       MerchT 1719]
    2.30               ParsT 189
    11.25              Mel 1668(2858)
    ?<13.1-20          T&C 1.1394ff., 1757>
    [17                BD 1118
                       ParsT 639]
    [18.16             HF 1245
                       MerchT 1719]
    [20.22             HF 1245
                       MerchT 1719]
I KINGS = III KINGS (Vulg.)
    [10.13             FrT 1510-2]
    [11.1ff.           KnT 1942]
    <11.12             MerchT 2300>
    [18-20             SumT 2116]
    [19.8                  1890]
II KINGS = IV KINGS (Vulg.)
    <24-25             MkT 2143(3335)>
TOBIAS
    4.20               Mel 1118(2308), <1162(2352)>
    6.17               ParsT 906
JUDITH
    [passim            MLT 940
                       MkT 2551(3741)-74(64)]
    [8ff.              Mel 1098(2288)]
ESTHER
    [2, 5              MerchT 1744-5]
    [7ff.              Mel 1100(2290)]
JOB
    1.12               FrT 1491
    1.21               <ClT 871-2>
                       Mel 1000(2190)
    2.6                FrT 1491
    <3.3               Rom 468-9
                       ClT 902-3>
    10.20-2            ParsT 176, 211, 217, 223
    <12.12             Mel 1164(2354)>
    ?<13.15            SecNT 420>
    <20.25             ParsT 191>
    <21.12             MLT 1132-4>        + INNOCENT
    33.26              ParsT 134
    40.4               ClT 932
    42.1-6               "
    [42.6              ParsT 143]
```

PSALMS
1.1	Mel 1198(2388)
4.5	ParsT 540
<7.12	ABC 29>
[8.1-2	PrT 453(1643)-54(44)]
10.5	ParsT 204
<10.9	FrT 1657>
11.14	Mel 1171(2361)
<12.4	ParsT 134>
12.5	Mel 1197(2387)
17.20	MancT 345
20.4	Mel 1735(2925)
26.28	MancT 345
<30.3, 9	MerchT 1401>
32.5	ParsT 309
<34.14	Mel 1692(2882)-93(83)>
<37.7	ParsT 500>
<37.16	Mel 1630(2820)-31(21)>
44.1-2	SumT 1934
<44.20-21	ParsT 1062>
55.15	ParsT 442
<57.4	MancT 340>
?<69	ParsT 273>
75.6	193
77.5	716
<84.11	T&C 3.1282>
96.10	ParsT 307
<104.2ff.	MLT 813-6> + BOETHIUS
107.34	ParsT 220
<114.9	SumT 2075>
119.3	ParsT 125
126.1	Mel 1304(2494)
<145.9	ParsT 582>
<147.3	PardT 916>

PROVERBS
1.28	ParsT 168
6.26-9	854
7.17	MancT 344
7.26	ParsT 854
8.17	709
10.19, 31	MancT 335 + Disticha Catonis
<11.14	Mel 1171(2362)>
11.22	<WBT p784-5>
	ParsT 156
12.4	ParsT 134 + Job
12.5	Mel 1197(2387) + PUBLILIUS SYRUS
13.7	GP 478-9
13.11	Mel 1579(2769)
13.24	PhysT 98
<14.13	T&C 4.836
	MLT 424> + INNOCENT
<14.20	MLT p115>

PROVERBS (cont.)

14.29	Mel 1513(2703)
15.4	ParsT 629
<15.15	MLT p118>
15.16	Mel 1628(2818)-29(19)
15.18	1514(2704)
16.6	ParsT 119ff.
16.7	Mel 1719(2909)
16.8	1628(2818)
16.24	1113(2303)
16.29	ParsT 614
16.32	Mel 1515(2707)
17.1	ParsT 633
<17.14	Mel 1039(2229)>
<17.17	Rom 5513>
17.22	Mel 995(2185)
18.9	ParsT 688
19.7	MLT p120 + Tristia
19.11	Mel 1512(2702)
<19.14	MerchT 1311> + ALBERTANUS
19.19	Mel 1539(2729)
<20.1	PardT 549> + JEROME
20.3	Mel 1485(2675)
20.4	<Mel 1593(2783)>
	ParsT 688
21.9	Mel 1087(2277)
	<WBT p778>
21.23	MancT 314
21.25	ParsT 688
22.1	Mel 1638(2828)
<22.17	1162(2352)>
<22.24	SumT 2085-8>
25.10	Mel 1638(2829)
25.16	1416(2606)-17(07)
25.18	ParsT 566
<25.20	WBT p376> + JEROME
<25.21	ParsT 569>
26.11	Rom 7286
26.17	Mel 1542(2732)
27.9	1158(2348)
27.15	ParsT 631
<27.20	Mel 1617(2817)>
[27.23	Rom 6453-4]
28.13	ParsT 127
28.14	Mel 1317(2507)-18(08), 1696(2886)
28.15	ParsT 568
28.20	Mel 1578(2768)
28.23	Mel 1177(2367), 1696(2886)
	ParsT 614
29.5	Mel 1178(2368)
<29.9	ParsT 664>

PROVERBS (cont.)

<30.16	WBT p371> + JEROME
<30.21-3	WBT p362-70>
[31.1	PardT 585]
31.4	Mel 1194(2384)
[31.4-5	PardT 584-7]

ECCLESIASTES

1.18	ParsT 229
<3.1	T&C 3.855
	FrT 1475>
	ClT p6
<4.10	T&C 1.694-5>
5.3	ParsT 649
5.11	Mel 1653(2843)
7.4	Mel 1707(2897), 1710(2900)
	ParsT 539
<7.19	ParsT 712>
7.28	Rom 5534
	MerchT 2247-8
	Mel 1057(2247)
9.1	Mel 1664(2854)
9.10	ParsT 679
10.19	Mel 1550(2740)
<36.27	MerchT 1381-2> + ALBERTANUS

SONG OF SONGS (for MillT see Kaske)

<1.2-3	MillT 3339-43
1.14	3244
1.15-4.16	MerchT 2138-48
2.1	MillT 3268
2.5	3705
2.7	3712-3
2.8-9	3328-30, 3366-7
2.12	3706
2.13-4	3700 + JEROME
4.1-5	3233-70
4.1	3244
4.4	3266
4.10	3704 + JEROME
4.11, 14	3698-3700
5.1	3684, 3707
5.2	3702-3
5.5	3708
5.8	3705
5.10-2	3314-7
5.13, 16	3690-3
7.1	3259, 3263, 3267
7.4	BD 945ff.
7.7	MillT 3264
7.8-9	3261-2
8.5	3310-1>

WISDOM

<7.25	T&C 3.11>

ECCLESIASTICUS

3.26	Mel 1671(2861)
<4.30, 35	SumT 1989>
6.5	Mel 1740(2930)
6.6	1167(2357)
6.14	1161(2351)
6.15	1159(2349)
8.20	1173(2363)
<8.22	1143(2333)-44(34)>
9.14	1162(2352)
<10.15	ParsT 388>
<11.25	MLT 421-2> + INNOCENT
11.29	CkT p4331
12.10	Mel 1186(2376)
12.10, 11, 16	NPT 3329(4519)
13.1	ParsT 854
<13.24	Mel 1635(2825)>
<18.26	MLT 1132-8> + Job + INNOCENT
19.8	Mel 1141(2331)-42(32)
22.6	1045(2235)
<22.26-7	Rom 5523-9>
<23.11	PardT 649-50>
<23.12	ParsT 593>
23.22-6	MerchT 2250
<25.16	WBT p775>
25.17-26	MerchT 2250
25.24-5	WBT p651-2
25.30	Mel 1059(2249)
26.1-3	MerchT 2250
26.7	ParsT 854
26.7-16	MerchT 2250
27.26	NPT 3329(4519)-30(20)
<27.29	ParsT 640>
30.17	Mel 1572(2762)
30.25	Mel 995(2185)
<32.6	NPT p2800(3990)-01(91)>
32.19	MillT 3530
	Mel 1047(2237)
33.18-20	Mel 1754(2944)-56(46)
33.20-2	1060(2250)
33.27	1589(2779)
	MerchT 1381-2
36.21-4	MerchT 2250
<37.28-9	PardT 512>
40.19, 23	MerchT 2250
40.29	MLT p114-5
	Mel 1571(2761)
41.12	1639(2829)
42.9-14	MerchT 2250

ISAIAH

<1.1	HF 514>
<6.1	514>

ISAIAH (cont.)
    <11.1   ParsT 288>
    14.11   ParsT 198
    <14.12   MkT 1999(3189)-2004(3194)>
    <14.13-4   FrT 1413>   + GREGORY
    <14.19   ParsT 288>
    <19.18   839>
    53.5   281
    66.24   210
JEREMIAH
    4.2   PardT 635-7
                      ParsT 592
    6.16   ParsT text
    <48.10   680>
EZEKIEL
    18.23, 32   ParsT 76-7   + Timothy + Peter
    18.24   236
    20.43   141
    33.17   76-7
DANIEL
    passim   NPT 3128(4318)-29(19)
    [1-4   HF 515]
    [1-5   MkT 2143(3333)-82(72)]
    4.10-2   ParsT 126
    [5   MkT 2183(3373)-2238(3428)]
    [13   MLT 639
                      ParsT 797]

MICAH
    7.6   ParsT 201
ZECHARIAH
    10.5   ParsT 434
    13.1   ABC 177
I MACCABEES
    1.8   MkT 2655(3845)
    3.18-9   Mel 1661(2851)-63(53)
II MACCABEES
    ?[4-10   MLT 182-5]
    9.3-7, 8-12, 28 MkT 2575(3765)ff.
MATTHEW
    [1.20   ParsT 286]
    [2.18   PrT 627(1817)]
    [3.8   ParsT 115]
    <4.19   Rom 7490-4
                      SumT 1820>
    [5.3   1923]
    <5.5   ParsT 1080>
    [5.9   Mel 1680(2870)
                      ParsT 661]
    <5.13   SumT 2196>   + Mark
    5.14-6   ParsT 1036-7
    <5.19   GP 497-8>

MATTHEW (cont.)

[5.22	ParsT 623]	
5.28	842–5	
5.34	588–90	
[5.44	526, 623]	
[6.16	Rom 446–8]	
<7.3	RvT p3919–20>	
[7.7	ParsT 705]	+ John
[7.15	Rom 7010–2]	
[7.20	ParsT 116]	
<9.12	716>	
<12.32	485>	
<12.34	627>	
<12.36	648>	
<13.8	869>	
<13.24–30	MLT e1183>	
[13.42	ParsT 208]	
[14.15	MLT 502–4]	
<14.29	GP 695–6>	
<15.27	SecNT p59–60>	
[15.28	LGW 1879–82]	
19.5	[WBT p30–1]	
	ParsT 842–5	
?[19.11–2	WBT p77–82]	
[19.17	Mel 1079(2269)]	
<19.20–1	Rom 6595–7, 6653–60>	
[19.21	WBT p107–10]	+ JEROME
<20.11	ParsT 506>	
<21.7	435>	
<22.37–9	512>	
23.1–8, 13–5	Rom 6888–93	
<23.7–8	SumT 2187–8>	+ Mark
<23.14	Rom 6636–44>	
<23.15	7017>	
<23.27	?BD 629	
	SqT 518–9>	
[25.30	ParsT 208]	
?<25.40–6	1031–2>	
<25.43	376>	
<26.7	947>	
[26.41	1048]	
[26.75	994–5]	
<27.5	1015>	
<27.35	665>	

MARK

<1.7	SqT 555>	
<5.13	SumT 2196>	+ Matthew
<9.44	ParsT 864>	
?<10.18	MerchT 2289–90>	
<12.30–1	ParsT 512>	
<12.38–9	SumT 2187–8>	+ Matthew
[16.9	Mel 1075(2265)]	

LUKE
<1.38	ABC 109>	
<2.7	ClT 206-7>	
<5.10	Rom 7490-4>	+ Matthew
	SumT 1820>	
<7.32	RvT p3876>	
[7.37	ParsT 996]	
8.48	T&C 2.1503	
[10.7	SumT 1973]	
<12.2	HF 351-2>	
<12.46	ParsT 1000>	
15.17, 24	700-3	
16.19	SumT 1877	
	ParsT 413	
<18.13	986>	
[18.19	Mel 1079(2269)]	
?<23.24	T&C 3.1577>	
<23.41	Mel 1496(2686)>	
23.42	ParsT 700-3	
<23.46	RvT 4287>	+ John

JOHN
[1.1	GP 254]	
1.8	ParsT 349	
<1.9	Mel 1884(3074)-88(78)>	
<2.1	WBT p10-3>	
[2.1-11	ParsT 919]	
3.15	565	
[4.6-30	WBT p14-9]	
<4.34	SumT 1845>	
6.9	WBT p145-6	+ JEROME
[8.3-8	Mel 1033(2223)]	
[8.11	ParsT 889]	
<8.32	Truth 7>	
[8.34	ParsT 142]	+ II Peter
<10.12	GP 514>	
[10.14	Rom 6452-4]	
[11.35	Mel 987(2177)]	
<12.3	ParsT 947>	
[12.4-8	502]	
<12.6	FrT 1350-1>	
<14.18	PrT 669(1859)>	+ Hebrews
<16.24	ParsT 705>	+ Matthew
<18.38	Buk 2>	
[19.19	ParsT 284]	
<23.46	RvT 4287>	+ Luke

ACTS
<4.5	Truth 11>	
4.12	ParsT [287], 597	
<8.9	HF 1274>	
<8.17-24	ParsT 781-3>	
<13.8	HF 1274>	
<20.33-5	Rom 6679-81>	

ROMANS
    [1.26-7   ParsT 910]
    5.12   322
    <7.4   ABC 38>
    7.24   ParsT 344
    <8.13   1080>
    ?<8.26   KnT 1260>
    <8.28   Frank1T 886>
    [11.33   Mel 1406(2596)]   + I Corinthians

I CORINTHIANS
    <1.24   PrT p472(1662)>
    ?<2.9   T&C 4.1695>
    3.17   ParsT 879
    [4.5   Mel 1406(2596)-07(97)] + Romans
    6.10   ParsT 619
    6.13   PardT 522-3
    [7.1   WBT p87]
    [7.4   p158-9]
    [7.6   p84-5]
    [7.7   p81, 103-4]
    <7.9   p46, 52   + JEROME
                           Buk 18>
    <7.20   WBT p147-8>
    [7.25   p64-5]
    7.28   p[51], 154-6
                           Buk 18
    [7.39   WBT p47-50]
    [10.13   FrT 1659-62]
    <11.3   ParsT 922>   + ST. AUGUSTINE
    <13.4-5   657>   + JEROME

II CORINTHIANS
    [1.12   Mel 1634(2824)]
    <3.2   PhysT 107-8>
    [3.6   SumT 1794]
    [4.17   Mel 1510(2700)]
    <6.10   Rom 6964>
    7.10   ParsT 725
    <8.9   WBT 1178-9>
    11.14   ParsT 895
    11.25-7   343
    <12.2   HF 981-2>

GALATIANS
    5.17   ParsT 342, 459
    5.19-21   867

EPHESIANS
    <1.4   T&C 1.1004-5>
    <2.3   ParsT 313>
    <2.14   642>
    ?<4.5-6   SecNT 201>
    4.28   Rom 6665
    5.4   ParsT 651
    5.5   748

EPHESIANS (cont.)
<5.18	PardT 483-4>
<5.23-33	ParsT 922-3>
5.25	[WBT p160-1]
	ParsT [922], 929 + I Corinthians
<5.25-31	MerchT 1384>
<5.32	1319>
	ParsT 918>

PHILIPPIANS
2.10	ParsT 598
3.18-9	[PardT 529-33]
	ParsT 819—20

COLOSSIANS
<2.14	ABC 59-61>
3.12	ParsT 1054
3.18	634

I THESSALONIANS
4.11-2	Rom 6661-5

II THESSALONIANS
<2.1-12	Rom 7009, 7155, 7191>

I TIMOTHY
1.4-7	ParsT p32-4
<2.4	75> + I Peter + Ezekiel
[2.9	WBT p342-5]
<4.4	Mel 1553(2743)> + ALBERTANUS
4.7	ParsT p32-4
<5.6	PardT 547-8>
[6.8	SumT 1881-2]
6.10	[Mel 1130(2320), 1840(3030)]
	PardT p334
6.10	ParsT 739

II TIMOTHY
<2.20-1	WBT p103-4>
2.24	ParsT 630
<3.16	Ret 1083>
4.4	ParsT p32 + I Timothy
<4.7-8	SecNT 386-91>

HEBREWS
<4.13	ParsT 1062>
[11.19	ABC 169] + Genesis
<13.5	PrT 669> + John

ST. JAMES
1.4	Mel 1517(2707)
1.5	1119(2309)
1.13	ClT 1153-4
1.14	ParsT 348
<1.22	SumT 1935-7>
<1.23-4	WomUnc 8-9>
2.13	Mel 1869(3059)
<2.17	SecNT p64>
<2.19	MLT 641>
	ParsT 599>

ST. JAMES (cont.)
     <5.12   PardT 633>
I PETER
     2.21-3   Mel 1502 (2692)-04(94)
     3.1-6   ParsT 930-2
     5.6   988
II PETER
     <2.4   MLT 361> + Jude + Revelation
                               + Nicodemus
     2.19   ParsT 142 + John
     <2.22   Rom 7286>
                   ParsT 138>
     <3.9   ParsT 75> + Timothy + Ezekiel
I JOHN
     1.8   ParsT 349
     3.15   565
     <3.20-1   ABC 20>
JUDE
     ?<6   MLT 361>   + II Peter
                                   + Revelation
                                   + Nicodemus

REVELATION = APOCALYPSE
     2.5   ParsT 136
     3.16   687
     [3.20   289]
     4.6   HF 1383-5
     6.8   Rom 7391-6
     <7.1-3   MLT 491-4>
     9.6   ParsT 216
     13   Rom 7009, 7155, 7191
     <14.1   WBT p105>
     14.3-4   PrT 579(1769)-85(75)
     17.4   ParsT 933
     ?18.16   933
     ?<20.1-2   MLT 361>   + II Peter   + Jude
                                      + Nicodemus
     <21.2   ParsT p51>
     21.8   ParsT 841, <867>
NICODEMUS
     <passim   MLT 361>   + II Peter   + Jude
                                     + Revelation

BIBLIS see BYBLIS.

BILYEA, the wife of Duillius the Roman general who won a naval
    victory against the Carthaginians in 260 B.C.; the story told
    here is, of course, from JEROME, Adv. Jov. 1.46.
        FranklT 1455

BISYNESSE, i.e. caution or carefulness, one of the personifications
    on the wall of the temple of Venus; Tes. 7.52.
        KnT 1928

BLACK in BD see JOHN OF GAUNT.

BLACK MONKS see BENEDICTINES.

[BLANCHE, Blanche of Lancaster, duchess of Lancaster and first wife
    of JOHN OF GAUNT, died in 1369. BD is taken to be a poetic
    record of her death and her husband's grief.
        BD 1318
    White
        BD ?780, ?905, ?942, 948, 955, 1318
    lady
        BD 77, 95, 101, 108, 117, 477, 482, 773, 858,
            948, 966, 1054, 1088, 1110, 1151, 1179, 1224,
            1228, 1267, 1268]

BOAR see ERYMANTHIAN BOAR.

<GIOVANNI BOCCACCIO, 1313–1375, the illustrious Florentine poet,
    never named or acknowledged by Chaucer. The dates of his
    various compositions, being disputed, are given in a generally
    accepted order of composition. Chaucer's failure to mention
    Boccaccio has occasioned a great deal of comment. See Hamm
    80–1, Louns 2.225–36, Cummings, CCS 149–55, Pratt, Pratt in
    S&A [KnT]. Boccaccio probably composed in the following order:
    Filocolo, Filostrato, Teseida, Ameto, Amorosa Visione,
    Fiammetta, Ninfale Fiesolano, Decameron, Corbaccio, Vita di
    Dante, De Montibus, Sylvis . . . , De Casibus Virorum Illustrium,
    De Claris Mulieribus, De Genealogiis Deorum.
    Filocolo
        1.4–7   T&C 1.274ff.
        1.5–6   1.232–52
        1.96–8   1.232–52
        1.120   5.561–81, 671–2
        1.124   5.551–2
        1.165–6   3.1192–3
        1.173   3.1436–42, 1464–70
        1.188   4.813ff.
        1.220   1.780–2
        1.238   2.542–50
        1.259–60   3.808
        1.266   4.327–9
        1.267–75   2.1093ff.
        1.297   LGW 1895   + Heroides   + Aen.
        2.165–6   T&C 3.1192–3
        2.175   3.797
        2.222   3.1464–70
        2.276   2.542–50
        2.376–8   5.1786
    Filostrato
        1.5, 6   T&C 1.21–3
        1.6   1.29–30, 31–56
        1.7–16   1.57–140

40

Filostrato (cont.)

1.17-25	1.148-213
1.26	1.267-73
1.27-32	1.281-329
1.32-7	1.351-92
1.38-51, 53-7	1.421-53
2.1	1.421-53
2.1, 16	3.234-8
?2.2	2.323-90
2.2-10	1.568-630
2.11, 13	1.666-75; 2.1095-9
2.12	1.680-6
2.13, 15	1.701-28
2.13	1.715-21; 3.337-43
2.16	1.676-9
2.16-7, 20-2	1.860-9
2.23	1.897-903
2.24, 25, 27, 28	1.967-1001
2.29-34	1.1009-64
2.32	3.694-7
2.35	2.265-6
2.36	2.274-82
2.37	2.225-6
2.37-45	2.293-308
2.43	2.344-50, 391-4, 554-88
2.46	2.316-22
2.47-8	2.407-20
2.48	2.355-7
2.49	2.113-9
2.52	2.447-8
2.54	2.391-4, 398-9
2.56	2.501-9
2.56-7	2.519-25
2.59	2.533-9
2.61	2.540-1
2.62-4	2.554-88
2.66	2.468
2.68, 69, 75,	
73-5, 75-8	2.757-84
2.68	2.596-603
2.69.1	2.743-9
2.69.2	2.750-6
2.70	2.733-5
2.71-8	2.645-65
2.73-5	2.750-6
2.79	2.937-8, 939
2.79.7-8	2.960-6
2.80-1, 89	2.967-81
2.82	2.615
2.83	3.470-4
2.84.5-8	3.477, 481-2
2.85.1-4	3.868-9

Filostrato (cont.)

2.90–1	2.995–1010
2.91	2.1023–9
2.93–5	2.1044–64
2.96–8	2.1071–94
2.96–107	3.127–47
2.98.4–6	3.475–6
2.101	3.136
2.102	3.475–6, 134–40
2.103	3.141–7
2.103.1–2	3.475–6
2.103–6, 100, 102, 107	2.1071–94
2.105	3.477
2.108–9	2.1100–6
?2.109	2.1120–4
2.109	2.316–36, 1208–11
2.109–13	2.1125–62
2.114	2.1173–6
2.117.3–8	3.465–7
2.118	2.1195–7, 1198–1200
2.119	2.1205–7
2.120–8	2.1212–6
2.121	2.480, 708, 945
2.121.1	3.477, 481–2
2.123, 125	2.722–8
2.125	2.719–21
2.128, 129, 130–43	2.1317–72
2.128	2.1305
2.129	2.1239
2.130, 133, 134	3.484–90
2.133	3.945
2.138	3.800
2.139	3.945
2.140–3	2.1492–1536
2.140	3.582–8
3.4	3.540–6; 4.947–50
3.5–10	3.239–87
3.9	3.330–2, 333–5
3.10.1	3.336
3.11–5	3.344–78
3.16–20	3.386–427
?3.17, 19, 20, 23	3.517–8
3.20	3.435–41
3.21	3.519–39, 568–81
3.23	3.698–700
3.24	3.547–53
3.25	3.601
3.27	3.666–93
3.29	3.955
3.30	3.1252
3.31–3	3.1310–23
3.32.7	3.1205, 1230–2

Filostrato (cont.)

3.32.8	3.1221
3.34-7	3.1338-65
3.38-9	3.1373-86
3.40	3.1009-71
3.40-1	3.1394-1414
3.42-3	3.1415-28
3.44	3.1443-9
3.44-8	3.1471-92
3.50-6	3.1513-55
3.56-60	3.1590-1624
3.61-5	3.1639-80
3.70	3.1695-1701
3.71, 72, 84, 72, 73	3.1709-43
3.74-9	3.701-4, 1-42
3.74-89	3.1254-74
3.83	3.129-35
3.90-3	3.1772-1806; 1.1079-85
3.94	4.1-10
4.1-11	4.29-119
4.12-6	4.127-68
4.17, 22, 23, 26-36	4.211-32
4.18-21	3.1092
4.27	4.239-41 + VIRGIL + DANTE
4.38-41	4.330-50
4.43	4.330-50, 356-7
4.44-6	4.365-85
4.47-8	4.393-406
4.49	4.414-7
4.52, 54, 56-8, 60-5,	
67, 68, 70-5	4.453-624
4.76	4.631-7
4.77-89, 92, 93,	
88-90	4.645-787
4.95-6	4.799-821
4.95	4.822-6
4.96-7	4.841-7, 813-21
4.98-107, 106	4.848-926
4.108	4.939-45
4.109-110	4.1107-71
4.119-27	4.1177-1253
4.121-2	4.1172-6
4.131, 133-4	4.1310-48
4.134-5	4.1359-65
4.137-40	4.1422-9
4.141-2	4.1464-75
4.142-6	4.1478-1537
4.146	4.1541-2
4.147-52, 154-60, 158	4.1555-1659
4.154-5, 159-61	4.1275-8
4.160, 161-3	4.1555-1659
4.164-7	4.1667-1701

Filostrato (cont.)

5.1-6, 9-13	5.15-91
5.12	5.120-3
5.14-21	5.190-231
5.21	5.232-45
5.22	5.124-6, 280-2, 283-7
5.22-3	5.288-97
5.25	5.172-3, 232-45
5.26-8	5.246-73
5.29-32	5.330-64
5.33-8, 40-62, 67,	
69, 68, 70, 71	5.389-693
6.1	5.94-5
6.1, 6	5.389-693
6.1-6	5.708-43
6.7	5.750-6
6.8, 10, 11	5.764-98
6.9	5.841-7
6.10-2, 14-25	5.92-175
6.12-25	5.855-945
6.26-7	5.953-7
6.32-8	5.1015
6.33	5.764-98, 804
7.1	5.1100-1
7.1-6, 18-33, 37, 40-1,	
43, 48, 49-52,	
53-9, 74	5.111-1365
7.24-7	5.1443-9
7.27	5.1513-9, 1247-53
7.60-72	5.1373-86
7.73, 75-7	5.1394-1439
7.77-8	2.1396-8
7.78	2.1541-3
7.80	1.1072-4
7.82	2.1541-3, 1396-8
7.83-5	2.1571-86, 1665-73
7.89ff.	5.1520-33
7.99	Gent 5-7
7.105	T&C 5.1394-1439
8.1-5	5.1562-89
8.5-26	5.1632-1764
8.9	1.31-56
8.27-9	5.1800-6
9-10	5.1040-1
9.3	A&A 20
Teseida	
1.1-3	A&A 1-21
1.1	T&C 3.1807-13
1.2	LGW 417ff.
1.3	HF 518
	T&C 3.1807-13

Teseida (cont.)

7.23-8	2371-2417	
7.27	T&C 5.295-322	
7.29-37	KnT 1971-2022	+ STATIUS
7.32	1982	
7.35	2002	
7.37	2017	
7.39-41	2423-35	
7.43	?T&C 3.720-1	
	KnT 2219-24	
7.43-9	2221-60	
7.45-9	2227-58	
7.50	1936-7	
7.53ff.	1918ff.	+ Aen.
7.51-60	PF 183-259	
7.55-7	KnT 1925-9	
7.61-2	PF 281-9	
7.63-6	260-76	
7.65	T&C 5.809-12	
7.66	5.207-10	
7.67	KnT 2438-41, 2445-6	
7.71-2	2275-83	
7.74-7	2290-9	+ STATIUS
7.78-81	2297-2313	
7.84-5	2317-25	
7.88-93	2331-65	
7.92	2340	+ Aen. + Meta. + DANTE
7.94	T&C 5.274-8	
7.96-100	KnT 2506-31	
7.99	2202-5	
7.106	1638-46	
7.108-10	1887-94	
7.113	2571-5	
7.114	2581-3	
7.119	1641-2	
8.81	T&C 2.197ff.	
8.124-6	KnT 2680-3	
9.1	T&C 5.1	
9.1-3	5.1807-27	
9.7-8	KnT 2686-91	
9.44	1329	+ Meta. + STATIUS + DANTE
9.48-9	2694-7	
?9.52-3	FranklT 865-7	
10.39	KnT 1329	+ Meta. + STATIUS + DANTE
10.55	2765-6	
10.88	T&C 3.1702-8	
10.89	5.295-322	
10.93-8	5.295-322	
10.96	4.300	

De Claris Mulieribus
    8   LGW 2654   + De Gen. Deor.
    22   MkT 2095(3285) + Hero. + Meta.
    86   LGW 580, 590, 594,
                           595, 650-62
    ?98   MkT 2247(3437)-74(64)
De Genealogiis Deorum
    2.22   LGW 2654
    3.6-9   T&C 4.22-4
    ?5.30   MancT 116
    5.48   A&A 5
    6.6   T&C 4.120-6   + SERVIUS   + OVID
    8.1   5.1527-33
                      LGW 510
    9.15, 19   T&C 5.1464-84
    9.21   T&C 5.1480-1
    10.48   LGW 2176-8, 2404   + "CEFFI"
    10.49   HF 416-20
                      LGW 2171-4
    11.25   HF 391
                      LGW 2423   + "CEFFI"
                                       + Ovide Moralisé
    11.26   1886, 1896-9
    11.29   2099, 2171-4
    11.30   HF 416-20
    13   T&C 3.1428
    13.1   3.1450-60;
                           5.1527-33
    13.23   HF 1573-9
RIME
    Sonnet 95   T&C 2.1-3>

BOETHIUS (Boece), Anicius Manlius Severinus Boethius, c. 480-524,
    consul in 510, magister officiorum 520-22; he was imprisoned
    on a charge of treason in 522 and executed in 524. While in
    prison he produced the Consolatione Philosophiae, one of the
    most important philosophical treatises for the Middle Ages.
    For its importance to Chaucer see Hamm 86-7, Louns 2.266-7,
    Skeat 2.xxviii-xxxvi, Jefferson, Patch, and Kottler; for its
    particular importance in T&C see Meech. Chaucer's real
    indebtedness will depend on editions of the French translation
    (see Lowes) and the edition of the medieval version (by Kottler).
        Rom [5409], 5661
        HF 972
        Bo 1.p4.78 gloss
           5.m4.20 gloss
        LGW 425(413)
        [KnT 1163]
        [MLT 480]
        NPT 3242(4432), 3294(4484)
        WBT 1168

```
          Ret 1088
          Adam 2
De Musica
     1.3                          <HF 765, 788>
                                  NPT 3294(4484)

Consolatione Philosophiae (Boece de Consolacione)
     general                      Ret 1087
     [1.p5.8-25                   Rom 5661
     2.p8                             5409
     3.m12.52-3                   KnT 1163-4
     4.m1.1-6                     HF 972-8
     4.p6                         MLT 480
                                  NPT 3242(4432)
     5                               "    "
     5.p1.12-21                   Rom 5659-61]
     <1.m1.15-6                   MerchT 1849
          .19-21                  T&C 4.503-4
          p1.12-9                 HF 1368-76
          .68                     Rom 682
          p2.19-20                T&C 1.730-1
          m3.4-8                      2.766-7
          .13-7                       2.767-9
          m4.10-2                 HF 535
          p4.2-3                  T&C 1.730-1
          .4-6                        1.857
     ?    .12-3                       1.837
          m5.1-4                  MLT 295-315
     ?    .8-10                   T&C 3.624
          .31-3                   FranklT 865-7
          .31-7                   KnT 1303-12
                                  ?MLT 813-6
          .31-43                  FranklT 879
          .43-52                  MLT 813-6
          .52-4                   FranklT 879
          p5.8-25                 Truth 17ff.
          .23-5                       17
     ?    .63-4                   HF 1545-8
     ?    m6.15-21                FranklT 1031
          m7.13ff.                Truth 20
     2.p1.10-4                    MkT 2446(3636)
          .14-20                  MerchT 2058, ?2062
          .16-20                  T&C 4.3-5
          .58                     MkT 2766(3956)
          .68-73                      2724(3914)
          .91-4                   Truth 15
          .95-100                 Fort 43-4
          p1.111-5                T&C 1.848-50
     ?    .111-3                      1.838-9
          m1.7-8                  Fort 1
          .7-16                   T&C 1.839-40
          .11-4                       4.6-7
          p2.1-14                 Fort 25
          .4-51                       57-63
```

<u>Consolatione</u> <u>Philosophiae</u> (cont.)

	.9–13	T&C 4.392–3		
	.12–4	4.392		
	.19–20	T&C 1.841		
	.19–23	Fort 29–31		
	.51–2	46		
	.51–4	MkT 2397(3587)		
	.51–7	KnT 926		
		Truth 8–9		
	.54–7	Fort 45–6		
	.58–63	MkT 2727(3917)–39(29)		
?	.60–1	KnT 1946		
	.70–2	MkT 1973(3163), 2761(3951)		
	.70–3	T&C 4.271–2		
	.72–3	Fort 29–31		
	.72–6	LGW 195		
	.74–6	WBT p170		
?	.81–3	T&C 1.851–4		
	.83–6	1.843–4		
	.84–5	4.392		
		NPT 3000(4190)		
	m2.	Rom 5706		
	p3.75–9	T&C 1.846–7		
	.87–8	Fort 71		
?	m3.1–3	T&C 5.278		
	.1–6	5.212		
?	.20–3	ParsT 471		
	p4.	T&C 4.836		
	.4–5	1.857–8		
	.5–9	3.1625–8	+ AQUINAS	+ DANTE
		?4.481–2		
	.7–9	Rom 4137–40		
	.54	Fort 38		
	.66–9	Truth 8–9		
	.75–7	T&C 3.816		
	.75–8	3.813–36		
	.96–101	5.763		
	.109–10	Fort 25–6		
	.109–13	T&C 4.446		
	.118–9	3.813		
		MkT 2347(3537)		
	.118–27	T&C 3.813–36		
?	.123–4	4.835		
	.134–8	1.891–3		
		4.1587		
		Fort 13–4		
	p4.135	Fort 13		
	.150–62	T&C 3.820–33		
		MkT 2139(3329)		
	.180–1	T&C 3.836		
	p5.15–6	Truth 3		
	.27–8	Sted 5		

Consolatione Philosophiae (cont.)

.75-7	Truth 2		
.122	KnT 1225-6		
.179-82	WBT 1191-4		
m5.	FormAge passim		
p6.20-7	Gent 5-7		
m6.8-23	MkT 2465(3655), 2479(3669)		
p7.61-3	WBT 1140		
.71-3	T&C 2.42		
p8.32-6	Fort 50		
.32-48	WBT 1203	+ Rom	
.36-41	Fort 34, 51		
m8.	Sted passim		
.4-26	T&C 3.1744-68		
.8-16	KnT 2991-3		
?3.m1.5-6	T&C 1.638		
	3.1219-20		
p2.	KnT 1251-67		
.8-11	T&C 3.1691-2		
	?5.763		
.19	KnT 1225-6		
.77-80	MerchT 2021		
.78	GP 336		
? .78-80	T&C 3.1691-2		
? .83-5	KnT 1266		
.86-7	1262-3		
m2.1-7	MancT 160-2		
.21-31	SqT 611		
	MancT 163		
.39-42	SqT 608		
p3.	Lady 43-5		
.33-6	PF 90-1		
p4.37ff.	Gent 5-7		
? .37-40	Sted 5		
.64-9	WBT 1140		
p5.24-30	KnT 2028-30		
.27-46	WBT 1187		
.66-70	MkT 2244(3434)		
.68-70	MerchT 1784, 1793		
p6.	Gent passim		
.32-51	WBT 1109-16		
	Gent 15ff.	+ RR	+ DANTE
m6.	19-20	+ DANTE	
.8-9	WBT 1109-16		
.10-4	1170		
p7.4-7	ParsT 472		
p8.44-6	BD 1057		
? m8.1-3	KnT 1266		
? p9.118-21	CYT 958		
m9.11-4	LGW 2228-30		
	?FranklT 877-80		
.19-20	PF 380		

Consolatione Philosophiae (cont.)

	p10.25–30	KnT 3005–10		
	m10.15–7	FormAge 30		
	.62ff.	T&C 1.960–1		
	.75–90	4.767–8		
?	.134–9	PF 380	+ ALANUS	
	p11.50–4	SumT 1968–9		
	.132–50	HF 730–46		
?	m11.9–11	T&C 4.200		
	.51ff.	Truth 17ff.		
	p12.156	HF 1920		
	.205–7	GP 741–2		
	.205–8	Sted 4–5		
	m12.36–8	T&C 5.212	+ Aen.	+ Meta.
	.38ff.	3.593		
	.40–2	1.786		
4.p1.		Truth 17ff.		
	.41–6	WBT p100		
	.64ff.	Truth 20		
	m1.	MLT 295–315		
		Truth 17ff.		
	.7–9	MLT 295–9		
?	.23–7	T&C 5.1809		
	p4.	Truth 17ff.		
	.186–8	PF 599		
	m5.8–9	SqT 258		
	p6.	HF 1526ff.		
		T&C 5.1541–7		
	.36–51	KnT 2994–9		
	.43–195	T&C 3.617–23		
	.51–6	Fort 65ff.		
?	.51–60	KnT 3003–4		
?	.57–60	T&C 1.1065–71		
	.60–3	Fort 66		
	.60–284	T&C 3.617–20		
	.82–6	1.1065–9		
	.87–97	3.617–20		
	.89–101	FrT 1483–91		
		?MerchT 1967–9		
?	.107–110	T&C 5.1541–4		
	.165–70	MLT 481–3		
?	.216–21	KnT 1251–4		
	.217ff.	T&C 2.527		
	.221–4	MLT 481–3		
	.281–4	FranklT 886		
	m6.	T&C 4.618		
		KnT 1163–8		
	m7.28–62	MkT 2095(3285)–2110(3300)		
5.p1.		Truth 17ff.		
	m1.18ff.	T&C 1.953–4		
	.18–23	3.617–20		
		Fort 65ff.		

Consolatione Philosophiae (cont.)
```
            p2.               Truth 17ff.
              .67-8           T&C 4.958-9
            p3.5-19           NPT 3243(4433)
              .7-10           T&C 4.960-6
              .8-12           NPT 3234(4424)
              .8-25           T&C 4.963-1078
              .10-2               4.974-80
              .12-7               4.981-7
              .17-9               4.988-94
              .22-6               4.995-1001
              .26-9               4.1002-8
              .28-99              4.963-1078
              .30-4               4.1009-15
              .35-9               4.1016-22
              .37-48          NPT 3243(4433)
              .39-41          T&C 4.1023-9
              .41-5               4.1030-6
              .45-51              4.1037-43
              .51-3               4.1094-50
              .53-8               4.1051-7
              .58-62              4.1058-64
              .62-5               4.1065-71
              .66-71              4.1072-8
            m4.               Truth 17ff.
              .1-23           T&C 3.1499
              .11-4               1.365
                              MerchT 1582
              .36-7               1582
            p4.35-49          NPT 3243(4433)
        ?     .64-6           ParsT 212
            m5.20-3           Truth 19
            p6.168ff.         T&C 2.622-3>


book:   the, our, a, thine own,
        Rom 6636              = Matthew
        BD 47, 48, 52, 57     = Meta.
        HF 426, 429           = Aen.
            712               = Meta.
        LGW 510(498)
            1022              = Aen.
            1721              = Fasti
        Mel 1144(2334), 1162(2352), 1164(2354), 1177(2367),
            1326(2516)
            1174(2364)        = CICERO
            1183(2373)        = PUBLILIUS SYRUS
            1328(2518)        = SENECA
            1330(2520)        = ALBERTANUS
        NPT 3064(4254)
        MerchT 2300           = I Kings
        SecNT 202             = Ephesians
```

ParsT 680	= Jeremiah
869	= Matthew
900	= I Samuel ?
918	= Ephesians
Ret 1083	= II Timothy ?

books: old books, as books tell, in books; cf. LOLLIUS.
    T&C 1.788

3.91, 1199	
.1773	= Filostrato
5.790, 1563, 1753	
.1478, 1481	= STATIUS
.799	= GUIDO

BOOK OF KINGS see BIBLE.

BOÖTES (Boetes), a constellation of the northern hemisphere of
    which the brightest star is ARCTURUS.
        Bo 4.m5.5, 7

BOREAS, or Aquilon, the north wind.
        Bo 1.m3.12; m5.24   = Boreas
           1.m6.11; 2.m3.15   = Aquilon

BOUNTY (Bountee), the personification of feminine generosity.
        Pity 38, 68, 72
        Lady 24

BRADWARDINE, Thomas, c. 1290–1349, doctor profundis, educated in
    Merton College, Oxford where he became a professor of divinity.
    He became Chancellor at St. Paul's in 1337 and archbishop of
    Canterbury in 1349. He was principally known for his De Causa
    Dei contra Pelagium.
        NPT 3242(4432)

BRISEIS (Breseyde, Brixseyde), the slave of Achilles who was
    surrendered by Agamemnon in place of his prize, Chryseis;
    thus, she was the cause of the wrath of Achilles. Hero. 3,
    20.69; Amores 1.9.33, 2.8.11.
        HF 398
        MLT 171

BROCK (Brok), actually a badger, but the name was applied to a
    gray horse.
        FrT 1543

BRUTUS (Brutes),
    (1) Marcus Junius, 78?–42 B.C., the husband of Portia, the
        daughter of Cato; although he joined the Pompeians he was
        pardoned by Caesar, made governor of Cisalpine Gaul in 46
        and praetor in 44. His complicity in the murder of Julius

Caesar resulted in his suicide; cf. Silverstein for Brutus
Cassius.
Bo 2.m7.19
LGW 1862
MkT 2697(3887) = Brutus Cassius!, 2706(3896)
FranklT 1449
(2) traditionally, the grandson of Aeneas, and the eponymous
founder of Britain.
Purse 22

BUKTON, either Robert or Peter. Robert Bukton (d. 1408) of Suffolk
was one of queen Anne's esquires (1391) and sat in parliament.
Peter Bukton (1350-1414) of Holderness in Yorkshire served in
John of Gaunt's army in 1369 and was in Richard's service in
1381. In 1386 he testified with Chaucer in the Scrope-Grosvenor
trial. From 1390-93 he was with the Earl of Derby in Prussia.
Peter Bukton is probably the recipient of Chaucer's poem.
Buk 1

WHITE BULL see TAURUS.

BUSIRIS, son of Neptune, brother of ANTAEUS, and king of Egypt who
sacrificed strangers to prevent drought. He was killed by
HERCULES who allowed himself to be led to the altar but broke
loose. Hoffman 188-9 suggests that the confusion with Diomedes's
horses is due to scholia on Ibis; cf. Skeat 5.232 and Shannon
312-7.
Bo 2.p6.66
MkT 2103(3293)

BYBLIS, daughter of Miletus and Cyanee, whose illicit passion for
her brother Caunus drove her insane after he rejected her
proffer of love; Meta. 9,450-665.
PF 289

BYGYNE see BEGUINE.

C

CACUS, the three-headed shepherd, son of Vulcan and Medusa, in the
Aventine forest. He stole the cattle of Geryon from HERCULES,
who traced Cacus to his cave, removed the giant boulder and
beat Cacus to a pulp; Aen. 8.207-8, 8.217, 233ff.; Livy 1.7;
Fasti 1.545ff.
Bo 4.m7.52, 54
MkT 2107(3297)

CADMUS (Cadme), the son of Agenor, the brother of Europa, and the
uncle of Minos. Cadmus founded Thebes: his companions were
killed by a dragon which Cadmus then killed and planted the

teeth from which sprang a race of giants who fought until only
five survived. Cadmus married HARMONIA, daughter of Mars and
Venus, and gave her the necklace of Vulcan; META. 3.1ff.
       KnT 1546, 1547

<CAECILIUS BALBUS, according to Webb ed. of Policraticus 1.p. 222.n1,
"auctore alias ignoto."
       Mel 1473(2663)>

CAESAR (Cesar).
       LGW 360(336)

CAESAR AUGUSTUS, i.e. Octavian, 63 B.C.-14 A.D., the first of the
Roman emperors; De Casibus 6.15 or De Claris 86.
       BD 368   = Octovyen
       LGW 592, 595, 663   = Cesar
           624   = Octovyan
       Astr 1.10.10   = Cesar Augustus
            .18   = Augustus Cesar

GAIUS CAESAR, i.e. Caligula (12-41 A.D.), emperor 37-41, the cruel,
prodigal, and insane son of Germanicus and Agrippina.
       Bo 1.p4.183

JULIUS CAESAR, 102?-44 B.C., the greatest of the Caesars, praetor
and pontifex maximus in 63, formed a triumvirate in 60, served
as proconsul in Gaul and Illyricum 58-49; he was victor in
the civil war 49-48 and assassinated in 44; JEHAN DE TUIM,
Hystore de Julius Cesar.
JULIUS
       HF 1502
       KnT 2031
       MLT 199, 400
       MkT 2673(3863), 2692(3882), 2695(3885), 2700(3890),
           2703(3893), 2711(3901)
CESAR
       MkT 2679(3869)
JULIUS CESAR
       Astr 1.10.9, 16

CAIN (Caym), the first-born of Adam and Eve, killed his brother
Abel and thereby became the first murderer; Genesis 4.1-16.
       ParsT 1015

CALCHAS (Calcas), the father of Criseyde. Homer's Calchas was the
most famous of the Greek soothsayers; the Trojan Calcas is due
to GUIDO, who substitutes him for Chryses.
       T&C 1.66, 71, 87, 92
            4.63, 64, 73, 134, 331, 333, 663, 761, [1368],
               [1381], 1466, [1471], [1478], [1509], [1629]
            5.149, [181], [190], 508, [694], 845, 846,

897, [904], [964], [1125], [1126], [1136],
[1284], 1575

CALLIOPE (Callyope, Caliope, Caliopee), the chief of the Muses;
occasionally in late authors the Muse of epic poetry. She was
also considered the mother of ORPHEUS; Meta. 5.338-661,
Purg. 1.7-12, Par. 23.97-111.
        HF [1399], 1400
        [Bo 3.m12.23]
        T&C 3.45

CALLISTO (Calistopee, Calyxte), the daughter of Lycaon and
companion of Diana, she bore Arcas to Jupiter. She was
transformed into a bear and almost shot by Arcas but Jupiter
translated them into stars; Meta. 2.381-530, Fasti 2.156,
Inf. 5.58-69, Tes. 7.61-2.
        PF 286
        KnT 2056

CALYPSO (Calipsa), the daughter of Atlas who kept Odysseus on
Ogygia for seven years; Odyssey 1, Ex Ponto 4.10.13, Ars Amat.
2.125-6. Shannon 90.
        HF 1272

CAMBALO (Cambalus), the younger son of Cambiuskan. The name is
unexplained.
        SqT 31, 656, 667

CAMBIUSKAN (Cambyuskan), probably Genghis Khan, 1162-1227, the
founder of the Mongol Empire.
        SqT 12, 28, 42, 58, 266, 345, 661

CAMBYSES (Cambises), the son of Cyrus, succeeded by Darius. He
became sole king in 529 B.C.; after successfully invading
Egypt in 525 he suffered reverses in Ethiopia whereupon he
committed suicide in 522; probably from SENECA, De Ira 3.14.
        SumT 2043

CANAAN, the son of Ham who was cursed to slavery by Noah, whose
nakedness he revealed; Genesis 9.26.
        ParsT 766

CANACE,
        (1) the daughter of Aeolus and sister of Macareus. Canace
            was impregnated and deserted by Macareus; she exposed the
            child to wild beasts and committed suicide; Hero. 11.
            LGW 265(219)
            MLT 178
        (2) the daughter of Cambiuskan. The name is unexplained.
            SqT 33, 144, 178, 247, 277, 361, 384, 410, 432,
                449, 475, 485, 631, 633, 635, 638, 651, 669

CANANEE, the Canaanite woman whose daughter was healed by Jesus; Matthew 15.22ff.
      SecNT p59

CANCER (Cancri, Cancro), the Crab, the fourth sign of the zodiac.
      Bo 1.m6.1, 4
      T&C 3.625
      MerchT 1887, 2224
      Astr 1.8.3; 17.3, 4, 6, 10, 11; 20.2
          2.6.17; 15.2; 16.3, 4, 7; 28.32, 36

CANDACE, the fictitious Indian queen who tried to win Alexander the Great; Wars of Alexander 5075ff., and see Wells [65].
      PF 288
      WomUnc 16

CANIUS (Canyus), Julius, the stoic condemned by Caligula. His death is described by SENECA in De Tranquillitate 14.
      Bo 1.p3.56; p4.182, 186

CANON (Chanoun), a clergyman attached to or enrolled in a cathedral chapter; canons lived according to rules but they were secular clergy.
      CYT p573, 685, 687, 700
          720

CANONS REGULAR (Chanouns Regulers), i.e. members of orders who followed the rules of their founder but lived less strictly than monks.
      Rom 6694

CANON'S YEOMAN (Chanons Yeman), the companion of the CANON.
      CYT p618, 627, 640, 652, 684, 686, 691, 692, 703

CAPANEUS (Cappaneus, Campaneus), one of the Argive chiefs, one of the seven against Thebes who mounted a scaling ladder and was struck dead by Jupiter's thunderbolt. Capaneus was the son of Hipponous by Astynome, daughter of Talaus and sister of ADRASTUS; Evadne was his wife. See Theb. 10.897-939, Tes. 2.28-34. A&A and T&C are probably due to Theb.
      A&A 59
      T&C 5.1504
      KnT 932

CAPRICORN, the tenth sign of the zodiac, see Wood 94-5.
      FranklT 1248
      Astr 1.8.4; 17.10, 46, 47, 49, 52; 21.91, 92
          2.1.23; 6.17; 15.2; 16.2, 5; 28.23, 26,
            38, 40; 40.3, 18, 22, 43, 47, 76

CARIBDIS see CHARYBDIS.

CARMELITES, the White Friars, one of the mendicant orders. There
was a curious story that Elias established a community of
hermits on Mt. Carmel which existed without break until the
Christian era. This Jewish Carmelite order consisted of sons
of the prophets and the Essenes who were present at St. Peter's
sermon on Pentecost and were converted and built a chapel to
the Blessed Virgin Mary: Historically the order was founded in
the middle of the 12th cent. by Berthold of Calabria and
received its rule from Albert of Vercelli, Patriarch of
Jerusalem, in 1210. They were recognized as mendicants by
Gregory IX in 1229 and had migrated to England by 1240.
See Knowles 1.196-9.
> Rom 7460
> [GP 210]

CARMES see CARMELITES.

CARPENTER, one of the five guildsmen among the pilgrims.
> GP 361

CASSANDRA (Cassandre), the daughter of Priam and HECUBA who became
Agamemnon's prize. The Cassandra of T&C is Chaucer's substitution for Filo. 7.86ff.; cf. Hero. 5.113ff., 16.127ff.
and BENOÎT 26113ff.
> BD 1246
> T&C 3.410
>> 5.[1450], 1451, 1456, 1534

CASSIODORUS (Cassidore, Cassidorus), Flavius Magnus Aurelius,
c. 480-575, served as advisor to Theoderic the Great and
magister officiorum in 526. In 540 Cassiodorus became a
Benedictine in one of the monasteries he founded in Calabria.
The Variae (540) and the Institutiones (543-55) are his
principal works; see Manitius 1.36-52. The use of the Variae
in Mel is due to RENAUD DE LOUENS; see S&A 560ff. The following
separation into Variae and Epistolae is not altogether convincing.
> Mel 1196(2386), 1348(2528), 1438(2628), 1527(2717),
>> 1564(2754), 1642(2832)

[Variae (MGH Auct. Ant. 12[1894])	
1.4	Mel 1438(2628), 1642(2832)
.17	1348(2538)
.30	1528(2718)
3.12	1642(2832)
9.13	1564(2754)
.22	1642(2832)
10.18	1196(2386)]
<Epistolae	
1.23	Bo 1.p4.93
3.29	1.p4.93
4.30	1.p4.101

<Epistolae (cont.)
    5.3 & 4   3.p4.23
     .40 & 41   1.p4.103
     .41   1.p4.115
    8.16   1.p4.115
     .28   1.p4.56>

CASSIUS see BRUTUS.

CASTOR and POLLUX, the Twins, the constellation Gemini.
    HF 1006

CATO (Catoun), either Marcus Portius, consul in 195 B.C., or Cato
    Uticensis (95-46 B.C.). The reference in Bo 4 is surely Cato
    Uticensis; Phars. 1.126.
        Bo 2.m7.19
           4.p6.234

CATO (Catoun), the supposed author of a collection of sayings
    probably begun in the second cent. and expanded on throughout
    the Middle Ages. The Disticha Catonis was an element in the
    very popular Liber Catonianus, one of the most important of
    mediaeval collections; see Hazelton, Hamm 87, Louns 2.358-61.
        MillT 3227
        Mel 1181(2371), 1216(2416), 1306(2496), 1489(2679),
            1594(2784), 1602(2792), [1605(2795)]
        NPT 2940(4130), 2971(4161), 2976(4166)
        MerchT 1377
        CYT p688
        [ParsT 661]
    Disticha Catonis
        [1.2   Mel 1594(2784)]
        < .3   T&C 3.292-4>   + ALBERTANUS
        < .12   MancT 325-8, 359>
        [.17   CYT p688-91]
          .38   <T&C 4.1584
                      FranklT 771-5>
                      [ParsT 661]
        [2.31   NPT 2940(4130)
         3.4   Mel 1181(2371)
          .14   1216(2416)
          .21   1605(2795)
          .23   MerchT 1377
         4.13   Mel 1306(2496)-07(97)
          .16   1602(2792)
          .39   1489(2679)]

CATULLUS, Gaius Valerius, c. 84-c. 54 B.C., the greatest of the
    Roman lyric poets. Shannon's suggestions, 364-70, are highly
    unlikely: Catullus was virtually unknown during the Middle
    Ages.
        Bo 3.p4.11

Carmina
[52
<64.58
.143-8
.188-248
.214

Bo 3.p4.11
LGW 2075
HF 269-85
LGW 1891-3
    2075>

CAYM see CAIN.

ST. CECILIA (Cecilie, Cecile), died c. 176, the patron saint of
   music and of the blind, commemorated 22 November. According
   to Fortunatus (bishop of Poitiers, d. 600) she perished in
   Sicily under Marcus Aurelius c. 176; traditionally she was
   martyred under Severus c. 230. Chaucer used the Legenda Aurea
   of JACOBUS DE VORAGINE; S&A 668-71.
        LGW 426 see LIFE OF ST. CECILE
        SecNT p28, 85, 92, 94, 99, 115
            120, 169, 176, 194, 196, 218, 222, 275, 284, 319,
            379, 382, 407, 412, 422, 450, 493, 550
        CYT p554

CEDASUS see SCEDASUS.

<FILIPPO "CEFFI," an early 14th cent. translator of Ovid's Heroides;
   see Meech PMLA 45.
       Epistole Eroiche (ed. Bernardoni, Milan, 1842)
           p.9   HF 388   + Hero. 2 + RR 13211-4
                    LGW 2404-6, 2424-5
           .10   2510-2, 2522-4   +   2.78; 2.43-4
           .11   2394-2400, 2446-51   +   2.75-6
                        2525-9   +   2.49-51
                        2536
                        2544-9   +   2.75-8
           .31   2096-2100, 2103ff.,
                            2176-8
           .45   T&C 1.659-65   +   5.151-2
           .63   LGW 1354-65   +   7.1-8
           .111   1670-7   +   12.11-2
           .132   2562-4, 2570-2, 2575
                            2656-60
           .133   2610-2   +   14.25-6
                        2613-7   +   14.27, 29-30
                      - 2682   +   14.35
           .134   2706-7   +   14.67-8>

CENOBIA, CENOBIE see ZENOBIA.

CENTAUROS (Centauris), probably a reference to Pholus, the centaur
   slain by HERCULES after the labor of the Erymanthian boar.
   Hercules also inadvertently killed CHIRON. The references are
   certainly not to NESSUS. See Shannon 312-7 and Hoffman 189-90;
   Meta. 9.191-2, Hero. 9.98-100.

Bo 4.m7.29
MkT 2099(3289)

CERBERUS, the three-headed watchdog of Hades, the son of Typhon
and Echidna. The Lernean hydra and Orthrus were also offspring
of Typhon and Echidna; Echidna was the mother by Orthrus of
the Theban sphinx and the Nemean lion; Meta. 7.404-24.
Bo 3.m12.31
4.m7.36
T&C 1.859
MkT 2102(3292)

CERES, identified with Demeter and probably representative of the
generative power of nature. The passage in T&C is not in Filo.;
but see Tes. 7.65.
PF 276
T&C 5.208

CESIPHUS see SISYPHUS.

CEYX (Ceys, Seys), the son of LUCIFER and husband of ALCYONE. Ceyx,
the ruler of Trachis, against the entreaties of Alcyone undertook a voyage to the oracle at Claros. Half-way in the journey
the ship sank in a storm and Ceyx drowned. Juno ordered
Morpheus to appear in the guise of Ceyx to Alcyone in order to
allay the shock of his death. The grief-stricken Alcyone went
to the shore from which Ceyx departed and was turned into a
bird; Meta. 11.410-748. See Wimsatt.
BD 63, 75, [91], [94], [111], [121], 142, 220,
229, 1327
MLT 157

CHARITY (Charite), an epithet for the GOD OF LOVE.
T&C 3.1254

CHARLEMAGNE (Charles), king of the Franks 768-814, the center of a
group of medieval romances, one of the Nine Worthies; see
Wells. The reference is indirect and represents general
familiarity with the Roland legend.
MkT 2387(3577)

CHARMS, the personification of idealized feminine attributes
depicted on the walls of the temple of Venus; not in Tes. 53.
KnT 1927

CHARYBDIS (Caribdis), the dangerous whirlpool opposite Scylla on
the straits of Messina; Aen. 3.420, 558 or Meta. 14.75.
Rom 4713
T&C 5.644

CHASTITY (Chastite), the personification of sexual continence.
Rom 3043, 3051, 3055, 3668, 3670, 3699, 3847

62

CHAUCER. [First person authorial intrusions and headings are not
    listed.]
      MLT i47

CHAUNTECLEER, the beast-hero of the tale whose "clear voice" almost
    leads to his downfall.
      NPT 2849(4039), 2875(4065), 2883(4073), 2886(4076),
         3185(4375), 3191(4381), 3219(4409), 3223(4413),
         3230(4420), 3269(4459), 3282(4472), 3322(4512),
         3331(4521), 3335(4525), 3339(4529), 3343(4533),
         3354(4544), 3361(4551), 3419(4609), 3448(4639)

"CHAUNTE-PLEURE", a proverbial song with the message that all joy
    ends in woe; Skeat 1.537.
      A&A 320

CHICHEVACHE, a proverbial cow which feeds on faithful wives;
    Skeat 5.351-2.
      ClT 1188

CHIRON, the centaur son of Saturn and Philyra, the wise and just
    tutor of Asclepius, Jason, and Achilles. He was inadvertently
    killed by HERCULES and translated into a constellation. The
    combination with Aeacus is probably due to Ars Amat. 1.17;
    cf. Meta. 2.630ff. and 6.126.
      HF 1206

CHORUS, in Bo the north-east wind (Caurus); Chorus as a sea-god
    is probably a confusion of Aen. 5.823-5. See Skeat 3.344,
    Clogan.
      Bo 1.m3.7
        4.m5.23
      LGW 2422

<CHRÉTIEN DE TROYES, fl. in the last half of the twelfth cent., the
    author of several sophisticated romances dealing mainly with
    Arthurian themes. He was patronized by Marie de Champagne and
    Philip of Flanders. His attributed "Muance de la hupe et de
    l'aronde et del rosignol" was incorporated in the Ovide Moralisé,
    ed. separately by De Boer as Philomena (Paris, 1909) and analyzed
    by Lowes PMLA 33.
    Érec et Énide
        61-2   MerchT 2315
    Ivain
        1492ff.   Rom 3205ff.
        4632ff.   2088ff.
    Cligés
        5180ff.   Rom 2421ff.
    Perceval
        3810ff.   Rom 2088ff.>

CHRIST see JESUS CHRIST.

CHRISTMAS, the date in the Christian calendar on which the birth
of Christ is celebrated.
   MLT 126
   PrT 1730
   FranklT 1255=Noel

ST. CHRISTOPHER (Cristopher), the patron of ferrymen, a legendary
saint who shields persons from hidden dangers, was probably
born in Syria, preached in Lycia, and was martyred in 250.
In Legenda Aurea, Christopher was a giant seeking a master who
was stronger; he was baptised and decided on charity by carrying
wayfarers across a river. He met his Master, of course, when
he carried the Christ child. His day is 25 July.
   GP 115

CHRYSIPPUS (Crisippus) of Soli in Cilicia, c. 280-204 B.C., the
philosopher who completed and systematized the stoic doctrine.
See JEROME, Adv. Jov. 1.48; Hamilton, p. 109n., suggests
   CICERO, De Divinatione.
   WBT p677

CIBELLA see CYBELA.

CICERO, Marcus Tullius, 106-43 B.C., the famous Roman orator,
philosopher, and statesman. He was known to the Middle Ages
mainly in bits and pieces; his works were important mainly for
their style and the De Re Publica exerted special influence
because it contained the Somnium Scipionis (Book 6); Lowes,
Robertson.
Tullius
   Rom 4882, 5286
   PF 31
   Mel 1165(2355), [1174(2364)], 1176(2366), 1180
      (2370), 1192(2382), 1201(2391), 1339(2529)
      see SENECA, 1344(2534), 1347(2547), 1355(2545),
      1359(2549), 1360(2550), 1381(2571), 1387(2577),
      1390(2580), 1393(2583), 1585(2775), 1621(2811),
      1860(3050)
Marcus Tullius
   Bo 2.p7.59
      5.p4.3
Marcus Tullius Scithero
   FranklT p722
<De Inventione (before 81)
      2.53   T&C 5.745-9>   + AQUINAS   + DANTE
<De Oratore (55)
      2.69   WBT p757>   + MAP   + Gesta
                                                      Romanorum
De Re Publica (55)
      6   *HF 31
      [6   Bo 2.p7.59]

De Re Publica (55) (cont.)
　　　　<6   T&C 5.1807-27
　　　　.18   5.1812
　　　　.19-20   5.1814ff.>
De Divinatione (44)
　　　　2.60   *Bo 5.p4.3
　　　　<1.13.23   T&C 2.1347, 1349?
　　　　2.21.48
　　　　.59.121   >
<Disputationes Tusculanae (45-44)
　　　　2.18   Bo 4.p7.86
　　　　.22   1.p3.54
　　　　3.30.73   Mel 1174(2364)
　　　　5.21.6   Bo 3.p5.23>
<De Natura Deorum (45-44)
　　　　2.20.53   Bo 1.m5.13
　　　　3.82   1.p3.54>
[De Senectute (45-44)
　　　　6.17   Mel 1165(2355)]
De Amicitia or Laelius (45-44)
　　　　<general   Scog 47
　　　　5 & 6   Rom 5201
　　　　6   5281>
　　　　[12, 13, 17   5286]
　　　　<13, 17   5201
　　　　14   5311ff.
　　　　25.91   Mel 1176(2366)>
De Officiis (45-44)
　　　　<1.16   WBT p333-6>   + Ars Amat.
　　　　[1.21.73   Mel 1344(2534)
　　　　.25.88   1860(3050)-61(51)
　　　　.26.91   1180(2370)
　　　　2.5   1355(2545), 1359(2549), 1360
　　　　 (2550), 1381(2571), 1387(2577),
　　　　 1390(2580), 1393(2583)
　　　　2.5.18   1201(2391)
　　　　.7.25   1192(2382)
　　　　2.15.55   1621(2811)
　　　　3.5.21   1585(2775)-88(78)]
　　　　<3.99   Bo 2.p6.69>
<Epistola 6 ad Caecinum
　　　　general   Scog 47>

CILENIOS see MERCURY.

CIPIOUS see SCIPIO.

CIPRIDE see VENUS.

CIRCE, daughter of Helios and sister of Aeetes, the enchantress who
　　held Odysseus for a year; Meta. 14.8-74, 241-357 and RR 14404-6.

HF 1272
Bo 4.m3.4, 32, 36, 44
KnT 1944

CISTERCIANS, the Grey or White Monks; in 1098 St. Robert took a
    group of monks to Citeaux (built by Odo of Burgundy) where
    they tried to reproduce exactly the rule of St. Benedict,
    notably the return to manual labor. They particularly practiced
    farm labor and, in England, the wool trade.
        Rom 6695

ST. CLARE, St. Clara, 1194–1253, born in Assisi and devoted to
    St. Francis, she received the habit in 1212 and later became
    the abbess at St. Damians. There was a convent of the
    Minoresses of St. Clare in Aldgate whose sisters were vowed
    to silence. See Neville.
        HF 1066

CLAUDIANUS (Claudian), Claudius, an oriental Greek raised in
    Alexandria. He was in Rome 395–404 and probably died in 408.
    He was a famous stylist and panegyrist; the In Rufinum and
    Laus Serenae are early productions and the De Raptu dates from
    c. 395–7: Raby 1.88–98. Pratt contends that Claudian was
    known to Chaucer through the Liber Catonianus and that Chaucer
    did not know the In Rufinum; cf. Hazelton, and Hall. In De
    Raptu ?= Pratt's ascriptions.
        HF 449, 1509
        LGW (280)
        MerchT 2232
    <In Rufinum
        1.365   T&C 5.1020>   + PLINY
    De Raptu Proserpinae (?= Pratt)
        [1.4–6   HF 1.507–12]
        <?1.1–116   BD 170–1
        ?   HF 1511–2
        ?   KnT 2082, 2299
        ?   FranklT 1073–5
        ? .85–6   T&C 1.859
        ? .101–2   5.1020
        ? .142–78   HF 1507–12
          .225   T&C 1.9   + BOETHIUS
                                                    + DANTE
        ? .226   1.6–9
        ?   4.22–4
        ?   SqT 448, 550
          .282   HF 71–2
         2.107ff   PF 176–82
        ? .156–372   BD 170–1
        ? .162   HF 1507–12
        ? .219   T&C 1.6–9
        ?   4.22–4
        ?   SqT 448, 550

De Raptu Proserpinae (cont.)
```
    ? .284, 323        T&C 4.790
    ? .314-6                3.1600
    ? .330-50          HF 445-50
    ? .332             T&C 4.116-8
    ? .335, 337             5.211-2
    ? .336-7           BD 709
    ? .337             T&C 3.592-3
    ?3.80-90, 231-47   BD 170-1
    ?                  HF 1511-2
    ?                  KnT 2082, 2299
    ?                  FranklT 1073-5
    ? .390-1           T&C 3.1600
    ? .399             HF 1507-12
      .433             T&C 3.1807-10>     + Aen.    + Meta.
                                          + Tes.    + DANTE
    <Laus Serenae (ed. Birt, MGH, A.A., 10):  Pratt
       11-30, 140-59   LGW p(267-80)>
```

CLAUDIUS, Marcus Aurelius Gothicus, emperor 268-70, who won the
    name Gothicus after his victory over the Goths at Naissus in
    269; De Clar. Mulier. 98.
       MkT 2335(3525)

CLAUDIUS, the "false cherl" who assisted Appius in his designs on
    Virginia; see S&A.
       PhysT 153, [164], 179, [191], [198], 269

CLEMENCY (Clemence), one of the personifications which takes the
    place of the gods in dispensing mercy; Tes. 2.17 from Theb.
    12.482.
       KnT 928

CLEO see CLIO.

CLEOPATRA (Cleopatre, Cleopataras), Cleopatra VII, 68-30 B.C.,
    successor of Ptolemy Auletes to the throne of Egypt. After
    being expelled by Pothinus she was restored in 47 by Julius
    Caesar by whom she had a son, Caesarion. Her interest in
    Caesar was followed by her intrigue with Mark Antony; she
    committed suicide after his defeat by Octavian in 30. PF is
    a combination of Tes. 7.61-2 and Inf. 5.58-69; for LGW Chaucer
    probably used De Clar. Mulier. 86 and De Casibus 6.15.
       PF 291
       LGW 259(213), 566(542), 582, 601, 604, [607],
          [653], 669

CLERE LAUDE, the name given for one of Aeolus's trumpets; Louns
    2.382 cites ALBRICUS.
       HF 1575

CLERK, one of the pilgrims, a student at Oxford.
        GP 285, 840
        ClT p1, 21
            1212a

clerk or clerks: old, wise, great, certain, another, etc.
        Rom 378, 2839, 5660, 7146
        BD 53
        HF 53, 152, 175, 413
        PF 333
        T&C 1.644, 961, 1002   [T&C cf. LOLLIUS]
            3.292=CATO, 814, 852, 1199, 1691
            4.968, 972, 980, 1397
            5.1854
        LGW (278), 370
        KnT 1163=BOETHIUS
        MLT 480?=BOETHIUS
        Mel 1143(2333), 1395(2585)
        MkT 2121(3311), 2127(3317)   = OVID and BOCCACCIO
        NPT p2800(3990)   = <u>Ecclesiasticus</u>
            3235(4425)   = BOETHIUS, AUGUSTINE,
                                          BRADWARDINE
        WBT p44c, 125, 694
            1184
        ClT 933, 935
        MerchT 1293, 1362, 1427, 1972, 2021   = EPICURUS?
        FranklT 774, 885, 890, 1119
        CYT p646
        MancT 154, 314=<u>Proverbs</u>, 326=CATO?
        ParsT p57
                372
        Mars 275
        Astr 30, 85

CLIO (Cleo), the muse of history; <u>Theb.</u> 1.41.
        T&C 2.8 [9]

CLYTEMNESTRA (Clitermystra), daughter of Tyndareus and Leda, wife
    of AGAMEMNON and mother of Iphigenia, Orestes, and Electra.
    During Agamemnon's absence at the Trojan war Aegisthus had
    become her paramour. She welcomed Agamemnon with a show of
    welcome, and then, with Aegisthus, murdered him and CASSANDRA.
    Clytemnestra and her lover were later killed by Orestes and
    Electra. She is mentioned in <u>Adv. Jov.</u> 1.48.
        WBT p737

DE <u>COITU</u> <u>see</u> CONSTANTINUS AFRICANUS.

COLLATINUS (Colatyn), Lucius Tarquinius, was the cousin of
    Tarquinius Sextus. The name is derived either from LIVY 1.57
    or <u>De Civ. Dei</u> 1.19, 2.17; <u>Skeat</u> 3.331 and <u>Shannon</u> 220-8.
        LGW 1705, 1713, 1714, 1740, 1778

COLLE, in NPT the name applied to the widow's dog. Colle tregetour
   has not been satisfactorily explained; Skeat 3.273.
      HF 1277
      NPT 3383(4573)

COMPANY (Compaignye), one of the golden arrows in the quiver of
   the God of Love.
      Rom 958, 1862

CONIGASTUS (Conigaste). His reputation is due solely to the
   authority of Boethius although he is mentioned by CASSIODORUS.
      Bo 1.p4.56

CONQUEST, Chaucer's addition to the temple of Mars; Robin cites
   Bo 3.p5.
      KnT 2028

CONSOLATIO PHILOSOPHIAE see BOETHIUS.

CONSTANCE (Custance), the heroine of the tale based on TRIVET
   exemplifies the virtue of constancy; S&A.
      MLT 151, 184, 208, 226, 241, 245, 249, 264, 274,
           278, 319, 431, 438, 446, 536, 556, 566, 570,
           576, 583, 597, 601, 608, 612, 631, 651, 679,
           682, 684, 689, 693, 719, 797, 803, 817, 822,
           900, 906, 908, 912, 924, 945, 953, 970, 978,
           986, 1008, 1009, 1030, 1033, 1047, 1105, 1107,
           1125, 1129, 1141, 1145, 1147

CONSTANTINUS AFRICANUS (Constantyn), 1015-1087, a monk of Monte
   Cassino, one of the fathers of western medicine. An African
   by birth, when he came to the west he brought Arabic medical
   books which he translated into Latin. The date of the De Coitu
   is uncertain. See Thorndike 1.742-59, Bassan, and Delany.
      GP 433
      MerchT 1810
   De Coitu
      general   MerchT 1811

CONSTRAINT (Constreynaunce), the personification of enforced
   restraint.
      Rom 7436

COOK, one of the pilgrims who rivaled the Pardoner in vulgarity
   and the Miller in drunkenness.
      GP 379
      CkT p4325
         p4336 (Hogge), 4345, 4353, 4356   = Roger
      MancT p15, 20, 26, 46, 85, 88, 92

CORDYLERES see FRANCISCANS.

CORINNA (Corynne). The reference is disputed. Robin accepts
    Corinna the sixth cent. Theban poetess who was a contemporary
    of Pindar; cf. Louns 2.403-4, Shannon 15-28.
        A&A 21

[CORONIS OF LARISSA, the beautiful daughter of Phlegyas who was
    slain by Apollo because she was unfaithful; Apollo however
    saved their son ASCLEPIUS who learned medicine from the centaur
    CHIRON; Meta. 2.542-632.
        MancT 139]

CORPUS IURIS CIVILIS see JUSTINIAN.

COUPE-GORGE see CUT THROAT.

COURTESY (Curtesie, Curtesye), the personification of courtly
    demeanor.
        Rom 796, 807, 1251, 1802, 2985, 3890, 5853
        PF 219
        LGW 163
        Pity 68

COVETOUSNESS (Coveityse, Coveitise), depicted on the wall outside
    the garden of Mirth.
        Rom 181, 205, 208

CRAFT, one of the companions of Cupid; cf. Tes. 7.55.
        PF 220

CRASSUS, Marcus Licinius Crassus, c. 115-53 B.C., the triumvir
    put to death by Orodes (he was forced to swallow molten gold);
    Purg. 20.116-7, De Casibus 6 & 7. See Shannon 133-4.
        T&C 3.1391

CREON, the son of Menoeceus and brother of Jocasta. After the
    expulsion of Oedipus he served as regent for Polyneices and
    Eteocles but finally usurped all authority. After the civil
    war he refused burial to Polyneices. He was killed by THESEUS.
    See Hero. 12.53-4, Theb. 11, Roman de Thébes, and Tes. 2.12.
        A&A 64
        LGW 1661
        KnT 938, 961, 963, 986, 1002

CREUSA,
    (1) a daughter of Priam, wife of AENEAS and mother of Ascanius;
        Aen. 2.738.
        HF 175, 183
        LGW 945
    (2) the daughter of Creon; Meta. 7.391-6.
        [LGW 1661]

CRISEYDE, the heroine of T&C, the daughter of Calchas; for detailed
characterization see Meech.

 T&C 1.55, 99, 169, 176, 273, 392, 459, 874, 1010
  2.386, 449, 598, 649, 689, 877, 884, 897,
   1100, 1235, 1265, 1417, 1424, 1453, 1550,
   1562, 1590, 1603, 1606, 1644, 1678, 1724
  3.68, 85, 95, 193, 507, 638, 760, 799, 883,
   925, 981, 1054, 1068, 1070, 1112, 1126,
   1173, 1198, 1209, 1226, 1238, 1275, 1350,
   1372, 1420, 1448, 1473, 1492, 1498, 1548,
   1564, 1670, 1715, 1733, 1740, 1820
  4.15, 138, 149, 177, 195, 207, 212, 231,
   264, 273, 281, 292, 307, 310, 316, 347,
   378, 457, 472, 479, 611, [663], 666, 682,
   731, 766, 807, 810, 825, 829, 855, 868,
   875, 939, 962, 1082, 1090, 1147, 1165,
   1194, 1209, 1214, 1229, 1252, 1317, 1436,
   1527, 1655
  5.5, 16, 53, 57, 176, [192], 216, 228, 452,
   [465], [467], 504, 508, 516, 523, 528, 595,
   604, 687, 735, 775, 806, 843, 848, 864,
   872, 934, 948, 1021, 1031, 1113, 1123, 1143,
   1187, 1241, 1247, 1252, 1254, 1260, 1264,
   1315, 1404, 1422, 1437, 1573, 1587, 1661,
   1674, 1683, 1712, 1720, 1732, 1746, 1774,
   1833
 LGW 332(265), (344), 441(431), 469(459)
 WomUnc 16

CRISIPPUS see CHRYSIPPUS.

CROESUS (Cresus), the last king of Lydia, 560-546 B.C., who subdued
the Greek cities of Aeolia and Ionia (except Miletus); he
invaded Persia and was defeated by Cyrus but his life was
spared. His wealth was proverbial. See RR 6489ff. and Bo 2.p2;
cf. Wimsatt.

 HF 105
 Bo 2.p2.58, 60
 KnT 1946
 MkT 2727(3917), 2728(3918), 2759(3949)
 NPT 3138(4328)

CRUELTY (Crueltee), the personified opponent of Pity in Love.
 Pity 11, 26, 52, 64, 80, 90, 114

CUPID see GOD OF LOVE.

CUSTANCE see CONSTANCE.

ST. CUTHBERT (Cutberd), bishop of Lindisfarne, d. 686. Among the
miracles associated with the saint is one in which he is

rewarded for hospitality to angels. See Cline; cf. Bede, esp. 4.28-31.
    RvT 4127

CUT-THROAT (Coupe-Gorge), the razor which False Semblance bore in his sleeve when he was disguised as a friar.
    Rom 7420

CYBELA (Cibella), i.e. Ceres, the power of nature; FROISSART's Dittié 105ff. Cf. Meta. 10.565ff.and perhaps Theb. 6.563; see Clogan.
    LGW 531(519)

CYNTHIA see DIANA.

CYPRIAN, one of the enemies of Boethius because Boethius defended Albinus. Cyprian is mentioned by CASSIODORUS Epist. 5.40, 41; cf. Robin 799n.103.
    Bo 1.p4.103

CYPRIDE see VENUS.

CYPRIS see VENUS.

CYRUS (Cirus), Cyrus the Great, founder of the Persian empire. He overthrew Croesus in 547 then conquered Asia Minor and subdued the Babylonians; he died in 529. Chaucer probably used Bo but may have gotten details from Spec. Hist. 3.17 and De Ira 3.21.
    Bo 2.p2.59, 61
    MkT 2728(3918)
    SumT 2079

CYTHERUS (Atiteris), a name of doubtful identity; Skeat 3.269.
    HF 1227

D

DAEDALUS (Dedalus), the legendary Athenian craftsman who fled to Crete and there constructed the labyrinth for MINOS. Because he had given THESEUS the clue to the maze, Daedalus and his son Icarus were also confined to the maze. In their attempt to escape on wings of wax and feathers Icarus fell into the sea and drowned. Daedalus escaped to Sicily, where Minos pursuing him met with a violent death. See Meta. 8.183ff. although no specific source need be assumed; for LGW see Meech.
    BD 570
    HF 919, 1920
    Bo 3.p12.156
    [LGW 2010, 2021, 2026, 2141, 2150]

DALIDA see DELILA.

DAMASCIEN see ST. JOHN OF DAMASCUS.

DAMASUS I (St. Damasie), pope 366-384, protected and esteemed
    ST. JEROME and entrusted to him the preparation of the Vulgate.
    Damasus also showed great zeal in discovering and embellishing
    the tombs of the martyrs in Rome.
        ParsT 788

DAMIAN (Damyan), Chaucer's invention, January's squire and May's
    lover.
        MerchT 1772, 1789, 1866, 1869, 1875, 1898, 1900,
               1923, 1933, 1936, 1979, 2002, 2009, 2019,
               2093, 2097, 2120, 2150, 2152, 2207, 2210,
               2326, 2352, 2361, 2394

DANAS = DANAUS (Danao) and his brother AEGYPTUS were descendants
    of Io. The brothers quarreled and Danaus and his fifty
    daughters fled to Argos where Danaus became king. The fifty
    sons of Aegyptus pursued Danaus's daughters and forced Danaus
    to consent to the marriages. He consented by ordering his
    daughters to stab their husbands on the wedding night. All did
    except HYPERMNESTRA who spared her husband LYNCEUS; Hero. 14,
    De Gen. Deor. 2.22, "CEFFI" p. 133.
        LGW 2563, 2568, 2600

DANGER (Daunger), the personification of feminine restraint.
        Rom 3018, 3130, 3188, 3250, 3352, 3362, 3371,
            3388, 3393, 3395, 3437, 3475, 3503, 3509,
            3549, 3583, 3585, 3602, 3607, 3619, 3983,
            3999, 4040, 4043, 4091, 4101, 4207, 4482,
            5866
        PF 136
        T&C 2.1376
        LGW 160
        MercB 16, 26

DANIEL (Danyel), a prophet and hero in the Old Testament, the
    central figure in the book of Daniel. He is particularly
    famous for his escape from the lions' den and his interpreta-
    tions of the dreams of NEBUCHADNEZZAR. The account of Daniel
    in MLT is not in TRIVET.
        MLT 473
        MkT 2154(3344), 2166(3356), 2209(3399)
        NPT 3128(4318)
        ParsT 126

DANTE (Dant, Daunte), Alighieri, 1265-1321, the most famous of
    Italian poets. Dante lived in Florence until his exile in
    1302; the remainder of his life was spent in Ravenna. The
    Divina Commedia opens in 1300 although it was composed later;
    the Convivio dates 1304-8. See Hamm 81-2, Louns 2.236-48,
    Lowes, Schless, CCS 145-9.

```
        HF 450
        LGW 360(336)
        MkT 2461(3651)
        WBT [1125], 1126, 1127
        FrT 1520
    [Divina Commedia
        Inferno
            33                      MkT 2407(3597)
        Purgatorio
            7.121ff.                WBT 1126]
    <Divina Commedia
        Inferno
            1.64                    HF 482
            1.83                    PF 109
            2.1                        85
             .7-9                   HF 521
           ? .49                       600ff.
           ? .122                      557
             .127-32                T&C 2.967-71        + Filo.
            3.1                     PF 127
             .10-1                  HF 14-5
             .19                    PF 169
           ? .53-4                  HF 1926
             .55-7                     2034-40
                                    LGW 285
             .112                   T&C 4.225-7
             .127-9                 PF 155-6
            ?4                      T&C 4.788ff.
             .88ff.                 HF 1460
            5.4-6                   T&C 4.1187-8        + Aen.
           ? .28-33                 HF 1803
             .31-6                  PF 80
             .56                    MkT 2477(3667)
             .58-60                 MLT 358-9
             .58-69                 PF 283ff.
             .100                   T&C 3.5
             .121ff.                Rom 4137-40        not in RR
            6.12                    ABC 54-6
            7.67ff.                 KnT 1251ff.
             .73ff.                    1663ff.
             .78-80                 T&C 3.617-23
             .78-82                    5.1541-5
             .106                      4.1538-40
             .127                   ?HF 1654
                                    ABC 54-6
            9.37-51                 T&C 1.9
                                       4.22-4
            9.43ff.                 T&C 4.470-6
             .44                    HF 1511-2
           ? .64-70                 KnT 1979-80
            11.5                    HF 1654
                                    ABC 54-6
```

<<u>Divina Commedia</u> (cont.)
    <u>Inferno</u> (cont.)
        12.22   T&C 4.239
        13.31–4   KnT 2340   + <u>Aen</u>. + <u>Meta</u>.
                                        + <u>Tes</u>.
       ? .64   LGW 358
       14.8, 13   HF 482
     ?15.112   T&C 1.15
      16.1   HF 1521
        .3   1526ff.
     17.109–14   919
     18.85, 91ff.   LGW 1371–2
       .85ff.   1603–6
     20.126   T&C 1.1024
     30.1–2   5.599–601
      .1–12   4.1538–40
      .1–2, 22–3   KnT 1329   + <u>Meta</u>.   + <u>Theb</u>.
                                      + <u>Tes</u>.
     31.4–6   T&C 4.927
                   ?SqT 156, 236
     33.121ff.   ?LGW 2066ff.
                   MLT 784
    ?34.48   SumT 1688
    <u>Purgatorio</u>
        1.1–3   T&C 2.1–4
       .7–9   3.45
       .19   3.1257
       .20   KnT 1494
      ? .43   LGW 926
      ? .78ff.   249ff.
      2.17–24   HF 500ff.
       .26ff.   LGW (141ff.)
       .34, 37–9   232ff.
      7.121–3   Gent 15ff.   + Bo + <u>RR</u> + <u>Convivio</u>
      9.1–3   T&C 3.1464–70
       .13–5   2.64–71
       .19–20   HF 499ff.
      ? .28–30   534
     ?10.57   PF 518
     ?11.6   T&C 3.11
      12.20   A&A 211
      17.37   HF 458
       .91–3   T&C 1.976
       .94ff.   1.894–5
      18.19   1.976
      18.28   HF 742
       .34ff.   T&C 1.894–5
      19.4–6   3.1419–20
     20.106–8   3.1387–93   not in <u>Filo</u>.
       .116–7   "
      21.25   5.3
       .89   PF 1460

<<u>Divina Commedia</u> (cont.)
   <u>Purgatorio</u> (cont.)
      ?22.64-9   LGW 924-7
       25.79   T&C 5.3
       27.95   3.1255
       28.9-15   PF 201-3
       29.40   T&C 3.1809-10
         .108   2.925
         .132   5.745-9   + CICERO + AQUINAS
   <u>Paradiso</u>
       1.1   HF 81
        .8-9   A&A 8-14
     ? .11   HF 520ff.
        .13-27   1091-1109
        .20   1229
        .20-1   T&C 4.776
        .31, 36   A&A 15-20
        .61-3   HF 504-6
       2.49   T&C 1.1024
       4.10-2   PF 155-6
        .37ff.   HF 1068ff.
       8.1-3   T&C 3.1-2
        .7-8   3.1807-10
        .12   3.3
        .131-2   4.25
      10.128   4.623
      14.28-30   5.1863-5
      15.148   4.623
      18.21   5.817
        .87   HF 520ff.
      19.8   T&C 3.1693
      22.19   HF 925
        .93   T&C 2.908
        .128   HF 888
        .151   T&C 5.1807-27
      23.55-9   A&A 15-20
        .97-111   HF 1395-1405
     ?32.133-5   MLT 641
                        SecNT p64-70
      33.1-21   p36-51
        .14   T&C 3.1262-7
        .16   3.39-42
                        ?PrT 1664

<<u>Convivio</u>
       1.3   HF 2060
        .5   T&C 2.22-5
       2.4   3.617-23
        .5, 8, 9   Mars 164ff.
        .14   T&C 2.22-5
       3.81ff.   LGW 166
       Canzone
         34-7   WBT 1152-8
         112-6   1162-3

<Convivio (cont.)

4.3.45, 50, 54	Gent 15ff.	+ RR
4.3.101-4	5-7	+ Bo
.112-9	19-20	"
.7	WBT 1152-8	
.13.101-10	1191-4	
.13, 14	Gent 15ff.	+ Bo + RR + Purg.
.14.5	"	
? .15.19-38	WBT 1133-8	
.20	T&C 3.5	
.24-8,		
47-53	WBT 1162-3	
.47-57	Gent 19-20	+ Bo
.22	T&C 3.1691-2	
.27	5.745-9	+ CICERO + AQUINAS
.28	LGW 249ff.>	

DAPHNE (Dane), a nymph, the daughter of Peneus. She was loved and
pursued by APOLLO; at her own entreaty she was changed into a
bay-tree in order to avoid his embrace. Thus, the tree became
sacred to the god. See Meta. 1.452-567 and Smith for the
suggestion that her association with Diana and the OF form of
her name are due to FROISSART.
 T&C 3.726
 KnT 2062, 2064

DARES PHRYGIUS (Dares Frygius, Dares), a priest of Haphaestos in
Troy who supposedly survived the Trojan war and wrote an
account of it; a fifth cent. A.D. translation, De Excidio
Troiae Historia, was foisted on Cornelius Nepos. The material
in Dares and DICTYS which dealt particularly with Troilus and
Criseyde was incorporated in the works of BENOÎT, GUIDO, and
JOSEPH OF EXETER and hence came to Chaucer through BOCCACCIO.
See Griffin and Frazer.
 BD 1070
 HF 1467
 T&C 1.146
  5.1771
?De Excidio Troiae Historia

[general	T&C 1.146; 5.1771]
<24	NPT 3141(4331)ff. >
[34	BD 1069-70]

DARIUS (Daryus),
 (1) the Mede, not known in profane history, is modeled on
  DARIUS the Great, the successor of CAMBYSES; Daniel.
  MkT 2237(3427), 2648(3838)
 (2) Darius III, mentioned in connection with APELLES, was
  overthrown by Alexander the Great and murdered by Bessus
  in 330; GUALTIER.
  WBT p498

daughter of the king Creon see CREUSA.

DAUN BURNEL THE ASSE see NIGELLUS WIREKER.

DAVID, c. 1010-970 B.C., the king of Judah and Israel and founder
    of the Judaean dynasty at Jerusalem. He was the supposed
    author of the Psalms and had a medieval reputation as a prophet;
    see Psalms, I Samuel.
        MLT 935
        Mel 1100(2290), 1198(2388), 1303(2493), [1630(2820)],
            [1692(2882)], 1735(2925)
        SumT 1933
        MancT 345
        ParsT 125, 193, 204, 220, 307, 309, 442, 540,
            716, 955

DEATH (Deth, Deeth), a personification rarely used by Chaucer;
        Rom 4992, 5002, 5004
        T&C 4.250, 501, 503, 509, 909
            5.205
        PardT 675, 699, 710, 727, 753, 761, 772

DEATH OF BLAUNCHE THE DUCHESS (Deeth of Blaunche the Duchesse),
    an allusion to BD in the enumeration of Chaucer's works.
        LGW 418(406)

DECEMBER (Decembre), the last month of the year in the modern
    calendar.
        HF 63, 111
        FranklT 1244
        Astr 1.10.5, 15
            2.1.19; 44.5, 21, 43, 48, 51; 45.6, 26, 30

DECIUS ALBINUS (Albyn), a courtier defended by Boethius; Bo is
    the sole authority except for a mention in CASSIODORUS.
        Bo 1.p4.101, 217

DECIUS PAULINUS (Paulyn), a courtier defended by Boethius; Bo is
    the sole authority except for a mention in CASSIODORUS.
        Bo 1.p4.93, 94

DE COITU see CONSTANTINUS AFRICANUS.

DE CONTEMPTU MUNDI (Wreched Engendrynge of Mankynde) see INNOCENT
    III.

DECORATUS, seems to have been in the favor of Theodoric although
    Boethius thought ill of him; Skeat 2.438 cites CASSIODORUS 5.31.
        Bo 3.p4.23, 26

the decree or the BOOK OF DECREES, probably references to the
    compilation known as the Corpus Iuris Canonici which consisted

of the decretal collection made by Gratian in the 12th cent. together with the decretals of Gregory IX.
Decretum Gratiani
       <?1.86   GP 177-82]
       2.1.1.25   Mel 1404(2594)
       < ?   ParsT 931>
Decretum Gregorii IX
       <1.37.3   Mel 1269(2459)>
       [9.3.31.18   1850(3040)]

DEIPHOBUS (Deiphebus), son of PRIAM and HECUBA, who became Helen's husband after the death of Paris; Aen. 6.494-547 and Meta. 12.547. His involvement in the affair of Troilus is due to the tradition established by the Filo.
    HF 444
    T&C 2.1398, 1402, 1408, 1422, 1425, 1443, 1480,
          1486, 1496, 1514, 1540, 1542, 1549, 1558,
          1569, 1601, 1611, 1641, 1675, 1693, 1702
       3.204, 221, 226
       5.1652, 1654

DEJANIRA (Dianyre, Dianira), the daughter of Oeneus of Calydon, second wife of HERCULES whom he won by wrestling the river-god ACHELOUS. The centaur NESSUS, intending to violate Deianira, was killed by Hercules. Nessus advised Deianira to save some of his blood to be used to win back Hercules if he ever proved unfaithful. Deianira smeared some of the blood on a cloak and sent it to Hercules when she learned that he had fallen in love with Iole, daughter of Eurytus of Oechalia. The "shirt of Nessus" caused Hercules to immolate himself; Hero. 9, Meta. 9.1-272, De Casibus 1.18, De Clar. Mulier. 22, RR 9195.
    HF 402
    MLT 166
    MkT 2120(3310)
    WBT p725

DELIGHT (Delyte, Delite, Delit), the personification of concupiscence and physical gratification; in Rom an enemy of AGE and in PF a companion of Cupid. See Robertson.
    Rom 4979, 4983, 4987, 5857
    PF 224

DELILA (Dalida), the perfidious "wife" of SAMSON who betrayed him to the Philistines; Judges 16 and RR 9203-6, 16677ff. See Landrum, p. 98.
    BD 738
    MkT 2063(3253)
    WomUnc 16

DELPHINUS, a small constellation not far from Altair, the brightest star in the constellation Aquila, thought to resemble a dolphin; Skeat 3.265 cites Fasti 1.457, 2.117.

HF 1006

DE MARIA MAGDALENA (Origenes upon the Maudeleyne), i.e. the homily
     attributed to Origen and supposedly translated by Chaucer.
     LGW 428(418)

DEMETRIUS, is of uncertain identity. Skeat 5.283 notes that
     Demetrius is mentioned in Policraticus 1.5[400b-c] right after
     Stilbon [=Chilon] in PardT 603, but the exact Demetrius is
     conjectural. Skeat suggests Demetrius II Nicator of Syria,
     139-127 B.C., who was captured by Mithridates of Parthia.
     PardT 621

DEMOPHO(U)N (Demophon), a son of THESEUS and PHAEDRA, who at Thrace
     wooed and abandoned PHYLLIS; one of those who fought at Troy.
     See Hero. 2, De Gen. Deor. 11, RR 13174ff.; Shannon, Child,
     Meech, "CEFFI."
          BD 728
          HF 388
          LGW 264(218), 2398, 2405, 2427, 2462, 2486, 2496
          MLT 165

DEMOTION, a prince of Athens whose unnamed daughter killed herself
     rather than marry another when she learned that her betrothed
     had been killed; Adv. Jov. 1.41.
          FranklT 1426

ST. DENIS (Denys), St. Dionysius, the patron saint of France died
     272. He was the first bishop of Paris; his feast day is 9
     October. According to Gregory of Tours, Hist. Franc. 1.30
     he was sent into Gaul during the reign of Decius and suffered
     martyrdom at Catulliacus.
          ShipT 151(1341)

DE NUPTIIS MERCURII PHILOLOGIAE ET see MARTIANUS CAPELLA.

DE PLANCTU NATURAE (Pleynt of Kynde) see ALANUS DE INSULIS.

<DESCHAMPS, Eustace, 1346?-1404?, studied at Rheims and reputedly
     learned versification from MACHAUT. About 1360 he went to the
     University of Orleans to study law; he entered the king's
     service in 1367 as a royal messenger. By 1372 he was usher-at-
     arms to Charles V and he quickly became bailiff of Valois and
     Senlis, squire to the Dauphin and governor of Fismes. He hated
     the English, complained bitterly of his own misfortunes, and
     toward the end of his life railed against women in the Miroir
     de Mariage. His works were edited in ten volumes (1878-1901)
     for SATF by Saint-Hilaire and Reynaud; cf. Hamm 77, Louns 2.217,
     CCS 123ff., S&A. Deschamp's "Ballade" is responsible for
     Chaucer's reputation as "grant translateur."
     Lay de Franchise
          14, 27-30   LGW 44-9

Miroir de Mariage (cont.)

?3376–81	GP 449–52
3520–5	WBT p316–22
3600–8, 3620–2,	
3629–32	p387–92
3634–5, 3644–5	p233
3871ff.	p316–22
3920ff.	p393 + RR
8672–91	p337–9
9006–7	MerchT 1393–6
9063–7	LGW 301–4
9081ff.	268–9
9097–9100	276–7
	MillT p3154–6
9150–2, 9156–9	MerchT 1393–6>

DE SENECTUTE, OF AGE, see CICERO.

DESIRE (Desyr), the personification of affection; Tes. 7.56.
   PF 227
   KnT 1925
   Pity 101

DESPENSE, the personification of generosity; Tes. 7.55.
   KnT 1928

DESTINY (Destanye), another name for the FATES.
   LGW 2580

DIANA (Dyane), goddess of nature, the hunt, and fertility. Her
   association with Artemis and her designation as Cynthia are the
   reasons for her designation as the moon-goddess. Latona is
   the mother of Diana and APOLLO; Meta. 1.696, 8.260–546;
   De Gen. Deor. 9.15 & 19. See Meech, Root, S&A, Wood 264–8 and
   Chap. II.
      PF 281
      T&C 3.731
         4.1591=Lucina, 1608=Cynthia
         5.655=Latona, 1018=Cynthia, 1464
      KnT 1682, 1912, 2051, 2057, 2063, 2066, 2072,
      2085=Lucina, 2274, 2296, 2346, 2364
      FranklT 1045=Lucina, 1390

DIANIRA see DEJANIRA.

DICTYS CRETENSIS (Tytus, Dite), a supposed witness of the Trojan
   war whose "diary" was translated by Lucius Septimus in the
   fourth cent. A.D. as Ephemeris Belli Troiana. As with DARES,
   the account of Dictys passed to the Middle Ages through BENOÎT;
   Frazer 7–11 and Griffin.
      HF 1467
      T&C 1.146

DIDO, the queen of Carthage who committed suicide when she was
    abandoned by AENEAS. She was the niece and wife of SYCHAEUS
    and sister of PYGMALION; Aen. 4, Hero. 7, "CEFFI," RR 13174ff.,
    Inf. 5.58-69; Bradley, Hall.
        BD 732
        HF 241, 254, 287, 312, 318, 432, 444
        PF 289
        LGW 263(217), 927, 956, 993, 995, 1004, 1017,
            1124, 1157, 1201, 1237, 1290, 1309, 1330,
            1333, 1336
        MLT 164

[DIGESTA see JUSTINIAN.]

DIOGENES, the Cynic, fourth cent. B.C.
        FormAge 35

DIOMEDE,
    (1) the son of Mars and king of the Bistonians in Thrace,
        slain by HERCULES in his eighth labor. Diomede's horses
        were fed human flesh; when Hercules threw Diomede to them
        they became tame; perhaps Servius on Aen. 8.300.
        Bo 4.m7.40
    (2) the son of TYDEUS and leader of the men of Argos and
        Tiryns at the Trojan war; Meta. 13.100ff. See Meech
        99-132 for characterization.
        T&C 4.11
            5.15, 37, 46, 86, [88], 92, 106, 183, 771,
                799, 841, 844, 869, 956, 1010, 1024,
                1031, 1041, 1045, 1071, 1087, 1512, 1513,
                [1514], 1517, 1519, 1654, 1677, 1703,
                [1746], 1757

DIONE, by Jupiter the mother of VENUS; Aen. 3.19, Ars Amat. 2.593,
    3.3, 769, Amores 1.14.33, perhaps De Raptu Pros. 3.433 or Par.
    8.7-8 as suggested by Root.
        T&C 3.1807

[DIONYSIUS OF SYRACUSE, c. 432-367 B.C., the tyrant of Syracuse
    who seized power in 405; Tusc. Disp. 5.21.6, Horace Odes
    3.1.17, Persius Satires 3.40. Damocles, one of his courtiers,
    extravagantly spoke of Dionysius's happiness: Dionysius
    invited him to a sumptuous banquet at which Damocles sat under
    a sword suspended by a hair.
        Bo 3.p5.23]

DIOSCORIDES (Deyscorides), a Greek medical writer who fl. c. 50 A.D.,
    i.e. he was a contemporary of Pliny. He was the first writer
    to establish medical botany as an applied science as presented
    in his Materia Medica.
        GP 430

DISDAIN, one of the pillars which warns off the person who enters
the park of Venus.
PF 136

DISTRESS, one of the attendants of Age.
Rom 4997

DIVES, the rich man; Luke 16.19ff.
SumT 1877

doctor: the, some.
PhysT 117 = Augustine
ParsT 85 = Augustine [Pennaforte]

DOCTOR OF PHYSIC, one of the Canterbury pilgrims.
GP 411

[DOMINICANS, Friars Preachers or Black Friars, a mendicant order
founded by St. Dominic in 1215. An encyclical bull from
Honorius III in 1221 ordered bishops to give the friars
facilities to preach and hear confession. The Black Friars
were established in England, at Oxford, in 1221.
Rom 6338, 7454
GP 210]

DONEGILD, the perfidious mother of Alla. The original form of her
name is doubtful.
MLT 695, 740, 778, 805, 896

DORIGEN, the heroine of the tale; the source and pronunciation
of her name are uncertain.
FranklT 815, 919, 926, 936, [967], [974], [1009],
1090, 1457, 1469, 1488, 1500, 1542, 1551,
1598

the dragon see LADON.

DRAGON see TAIL OF THE DRAGON.

DREAD (Drede), in Rom the watchman of the north gateway of the
castle of Jealousy; in Pity one of the qualities dead in the
Lady.
Rom 3958, 3966, 3967, 3999, 4042, 4217, 4226,
4228, 4483, 5861
Pity 41

[DRUSUS, the son of Tiberius, poisoned by his wife LIVIA, at the
instigation of Sejanus, 23 A.D.; Valerii 4.3.
WBT p750]

BOOK OF THE DUCHESSE.
Ret 1086

[DU GUESCLIN, BERTRAND, c. 1320-80, one of the most famous warriors
of France. In 1366 he helped Henry of Trastamara unseat his
brother PETER the Cruel and was made constable of Castile and
count of Trastamara. In April 1367 he was defeated and captured at Najera by Peter's ally the Black Prince. He was
released for a large ransom and once more fought for Henry and
won the battle of Montiel in 1369. Henry was reinstated on
the throne after Peter was murdered in du Guesclin's tent.
In May 1370 Charles V sent du Guesclin back to France as
constable. Quite appropriately (i.e. to the Ganelon association) du Guesclin was a Breton.
     MkT 2383(3573)-85(75)]

DULCARNON, the medieval Latin corruption of an Arabic term "two
horned." Pandarus claims that it was the name for the 47th
proposition of the first book of Euclid, but "fleming of
wrecches" is a translation of Fuga miserorum which is a name
for the 5th proposition; Skeat 2.479-80, refers to Speght's
annotations which refer to NECKAM, De Naturis Rerum 173.
     T&C 3.[931], 933

DUN, like BAYARD, a common name for a horse; Skeat 5.435-6.
     MancT p5

<DUNS SCOTUS, JOHN, 1265-1308, known as the doctor subtilis, was
a Franciscan educated at Oxford where he later lectured,
c. 1290, and to which he returned after four years in Paris.
Scotus returned to Paris in 1302 and was transferred to
Cologne. His commentaries on the Bible and the works of
Aristotle were the most widely known in the later Middle Ages.
See Root for the ascription.
Expositio in Metaph. Arist.
     10.2.1.30   T&C 3.404-6>

ST. DUNSTAN, 908-988, in 943 became the abbot of Glastonbury and
was elevated to the see of Worcester in 957. In 959 he received the bishopric of London and in the same year became
the archbishop of Canterbury. He was the patron saint of
goldsmiths. He is often represented carrying a pair of pincers
in his right hand in reference to the legend that on one occasion at Glastonbury he seized the Devil by the nose with
a pair of red-hot tongs.
     FrT 1502

DYANIRA see DEJANIRA.

DYER, one of the five guildsmen.
     GP 362

E

EACIDES CHIRON see CHIRON.

ECCLESIASTICUS; cf. BIBLE and JESUS FILIUS SIRACH.
     [Mel 1635(2825)]
     NPT 3329(4519)
     WBT p651
     [SumT 1988]

ECHO (Ekko, Ecquo), the nymph rejected by NARCISSUS. She was
    changed into a repeating voice because she rejected Pan.
    See Meta. 3.356-406 and RR 1439 (Rom 1469)ff.
     Rom 1474
     BD 735
     ClT 1189
     FranklT 951

<Ecloga Theoduli, a tenth cent. strife between Pseustis, a shepherd
    from Athens, and Alithia, a maiden shepherdess descended from
    David. The contest was arbitrated by Fronesis. Obviously,
    Pseustis used pagan mythology and Alithia drew upon the Old
    Testament; equally obvious is Alithia's victory. See Raby
    1.228-9, and Hazelton for discussion of its inclusion in the
    Liber Catonianus.
     general   HF 1227-8
     65-8, 77-80, 217-9   589>

ECLYMPASTERYE see ENCLIMPOSTAIR.

EDDIPUS see OEDIPUS.

ST. EDWARD, probably Edward the Confessor, a bad but holy king
    who was crowned in 1043 and died in 1066.
     MkT p1970(3160)

EGEUS see AEGEUS.

EGISTE see AEGYPTUS.

EGLENTINE see PRIORESS.

ELCANOR, has not been satisfactorily identified. Skeat 3.253
    hesitantly suggests Elkanah, I Samuel 1.1, and Alcanor
    [Alcander], Aen. 10.338; Tatlock suggests the OF Cassiodorus,
    a continuation of the Sept Sages de Rome, which contains the
    story of Helcana-Helcanor, in which the heroine appears in
    twelve dreams.
     HF 516

ELD, one of the figures on the wall outside the garden of Mirth;
    the personification of Old Age which Reason contrasts with Youth.

Rom 349, 4941, 4948, 4955, 4963, 4967, 4989

ELEATICS (Eleaticis), the followers of Parmenides (born c. 510 B.C.)
and Zeno of Elea (fl. c. 460 B.C.).
    Bo 1.pl.66

eldest lady see EVADNE.
    KnT 912

ELEYNE see HELEN.

ELI (Helie), a member of the ancient priesthood founded in Egypt,
he was priest of the temple of Shiloh, the sanctuary of the
ark, and also judge over Israel. Since he was unable to
control his sons, Hophni and Phinehas, the Philistines overcame
the Israelites at the battle of Ebenezer where the ark was
taken and Eli's sons were slain. Eli, upon hearing, dropped
dead. The fall of his house was the fulfillment of prophecies
uttered against his corrupt house. See I Samuel 2.
    ParsT 897

ELIACHIM, the high priest who preached resistance to HOLOFERNES
and thereby brought about the siege of Bethulia; Judith 4.
    MkT 2566(3756)

ST. ELIGIUS (Loy), 588-659, became bishop of Noyon in 640 after
serving as coiner to Clotaire II and treasurer to Dagobert.
He was a famous worker in gold and silver and became the
patron saint of artists and smiths.
    GP 120
    FrT 1564

ELIJAH (Elye, Elie), a contemporary of Ahab (c. 876-853 B.C.) and
hero of a number of stories; notably his conference on Horeb
with Yahweh and his passing in a whirlwind. See I Kings 19.8
and II Kings 2.11.
    HF 588
    SumT 1890, 2116

ELISHA (Elise), the prophet anointed by Elijah; II Kings 2.
    SumT 2116

ELPHETA, the wife of Cambushkin. Her name is unexplained.
    SqT 29

ELYMAS see LIMOTE.

EMETREUS, the "king of India," one of Arcite's knights in the
contest with Palamon; he is not mentioned in Theb. or Tes.
    KnT 2156, 2638, 2645

EMILY (Emelye), the beautiful young sister of HIPPOLITA, beloved
    of PALAMON and ARCITE.
        A&A 38
        KnT 871, 972, 1035, 1046, 1061, 1068, 1077,
            1273, 1419, 1427, 1486, 1567, 1588, 1594,
            1686, 1731, 1737, 1749, 1820, 1833, 1860,
            2243, 2273, 2282, 2332, 2341, 2361, 2571,
            2578, 2658, 2679, 2699, 2762, 2773, 2780,
            2808, 2816, 2817, 2836, 2885, 2910, 2941,
            2956, 2980, 3098, 3103, 3107

EMPEROR see TIBERIUS CONSTANTINE.

ENCLIMPOSTAIR (Eclympasteyr), one of the sons of Morpheus, the
    source of the name is uncertain; perhaps, from FROISSART's
    Paradys d'Amours 28.
        BD 167

ENEYDOS see VIRGIL, AENEID.

ENOCH (Enok, Ennok), the father of Methuselah; Genesis 5.24.
        HF 588

ENVY (Envye), one of the Seven Deadly Sins. See Meta. 2.775ff.,
    Filo. 3.93, and Inf. 13-64 although no particular source need
    be sought.
        Rom 248, 281, 289, 301
        LGW 358(333)
        T&C 3.1805
        PhysT 114
        ParsT 484, 485, 487, 488, 489, 490, 491, 492, 505,
            515, 531, 533, 534, 555

EOLUS see AEOLUS.

EPHESIANS see BIBLE.
        [SecNT 202
        ParsT 918]

EPICUREANS, the followers of EPICURUS who, according to Lady
    Philosophy, perverted her true followers.
        Bo 1.p3.33, 44, 46

EPICURUS, 341-270 B.C., the Greek philosopher who counseled a
    rather stoic doctrine of enjoyment of virtue as the supreme
    good; during the Middle Ages his name and philosophy became
    synonymous with self-indulgence and the deadly sin of luxuria.
        Bo 3.p2.78
        [T&C 3.1169]
        GP 336
        [MerchT 2021]

EPISTLE OF OVID see OVID, HEROIDES.
    HF 379
    LGW (305), 1465, [1558], 1678, 2220
    MLT i55

EPISTOLA ADVERSUS JOVINIANUM see JEROME.
    *WBT p675
    ?SumT 1929

EPISTOLA VALERII see MAP.
    WBT p[669], 671, [714]

ERINYES (Herenus) see FURIES.

ERIPHYLE (Eriphilem), the wife of AMPHIARAUS, she was bribed by
    Polyneices (with the necklace of Harmonia) to persuade
    Amphiaraus to become one of the Seven against Thebes. She
    was killed by their son Alcmaeon. See Adv. Jov. 1.48 which
    was probably supplemented by Theb. 4.187-213.
    WBT p743

ERYMANTHIAN BOAR, one of the labors of HERCULES was to catch it
    alive, so he drove it into a snowfield, tired it out, and
    caught it in a net; Meta. 9 and Hero. 9.
    [Bo 4.m7.55]
    [MkT 2109(3299)]

ESCALIPHO see AESCULAPIUS.

ESON see AESON.

ESTATE, the regard for social station, a quality of the lady to
    which no appeal is available since Pity is dead within her.
    Pity 41

ESTHER (Hester, Ester), the Jewish cousin and foster-daughter of
    MORDECAI who became the queen of AHASUERUS. Esther and Mordecai
    frustrated the attempts of Haman to extirpate the Jews; Haman
    was replaced by Mordecai as grand vizier and Esther obtained
    permission for the Jews to destroy all who attacked on the day
    Haman had appointed for the destruction of the Jews. The day
    was celebrated by the feast of Purim; Esther.
    BD 987
    LGW 250(204)
    Mel 1101(2291)
    MerchT 1371, 1744

ESTORYAL MYROUR see VINCENT OF BEAUVAIS, SPECULUM HISTORIALE.

ETEOCLES and POLYNEICES, sons of OEDIPUS, were to rule Thebes
    alternately but Eteocles expelled his brother. This led to

the war of the seven against Thebes during which Eteocles and
Polyneíces killed each other and CREON seized control. The
passage in T&C represents a summary of the first two books of
Theb.; see Magoun.
      T&C 5.1489, 1507

ETHIC (Etik). Skeat 3.296 refers to the Nichomachean Ethics of
Aristotle while Robin suggests Policraticus 8.13 or Convivio
Cans. 3.81ff.; cf. Louns 2.387.
      LGW 166

EUCLID (Euclude), the Greek geometrician who fl. at Alexandria
c. 300 B.C. His principal work was the Elements in 13 books;
RR 16171.
      SumT 2289

EURIPIDES (Euripidis), c. 480-406 B.C., the Greek tragedian.
      Bo 3.p7.25
    [Andromache
      319-20   Bo 3.p6.4
      418-20   3.p7.25]

EUROPA (Europe), the daughter of Agenor, king of Tyre, whom Zeus
wooed in the form of a bull and bore her off to Crete where
she gave birth to MINOS and RHADAMANTHUS; Meta. 2.833-75 and
Tes. 3.5.
      T&C 3.722
      [LGW 144]

EURUS, the east or southeast wind.
      Bo 2.m4.4
         4.m3.1

EURYDICE (Erudyce), the wife of ORPHEUS; Georg. 4.454-527, Meta.
10.1-85 and 11.1ff.
      Bo 3.m12.59
      T&C 4.791

[EVADNE, the wife of CAPANEUS, one of the seven against Thebes;
Theb. 12.545 and Tes. 2.2-5, 25-95.
      KnT 912]

EVANDER, an Arcadian, the son of Carmentis and Mercury who migrated
to Italy and founded a colony; Aen. 8.190ff. and Fasti 1.543-86.
      Bo 4.m7.53, 55

EVANGELISTS, i.e. Matthew, Mark, Luke and John.
      MLT 666

EVANGILE, i.e. the Evangelium or Gospels.
      Rom 445=Matthew 6.16, 5453

MLT 666
Mel 1079(2269)=Matthew 19.17 and Luke 18.19

EVE, the first woman, the mother of mankind; Genesis.
        MLT 368
        [NPT 3257(4447)-58(48)]
        WBT p715
        MerchT 1329
        SecNT p62
        ParsT 325, 331, 332, 819   + ADAM

EXODUS see BIBLE.
        [MLT 488-90]
        ParsT 750

EZEKIEL (Ezechiel), the prophet, a priest in Jerusalem carried
    into Babylonia in the First Captivity 597 B.C.; BIBLE.
        ParsT 140, 143, 236

EZECHIE see HEZEKIAH.

F

FABRICIUS, Gaius Luscinus, third cent. B.C. Roman general who had
    a distinguished career as soldier and diplomat. In 285 he
    was one of the ambassadors to the Tarentines; in 282 he defeated
    the Bruttians and Lucanians. In 280 when the Romans were de-
    feated by Pyrrhus at Heraclea, Fabricius was sent to treat for
    ransom and exchange; Pyrrhus was so impressed with the fact
    that Fabricius could not be bribed that he released the
    prisoners without ransom. In 278 Fabricius was elected consul
    for the second time and was successful in negotiating terms
    of peace with Pyrrhus.
        Bo 2.m7.18

FAINT DISTRESS, one of the items in the scrip of Dame Abstinence.
        Rom 7403

FAIR RUTHLESS, another name for BOUNTY.
        Lady 28

FAIR SEMBLANCE, one of the arrows in the quiver of the God of Love.
        Rom 963, 1880

FAIR WELCOME, the captive of Jealousy liberated by the God of Love.
        Rom 5856, 7522, 7527, 7565, 7639

FALSENESS (Falsnesse), the personification of dissimulation.
        Rom 7448

FALSE SEMBLANCE (Fals-Semblant), the chief ally of the God of Love
    in the defeat of Jealousy and recovery of Fair Welcome.
        Rom 5848, 6049, 6136, 6140, 6219, 6473, 7297,
            7330, 7354, 7406, 7429, 7443, 7306, 7665

FAME, i.e. reputation in general, the discrimination of which is
    ascertained in the house of Fame; Aen. 4.173ff.
        HF 349, 703, 786, 844, 852, 1053, 1200, 1292,
            1311, 1357, 1404, 1406, 1603, 1728, 1769,
            1857, 1903, 2111
        T&C 4.659

BOOK OF FAME, the name given to HF in the list of works.
        Ret 1086

FATES, or Parcae or Wirdes, determine length of life and moment of
    death. They were considered the daughters of Night; Theb.
    1.632; 3.68, 556, 642; 8.59; 9.323. Cf. RR 19768ff.; Inf.
    33.126; Purg. 21.25, 25.79. The Fates, collectively or indi-
    vidually, are not named in Filo.; in the references above most
    of the references are to individuals. Clotho holds the
    distaff, Lachesis draws off the thread, and Atropos cuts the
    thread.
        T&C [3.733 = a fatal sustren]
            4.1208, 1546 = Atropos
            5.3 = Parcas, 7 = Lachesis
        LGW 2580 = Wirdes

his father see AEGEUS.
        LGW 2178

FEBRUARY, the second month in the modern calendar.
        Astr 1.10.3, 13, 17

FELONY, evil-doing, one of the personifications on the wall outside
    the garden of Mirth.
        Rom 165

field of snow see DU GUESCLIN.
        MkT 2383(3573)

FISH see PISCES.

FLATTERY (Flatery), the personification of unsolicited, extravagant
    praise; in PF one of the companions of Cupid and in KnT one
    of the figures on the wall of the temple of Venus. See Tes.
    7.56.
        PF 227
        KnT 1927

FLEGETOUN see PHLEGETHON.

FLEXIPPE, one of Criseyde's nieces; the origin of her name is
    unknown. Hamilton 94ff. suggests Plexippus in Meta. 8.440.
        T&C 2.816

FLORA, the goddess of flowers, whose festival was celebrated on
    28 April, often with license; Fasti 5.183ff. and RR 8411ff.
    where she is associated with ZEPHYRUS.
        BD 402
        LGW 171

wise folk,
        T&C 5.790 = ?

as writen folk biforn, cf. Genesis 4.19-23.
        SqT 551

FOOLHARDINESS, boldness; in PF one of the company of Cupid and in
    KnT one of the figures painted on the wall of the temple of
    Venus. See Tes. 7.56.
        PF 227
        KnT 1925

FORCE, one of the figures painted on the wall of the temple of
    Venus.
        KnT 1927

FORTUNA MAJOR, theta Pegasi and alpha, pi, gamma, delta, and eta
    Aquarii; Skeat 2.482. The reference is not in Filo.; Root
    suggests that it was from Purg. 19.4-6.
        T&C 3.1420

FORTUNE, the relative states of felicity or woe and the personifi-
    cation of determination of those states; a great deal of
    Chaucer's emphasis on Fortune is due to Bo. See Jefferson,
    Patch.
        Rom 4353, 5331, 5403, 5411, 5463, 5467, 5479,
            5489, 5494, 5517, 5543
        BD 618, 659, 673, 719, 811
        HF 1547, 2016
        A&A 44
        Bo 1.ml.23, 26; p4.11, 135, 136; m5.34; p5.62
            2.p1.11, 16, 22, 50, 58, 75, 82, 89, 93, 97,
                99, 109, 114, 115; ml.1, 7; p2.2, 68;
                p3.1, 64, 65, 67, 70, 88, 91; p4.138;
                p5.5, 71, 113; p6.90, 120; p8.3, 11, 12,
                13, 16, 18, 19, 22, 23, 26, 28, 30, 34, 36
            3.p1.12, 13
            .ml.18?
        T&C 1.138, 837, 841, 843, 849
            3.617, 1667, 1714
            4.2, 260, 274, 324, 391, 600, 1189, 1192,
                1588, 1628

        T&C 5.469, 1460, 1541, 1745, 1763
        LGW 589, 1609
        KnT 925, 1086, 1238, 1242, 1252, 1303-33[planctus],
            1490, 1861, 2682
        MLT 448
        MkT 1995(3185), 2001(3191), 2136(3326), 2140(3330),
            2189(3379), 2241(3431), 2244(3434), 2347(3537),
            2367(3557), 2376(3566), 2397(3587), 2413(3603),
            2445(3635), 2457(3647), 2478(3668), 2519(3709),
            2550(3740), 2556(3746), 2661(3851), 2669(3859),
            2678(3868), 2686(3876), 2694(3884), 2723(3913),
            2737(3927), 2759(3949)
        NPT p2782(3972)
            3403(4593)
        SumT 2020
        ClT 68, 756, 812, 898
        MerchT 1314, 2057
        SqT 577
        FranklT 1355
        PardT p295
        Fort 4, 8, 16, 24, 67

FRANCHISE, liberty or independence, one of the arrows in the
    quiver of the God of Love.
        Rom 955, 1211, 1238, 3501, 3507, 3575, 3592,
            3608, 5865

FRANCISCANS, or Friars Minor or Grey Friars, founded by St. Francis
    according to a rule inaugurated in 1209 in imitation of the
    gospel life of Christ, especially the life of poverty. In
    1223 Honorius III granted the bull officially establishing the
    order and by the following year it had spread into England.
    St. Francis died in 1226 and by 1232 (under Elias of Cortona)
    the order had been greatly extended but had also become very
    wealthy; consequently, by 1239 the order had divided into
    three parties: zealots or spirituals, moderates, and liberals.
    The English province was one of the poorest but most notable:
    Roger Bacon, Bartholomaeus Anglicus, Alexander Hales, Duns
    Scotus, and William of Occam. See Knowles.
        [Rom 6338, 7459
        GP 210]

FRANKLIN, one of the pilgrims, a landholder of free but not noble
    birth.
        GP 331
        SqT e675, 696, 699

FRIAR, one of the pilgrims. His name was Huberd but his order
    was not specified.
        GP 208, 269 = Huberd
        WBT p829, 832, 840, 844, 855

```
          FrT p1265, 1299
              1338, 1645
          SumT p1666, 1670, 1672, 1707
              1761
```

FRIARS MINOR see FRANCISCANS.

FRIARS DE PENITENTIA, or di Sacco or Croutched Friars or Sacked
    Friars, an order with several houses in England.
        Rom 7460

FRIAR WOLF, i.e. a wolf in shepherd's clothing.
        Rom 6424, 6428

FRIDAY, the sixth day of the week. The ill luck associated with
    the day is due, of course, to the crucifixion.
        KnT 1534, 1539
        NPT 3341(4531), 3351(4541), 3352(4542)

ST. FRIDESWIDE, an English abbess of the eighth cent. The church
    of the priory of St. Frideswide at Oxford became the present
    cathedral. As Cline notes, her presence in the MillT is due
    to her powers as a healing saint; Cline also suggests that
    she is a "local" saint.
        MillT 3449

a friend see AEACUS.
        LGW 2156

FRIEND, the personification intermediation, acts as intercessor
    with Danger.
        Rom 3346

<FROISSART, Jean, 1338-1410?, one of Chaucer's most important
    French contemporaries, perhaps acquainted with Chaucer, and
    one of Chaucer's unacknowledged sources. Froissart first knew
    England in the train of Philippa of Hainaut when she went
    there in 1356. Froissart's wanderlust persisted throughout
    his life. In 1360 he traveled to Avignon and returned to
    England the following year. In 1366 he traveled to Brussels
    and then to Brittany, then to Nantes where he met Richard.
    He accompanied the Black Prince to Dax but returned to England.
    Froissart escorted Lionel to Italy in 1369. From Milan he
    traveled to Venice where he was patronized by Peter of Cyprus.
    In the same year Peter was assassinated and Philippa died, so
    Froissart returned to Flanders and the patronage of the
    duchess of Brabant. See Hamm 77-8, Smith, CCS, and especially
    Wimsatt, Sypherd, and Lowes.
    Dittie de la Flour de la Margherite
        81-2   LGW 56-9
        96ff.   (58)
```
```

Dittie de la Flour de la Margherite (cont.)
```
     105ff.                    LGW 53
     159-62                       56-9
     162-6                        44-9
     166                          217
     187                          220
```
Le Joli Mois de May
```
     289-90                    LGW 53-5
```
Pastourelle
```
     17.66                     LGW 123
```
Tresor Amoreux
```
     615ff.                    HF 66ff.
```
Prison Amoreuse
```
     878-9                     LGW 40-3
```
Joli Buisson de Jonece
```
     786-92                    LGW 1
```
Paradys d'Amours
```
     1ff.                      BD 1-15          + MACHAUT
     7                            23
     13                           45
     14                           272-5
     15-18                        242-69
     19-22                        222-3
     28                           167
     31                           272-5
     358-60                    LGW 518
     916ff.                    BD 348ff.
     1621-2, 33-5              LGW 40-3
     1636-8                       (58), 247
     1685-92                   BD 1324-5
     1693-5, 1722-3               1330-4>
```

FURIES (Herynes), or Erinyes, the powers of punishment, especially
of crime against the ties of kinship, were the daughters of
Night. Their names were Alecto, Megaera, and Tisiphone and
they were usually depicted as winged and accompanied by snakes.
Chaucer refers to all three by name in T&C 4.24. See Aen.
12.845-7, Meta. 4.451-2, De Gen. Deor. 3.6-9, Tes. 1.58, and
3.1, Inf. 9.45-9.
      T&C 1.6, [9] = Tisiphone
          2.436
          4.22, [24]
      [LGW 2252]
      ?[Pity 92]

G

GABRIEL (Gabrielles), the heavenly messenger sent (1) to Daniel to
explain the vision of the ram and the he-goat and to communicate
the prediction of the seventy weeks [Daniel 8.16, 9.21],

(2) to announce the birth of John the Baptist to Zacharias and
(3) to announce the Messiah to the Virgin Mary [Luke 1.19, 26].
The reference here is obviously to the Annunciation.
    ABC 115

GAIUS CAESAR see CAESAR, GAIUS.

GALATEA (Galathee), the heroine of PAMPHILIUS DE AMORE; Hamm 100,
    Louns 2.370-2, S&A, and Garbaty.
        FranklT 1110

GALAXY (Galaxye), or Milky Way, from via lactea because of the
    appearance of massed stars; Skeat 3.263. See Meta. 1.168.
        HF 936, [937 = Milky Way]
        PF 56

GALEN (Galien), 129-199 A.D., was born at Pergamum and from c. 164
    until his death lived at Rome under Marcus Aurelius. After
    Hippocrates, he was the most famous physician of antiquity.
        BD 572
        GP 431
        ParsT 831   not in PERALDUS

GALLIENUS (Galien), Publicus Licinius Egnatius, the son of
    Valerian, was emperor 260-68. During his reign the empire
    was ravaged by pestilence, and the chief cities of Greece were
    sacked by the Goths. His generals rebelled and the period
    came to be known as the reign of the Thirty Tyrants.
    Gallienus was killed at Mediolanum (Milan) and succeeded by
    Aureolus. See De Clar. Mulier. for the brief reference;
    viz. 98.
        MkT 2336(3526)

GANELON (Genyloun), Count of Mayence, one of Charlemagne's
    paladins who, because of his jealousy, planned with Marsilius
    the ambush at Roncesvalles. For his perfidy he was torn to
    pieces by wild horses. In MkT he is compared with DU GUESCLIN.
        BD 1121
        ShipT 1941(1384)
        MkT 2389(3579)
        NPT 3227(4417)

GANYMEDE, the son of Tros, who was carried off by the eagle of
    Jupiter or by Jupiter himself to be cupbearer to Jupiter;
    Aen. 1.28 and Meta. 10.155-61. Cf. Steadman for the suggestion
    that the account is derived from PETRUS BERCHORIUS.
        HF 589

GAUDENTIUS, one of Boethius's accusers.
        Bo 1.p4.116

GAUFRED see GEOFFREY DE VINSAUF.

GAWAIN, King Arthur's nephew, was the model of courtesy; cf. Wells
    [25-38].
        Rom 2209
        SqT 95

the gayler see DAEDALUS.

GEMINI, the twins Castor and Pollux, the third sign in the zodiac.
        MerchT 2222
        Astr 1.8.3; 21.74
            2.3.34; 6.16; 28.24, 27, 36

GENESIS, cf. BIBLE
        [WBT p29]
        ParsT 755

GENIUS, the "priest" of Nature who excommunicates those who do
    not perform their rites to Venus.
        Rom 4768

GENTILESSE, the personification of the qualities of courtesy and
    nobility which distinguish and ennoble the possessor.
        PF 224
        Pity 68, 78

GENYLOUN see GANELON

GEOFFREY CHAUCER
        HF 729 = Geffrey
        MLT 147 = Chaucer

GEOFFREY DE VINSAUF, author of Poetria Nova c. 1210, about whom
    very little is known except that he was an Englishman who went
    to Rome; Faral 15-18, Louns 2.341, Friend, Raby 2.122-6, and
    Meech.
        NPT 3347(4537)
        Poetria Nova
            <43-5   T&C 1.1065ff.>
            [363-8   NPT 3347(4537), 3358(4548)-59(49)]
            <1780   LGW 249ff.>
        <De Arte Versificandi
            2.1.3   LGW 1896ff.>

GEOFFREY OF MONMOUTH (Gaufride), c. 1100-1154, was known to have
    been at Oxford c.1129 and became bishop of St. Asaph's in
    1151. His Historia Regum Britanniae, which professes to be
    a translation from a Celtic source brought from Brittany by
    Walter, archdeacon of Oxford, is largely responsible for the
    tradition of Brut as a descendent of Aeneas--hence the British

association with the story of Troy. For the importance of
the <u>Historia</u>, which dates from about 1139, in the Arthurian
legend see <u>ALMA</u> 72-93.
    HF 1470

GERLAND, one of the widow's dogs.
    NPT 3383(4573)

GERMANICUS, Germanicus Julius Caesar, Nero Claudius, 15 B.C.-19 A.D.,
    the nephew and adopted son of Tiberius and father of Caligula,
    GAIUS CAESAR.
    Bo 1.pr.183

GERVEIS, the blacksmith who furnished ABSOLON his weapon of revenge.
    MillT 3761, 3765, 3775, 3779

GESTA ROMANORUM, a Latin collection of anecdotes and tales probably
    compiled about the end of the 13th or beginning of the 14th
    cent.; <u>Louns</u> 2.317-20.

*MerchT 2284		
<?33	WBT p757	+ CICERO + MAP
146	MancT 226	+ CICERO + AUGUSTINE
		+ <u>Polycraticus</u>
174	MerchT 1786>	

old Roman gestes, the geste,

T&C 2.82	= <u>Theb</u>.
3.450	?
MLT 1126	?
WBT p642, 647	= VALERIUS MAXIMUS
SqT 211	= VIRGIL or BENOIT or GUIDO

GIB, i.e. Gilbert, a common name for a tomcat. In the sermon of
    False Semblance: False Semblance is equal to the nefarious
    methods of the cat.
    Rom 6204

GILBERTUS ANGLICUS, an early 13th cent. Englishman who studied
    medicine at Salerno and spent a great deal of time in France.
    His <u>Compendium</u> was one of the standard medical text-books;
    Bowden 201-2.
    GP 434

ST. GILES <u>see</u> ST. AEGIDIUS.

GILL, a common name for a female servant, the maid of John the
    carpenter.
    MillT 3556

GLADNESS, sang the carol for the company of Mirth in the garden
    of love.
    Rom 746, 848

GLASCURION, perhaps the 10th cent. British bard, the brother of
Morgan Hen, king of Glamorgan; Robin 785n.
HF 1208

GOD, the Supreme Deity. Some of the references are ambivalent and
are therefore listed separately; i.e., the allusions may be to
JUPITER or JOVE. For a discussion of the problem in T&C see
Meech.
Rom 42, 278, 434, 470, 505, 632, 798, 1027, 1158,
1255, 1339, 1490, 1500, 1542, 1948, 2135,
2421, 2581, 2627, 2732, 2805, 3027, 3210,
3500, 3643, 3667, 3838, 4267, 4274, 4277,
4522, 4561, 4589, 4824, 4921, 5207, 5647,
5682, 5692, 5693, 5752, 5773, 5780, 6001,
6274, 6281, 6308, 6432, 6433, 6533, 6542,
6561, 6578, 6590, 6606, 6653, 6702, 6767,
6799, 6802, 7196, 7232, 7233, 7375, 7591,
7683
BD 210, 370, 550, 665, 677, 680, 683, 755, 758,
814, 831, 838, 877, 1143, 1144, 1178, 1205,
1235, 1237, 1277
HF 1, 382, 576, 584, 629, 646, 700, 875, 970,
982, 1012, 1056, 1067, 1087, 1135, 1310,
1384, 1561, 1612, 1697, 1711, 1758, 1760,
1995
A&A 202
PF 14, 84, 199, 404, 560, 582, 595, 663
Bo 1.p4.45, 196, 200, 211, 262, 266, 286, 292
(gloss), 316; p5.20; m6.18; p6.14, 20, 28,
45, 88
2.m2.9; p5.134
3.m6.11; p9.193; p10.42, 43, 46, 48, 51, 53,
58, 62, 68, 74, 77, 79, 80, 85, 109, 125,
130, 147, 148, 245, 249; m10.10; p11.8,
179; p12.24, 27, 47, 56, 67, 87, 104, 107,
127, 129, 135, 142, 149, 166, 170, 172,
176, 188
4.p1.34, 49; m1.15, 17, 27; p2.233; p3.45,
127; p5.31, 32, 38, 45; p6.26, 49, 87, 96,
131, 136, 137, 216, 217, 223, 246, 248,
251, 252, 262, 273, 299, 304, 347, 352,
357; m6.3, 60
5.p1.41, 47; m2.6, 11, 13; p3.6, 8, 9, 12, 13,
24, 32, 36, 73, 78, 80, 87, 91, 118, 122,
123, 125, 147, 176, 182, 184, 185, 186, 187,
191, 200, 213; m3.3, 4, 7, 40; p4.2, 18;
p5.20, 103; p6.10, 57, 65, 73, 75, 86, 98,
102, 136, 158, 161, 164, 195, 199, 208, 229,
245, 277, 282, 294, 301
T&C 1.32, 40, 44
2.137, 381, 467, [500], 563, 1638

T&C 3.56, 378, 1326
      4.1162, 1212
      5.538, 1105, 1212, 1434, 1750, 1761, 1781,
         1787, 1795, 1798, 1805, 1839
LGW 10, 14(14), 186, 277(180), 286(189), (273),
      (278), (333), 456(446), 705, 1039, 1076,
      [2228-34], 2457
GP 573, 769, 854
KnT 1520, 1665, 2104, 3064, 3099, 3108
MillT p3132, 3164, 3165, 3172
         3281, 3325, 3369, 3427, 3454, 3491, 3526,
         3558, 3588, 3592, 3595, 3709, 3743, 3769,
         3792, 3795, 3815, 3838, 3854
RvT p3918
      4026, 4036, 4073, 4086, 4087, 4089, 4118, 4187,
      4247, 4252, 4270, 4322
CkT p4335, 4339
MLT i18
      156, 160, 169, 195, 245, 333, 334, 439, 476,
      477, 523, 602, 639, 733, 782, 813, 872, 873,
      907, 914, 938, 942, 943, 962, 1019, 1023,
      1060, 1146, 1155
      e1166, 1169, 1175, 1181
ShipT 113(1303), 115(1305), 125(1315), 135(1325),
         148(1338), 166(1356), 170(1360), 193(1383),
         207(1398), 219(1409), 226(1416), 264(1454),
         274(1464), 286(1476), 345(1535), 355(1545),
         380(1570), 383(1573), 385(1575), 393(1583),
         406(1596), 421(1611), 424(1614), 433(1623),
         438(1628)
PrT [p469(1659)]
      577(1767), 607(1797), 683(1873), 688(1878)
Thop 723(1913), 831(2021), 908(2098), 919(2109),
         922(2112), 936(2126)
Mel 982(2172), 1015(2205), 1034(2224), 1058(2248),
      1079(2269), 1080(2270), 1090(2280), 1100(2290),
      1106(2296), 1116(2306), 1118(2308), 1119(2309),
      1304(2494), 1405(2595), 1406(2596), 1407(2597),
      1446(2636), 1495(2685), 1625(2815), 1626(2816),
      1627(2817), 1628(2818), 1641(2831), 1657(2847),
      1658(2848), 1661(2851), 1663(2853), 1664(2854),
      1680(2870), 1714(2904), 1716(2906), 1717(2907),
      1719(2909), 1868(3058), 1873(3063), 1883(3073),
      1885(3075)
MkT p1897(3087), 1932(3122), 1943(3133), 1950(3140),
      1962(3152), 2008(3198), 2017(3207), 2041(3231),
      2046(3236), 2168(3358), 2177(3367), 2179(3369),
      2182(3372), 2210(3400), 2212(3402), 2213(3403),
      2219(3409), 2221(3411), 2225(3415), 2231(3421),
      2436(3626), 2523(3713), 2525(3715), 2590(3780),
      2599(3789), 2609(3799), 2615(3805), 2622(3812)

```
NPT  p2788(3978)
     2828(4018),  2894(4084),  2896(4086),  2909(4099),
     2917(4107),  2922(4112),  2943(4133),  2974(4164),
     3050(4240),  3054(4244),  3097(4287),  3120(4310),
     3159(4349),  3188(4378),  3203(4393),  3234(4424),
     3243(4433),  3248(4438),  3295(4485),  3408(4598),
     3425(4615),  3432(4622),  3433(4623),  3444(4634)
WBT  p5,  15,  28,  37,  39,  41,  44,  50,  60,  69,  78,  102,
     103,  128,  [150],  151,  164,  201,  207,  223,  385,
     401,  423,  450,  483,  489,  491,  493,  501,  504,
     525,  530,  539,  586,  596,  605,  621,  634,  663,
     693,  805,  823,  826,  833
     917,  1060,  1096,  1103,  1129,  1150,  1162,  1173,
     1178,  1202,  1242,  1264
FrT  p1270,  1276,  1292
     1435,  1443,  1483,  1555,  1564,  1578,  1585,  1612,
     1642
SumT p1673,  1702,  1707
     1717,  1723,  1747,  1749,  1772,  1784,  1787,  1807,
     1809,  1810,  1834,  1850,  1858,  1861,  1886,  1890,
     1892,  1913,  1937,  1941,  1948,  1972,  2006,
     2013,  2014,  2053,  2103,  2106,  2112,  2153,
     2169,  2177,  2193,  2197,  2202,  2205,  2207,
     2210,  2232,  2252,  2265
ClT  p7,  30
     133,  135,  136,  155,  157,  159,  206,  274,  395,
     423,  455,  491,  505,  611,  616,  718,  821,  830,
     839,  841,  852,  977,  1034,  1062,  1064,  1076,
     1088,  1096,  1151,  1171,  1212b
MerchT p1232,  1240
     1262,  1267,  1301,  1308,  1311,  1325,  1327,
     1352,  1353,  1367,  1373,  1401,  1404,  1423,
     1449,  1457,  1489,  1493,  1510,  1544,  1549,
     1621,  1629,  1660,  1665,  1671,  1688,  1707,
     1758,  1761,  1762,  1787,  1792,  1814,  1851,
     1874,  1974,  2113,  2125,  2165,  2175,  2195,
     2290,  2291,  2293,  2299,  2300,  2341,  2375,
     2377,  2385,  2392,  2418
SqT  458,  464,  469,  534,  573
     e679,  707
FranklT p1270,  1276,  1292
     1435,  1443,  1483,  1555,  1564,  1578,  1585,
     1612,  1642
PhysT  [19],  242,  248,  250,  278,  282
PardT  i304,  308
     p386,  457
     523,  555,  576,  633,  640,  647,  651,  654,  692,
     695,  701,  715,  726,  748,  750,  757,  766,  782,
     843,  904
SecNT  p38
     125,  135,  162,  207,  239,  267,  278,  335,  351,
     353,  357,  358,  378,  418,  508
```

CYT p583, 593, 641, 651, 665, 715
    723, 740, 839, 865, 1046, 1048, 1064, 1073,
    1176, 1243, 1274, 1327, 1351, 1357, 1361,
    1372, 1375, 1472, 1476, 1481
MancT p15, 21
    160, 221, 248, 318, 322, 331, 343
ParsT p20, 44, 72
    153, 155, 161, 168, 170, 176, 179, 184, 185,
    189, 191, 195, 198, 200, 201, 218, 220, 221,
    225, 236, 244, 252, 261, 262, 268, 282, 283,
    290, 291, 294, 296, 301, 302, 303, 304, 307,
    323, 326, 327, 328, 337, 338, 340, 356, 359,
    365, 366, 367, 368, 369, 370, 375, 378, 383,
    392, 430, 434, 435, 442, 443, 457, 458, 474,
    479, 487, 499, 500, 501, 515, 516, 517, 522,
    523, 544, 545, 561, 580, 581, 582, 587, 588,
    589, 592, 595, 596, 606, 607, 619, 625, 630,
    633, 643, 648, 661, 676, 679, 682, 683, 687,
    693, 699, 708, 712, 713, 718, 734, 740, 750,
    751, 760, 771, 772, 778, 781, 783, 789, 793,
    795, 798, 818, 832, 837, 838, 839, 842, 844,
    859, 860, 867, 879, 881, 882, 883, 893, 894,
    900, 921, 928, 970, 972, 983, 984, 985, 986,
    988, 989, 1005, 1026, 1030, 1039, 1043, 1045,
    1050, 1054, 1062, 1075, 1079
Ret 1084, 1092
ABC 27, 31, 108, 137, 138, 145
Pity 98
Mars 141, 142, 154, 218
Truth 19
Sted 27
Scog 37
Buk 15, 31
d'Am 58, 72, 83
Astr 36, 56, 107
Father (Fader, Fadir).
    Bo 3.p9.198; m9.1, 38
    PrT p472(1662)
    ClT 557
    SecNT 208, 326, 328
    ABC 52, 130
    Gent 1, 8, 9
Heaven's King.
    HF 1084
    MillT 3464
    MLT 458
    NPT p2796(3986)
    SecNT 542
Holy Ghost (Holi Gost, Goost).
    Rom 7103, 7181, 7216
    SecNt 328

Holy Ghost (cont.)
    ParsT 250, 311, 485, 695, 783
    Ret 1092
    ABC 114, 130
Judge (Juge).
    Mel 1458(2648)
    SecNT 389
King of Grace.
    SecNT 399
Lord.
    BD 1175
    HF 470, 1305, 1393, 1395, 2121
    PF 171, 379, 669
    T&C 1.877
        2.597, 694
        3.57, 82, 206, 956
        4.362
        5.82, 529, 1862
    MillT 3535
    MLT 762, 826?
    PrT 453(1643)
    Mel 1000(2190)
    WBT p384
    SumT 2118?
    MerchT 1258, 2162
    FranklT 876, 1000
    PardT 840
    SecNT 136, 207
    ParsT 131, 176, 309, 760?
Lord God.
    ParsT 75, 588
Trinity.
    PrT 646(1836)
    SumT 1824
    SqT e682
ambivalent allusions: GOD.
    A&A 277, 287, 311
    T&C 1.195, 276, 334, 400, 436, 459, 517, 519,
            526, 533, 552, 558, 571, 597, 612, 715,
            770, 826, 835, 917, 1005, 1027, 1041, 1047,
            1049, 1055
        2.85, 93, 96, 113, 114, 115, 123, 127, 133,
            155, 163, 182, 183, 213, 225, 243, 246,
            290, 309, 336, 364, 430, 431, 568, 577,
            582, 588, 590, 686, 744, 751, 958, 978,
            992, 995, 1004, 1019, 1060, 1107, 1126,
            1131, 1138, 1200, 1212, 1213, 1230, 1234,
            1237, 1261, 1263, 1272, 1274, 1282, 1317,
            1319, 1360, 1363, 1409, 1464, 1476, 1551,
            1561, 1565, 1676, 1686, 1690, 1713, 1728,
            1731, 1757

ambivalent allusions: GOD (cont.)
    T&C 3.12, 49, 61, 66, 73, 100, 102, 118, 120, 123,
        162, 240, 260, 265, 321, 335, 343, 372, 378,
        416, 474, 545, 609, 619, 663, 755, 761, 795,
        807, 813, 816, 849, 864, 869, 875, 878, 925,
        930, 941, 951, 966, 1027, 1040, 1048, 1053,
        1058, 1084, 1124, 1138, 1165, 1185, 1224,
        1246, 1277, 1289, 1290, 1301, 1349, 1357,
        1378, 1385, 1387, 1400, 1410, 1430, 1437,
        1456, 1470, 1481, 1501, 1503, 1509, 1512,
        1518, 1526, 1565, 1566, 1619, 1621, 1639,
        1645, 1649, 1765
    4.69, 109, 157, 325, 383, 407, 439, 498, 566,
        613, 693, 696, 723, 738, 895, 904, 963,
        974, 975, 986, 991, 993, 1011, 1046, 1062,
        1066, 1231, 1286, 1319, 1364, 1444, 1532,
        1556, 1561, 1600, 1604, 1619, 1647, 1652,
        1654, 1664
    5.124, 144, 153, 156, 159, 227, 333, 347,
        363, 392, 423, 430, 481, 486, 507, 522,
        608, 656, 707, 766, 959, 963, 983, 1004,
        1007, 1074, 1127, 1147, 1161, 1263, 1359,
        1363, 1392, 1411, 1604, 1631, 1702, 1706,
        1713, 1733, 1739, 1742
    LGW 755, 905, 910, 1538, 1571, 1625, 1726, 1731,
        1792, 2056, 2082, 2264, 2329, 2340, 2401,
        2512, 2533, 2538, 2651
    KnT 1084, 1127, 1252, 1282, 1317, 1599, 1800,
        1810, 1863, 2782
    MancT 248
    Mars 141, 142, 154, 218
ambivalent allusions: Lord.
    T&C 1.528, 803, 1025
    2.276, 464, 885, 943, 975, 981, 1053, 1753
    3.656
    4.1175, 1236, 1564
    5.502, 735

GOD OF LOVE see LOVE.

GOD OF SLEEP see MORPHEUS.

THE GODS, a general reference to the pantheon.
    Rom 5959
    BD 166, 230, 235, 1328   = gods of Sleep
    HF 172, 460, 594, 1002
    Bo 3.p12.134
      4.p3.49
    LGW (10), 387, 1360, 1639, 1891, 1920, 2222, 2264,
      2522, 2578
    Scog 3

GOLIATH (Golias), the giant of Gath defeated and killed by DAVID; I _Samuel_ 17.4-54. The account is not in TRIVET.
MLT 934

GOOD ADVENTURE, i.e. Good Fortune. Since the Lady enjoys good fortune she will not impair it by bestowing any thought upon her lover: _Skeat_ 1.527.
Lady 28

GOODELIEF, the name given his wife by Harry Bailly, the Host.
MkT p1894(3084)

GOOD-HOPE, cited by the God of Love as a necessary companion of the Lover (together with SWEET THOUGHT, SWEET LOOKING, and SWEET SPEECH).
Rom 2941

GORDON, Bernard, fl. at the beginning of the 14th cent., a professor of medicine at Montpellier. His _Lilium_, written c. 1305, while primarily a textbook of natural medicine, listed the remedies for the plague and discussed the efficacy of bleeding. See Bowden 201 and Thorndike 2.479ff., 856ff.
GP 434

GOVERNANCE, self-control, one of the attendants at the hearse of Pity.
Pity 41

GOWER, John, d. 1408, a contemporary and friend of Chaucer, who served as Chaucer's executor in 1378; see Fisher.
T&C 5.1856
[MLT 177]

GRACE, one of the qualities of Beauty withdrawn by Cruelty; i.e. Grace is necessary to the Beauty of Pity.
Pity 70

GRAUNSON _see_ OTES DE GRANSON.

ST. GREGORY, the Great, Gregory I, c. 540-604, was elected pope in 590 but tried to escape his coronation. He was one of the four greater doctors of the Western Church. After he accepted election he set about extending and strengthening the prestige and authority of the Roman see. Because he was responsible for the mission of Augustine to Britain in 596 he enjoyed great prestige in name as well as in his writings. Apparently Chaucer did not know his _Dialogues_ but seems to have made use of his _Moralium_ or Commentary on Job and at least one of his homilies on the Gospels. See Petersen, S&A, and Hazelton.
Mel _1497(2687)_
ParsT 92, 214, 238, 414, 470, 692, 828, 934, 1069

Moralium
   [3.18.60   ParsT 828
    9.63-6   175-230
    .66   214]
   <17.24   FrT 1413>   + Isaiah
   [34.19.36   ParsT 1069]
Homilies on the Gospels
   [2.40.3   ParsT 414, 934]

GRISEL, properly, a gray horse, i.e. an old man. Skeat 1.557.
   Scog 35 = Chaucer

GRISELDA, the epitome of patience; S&A.
   ClT 210, 232, 255, 274, 297, 335, 344, 365, 428,
     442, 466, 470, 537, 576, 752, 792, 948, 953,
     989, 1007, 1009, 1029, 1030, 1051, 1062,
     1143, 1147, 1165, 1177, 1182, 1187
   MerchT p1224

GROANING
GRUDGING, the harbingers of Old Age.
   Rom 5000

<GROSSETESTE, Robert, d. 1253, one of the most famous and most
  prolific of English intellectuals associated with Oxford, of
  which he became Chancellor in 1207; 1235-53 he was bishop of
  Lincoln. See Fleming.
  Epistolae
    ?48   GP 498-500>

<GUALTIER DE CHATILLON, fl. during the later half of the 12th
  cent., was archdeacon of Tournay. His Alexandreis, sive Gesta
  Alexandri Magni was based upon Quintus Curtius. ALANUS DE
  INSULIS contemptuously refers to Gualtier as Maevius in
  Anticlaudianus 1.167. See Louns 2.353-5, and S&A.
  Alexandreis
    general   MkT 2631(3821)ff.
    7.381ff   WBT p498
                 PhysT 16>

GUIDO DELLE COLONNE (Columpnis), a Sicilian judge who produced
  in 1278 a rhetorical Latin prose paraphrase of BENOÎT's Roman
  de Troie entitled Historia Trojana or, as it is now called,
  the Historia Destructionis Troiae. See Hamm 91, Louns 2.309-12,
  Root, Griffin, Shannon 208, Lumiansky, and Wells [72].
    HF 1469
    LGW 1396, 1464
  <Historia Destructionis Troiae (Strassburg, 1489)
    ?general   BD 326ff.
    ?passim   T&C 3.797   Orestes>Horestes>
                                     Horaste?
    Book I   LGW 1368ff. [ed. Griffin
    Book II   1580-1655   "   ]

<Historia Destructionis Troiae (cont.)

a5^{r}1	T&C 3.1809–10
c1^{v}2	2.616–8
e2^{r}1	5.799–805
e2^{r}2	5.806–26
e2^{v}1	2.158
e2^{v}1–2	5.827–40
e6^{r}1	1.68–70
e6^{r}1–2	4.1411
f5^{v}2	5.403
i1^{r}1	4.50–4, 57–8
i1^{v}1	4.137–8, 169–210
i2^{r}2	4.18–20, 813ff., 1415–21
i2^{v}1	5.189, 1002–3
i2^{v}1–2	5.1013
i3^{r}1	4.1397–8, 1404–11, 1478–82
i3^{r}2	4.18–20
i4^{v}	NPT 3141(4331) + DARES 24
	+ BENOÎT 15263
i6^{r}1	T&C 5.1548–61
i6^{v}1	3.540
k5^{v}–12^{v}	5.1751–6
k6^{r}2	3.1774–5
k6^{v}2–11^{r}1	5.1044–50
13^{v}	BD 1069 + BENOÎT
m1ff.	1117
m1^{r}1–4^{r}1	T&C 4.203–5>

GUILE, Fraud, one of the offspring of False-Semblance who is
recounting his deeds to the God of Love because he has just
been accepted in service.
      Rom 6112, 6198, 7402

<GUILLAUME DE GUILLEVILLE, a Cistercian of a house near Senlis
who wrote the Pelerinage de la Vie Humaine in 1331 from which
Chaucer translated the ABC; Skeat 1.58–61, 261–71.>

[GUILLAUME DE LORRIS, fl. about 1230 and died c. 1237, was the
author of the first part (to line 4058) of RR; see Fleming.
      MerchT 2032]

GUILLAUME DE ST. AMOUR, a professor at the Sorbonne toward the
middle of the 13th cent. who was a partisan of the secular
clergy in their controversy with the friars. His Tractatus
Brevis de Periculis Novissimorum Temporum was used by Jean de
Meun. It was condemned by Alexander IV in 1256 and Guillaume
was banished from France; Langlois.
      Rom 6763, 6778, 6781

<De Periculis

1(p.21)	Rom 6993–4
2(p.25)	6631

<De Periculis (cont.)
    (p.52)   Rom 6615
  4(p.12)   6875
  5(p.32)   6871ff.
 12(p.48)   6573, 6661ff., 6691
  (p.49)   6653
  (pp.49-51)   6685ff.
  (pp.50-1)   6552-3>

GUY DE WARWICK (Gy), an English metrical romance of the early 14th cent. based on an AN version; Wells [7].
    Thop 899(2089)

H

HABERDASHER, one of the five guildsmen among the pilgrims.
    GP 361

HABRADATES (Habradate), Abradates, king of the Susi who was killed in battle against the Egyptians, whereupon his wife, PANTHEA, killed herself with his dagger and fell upon his breast; Adv. Jov. 1.45 which is from Xenophon, Cyropaedia 7.
    FranklT 1414, 1416

HALI IBN ABBAS, 'Ali ibn-al-'Abbas al Majūsi, died 994. A Zoroastrian whose al-Kitāb al-Malaki (the royal book, Liber regius) was a medical treatise superseded only by IBN-SINA's āl-Qanūn. The most scientific parts of the Kitāb are devoted to dietetics and materia medica; Hitti 367.
    GP 431

HANNIBAL (Hanybal), 247-183 B.C., the son of Hamilcar Barca, was a successful Carthaginian general during the second Punic war 220-216, after which he set about restoring corrupt Carthage. His only defeat was suffered at the hands of Scipio at Zama in 202. Rome's demand for his surrender forced him to flee to ANTIOCHUS of Syria, then to Crete then to Prusias, king of Bithynia, at whose court he took poison.
    MLT 290

HARDINESS, one of the barons of Love who, with Security, assailed Dread.
    Rom 5861

HARPIES, the Stymphalian birds slain by HERCULES in his fifth labor; Meta. 9.187. Cf. Shannon 312-7.
    Bo 4.m7.33
    MkT 2100(3290)

HASDRUBAL, the king of Carthage who was killed when the Romans
    burned the city during the third Punic war in 146 B.C. His
    wife and her two sons burned themselves in despair; Adv. Jov.
    1.43.
        NPT 3363(4553)
        FranklT 1399

HATE, the first figure on the wall outside the garden of Mirth.
        Rom 147

he,

        SumT 1085 see SOLOMON.
        MerchT 2032 see GUILLAUME DE LORRIS.

HECTOR, son of Priam and Hecuba, husband of Andromache, father of
    Astyanax, and chief Trojan hero defeated by ACHILLES. To the
    Middle Ages he was one of the Nine Worthies. No particular
    source need be sought for his treatment.
        BD 328, 1065
        T&C 1.110, 113, 471
            2.153, 158, 171, 176, 183, 417 [644], 740,
                1450, 1481, 1627, 1698
            3.39, 193, 1775
            4.33, 176, 187, 193, 214
            5.1549, 1804
        LGW 934
        KnT 2832
        MLT 198
        NPT 3141(4331), 3142(4332), 3144(4334)

HECUBA, wife of PRIAM, mother of HECTOR, PARIS, CASSANDRA, TROILUS,
    POLYXENA and POLYDORUS. The reference in T&C 5 is not in Filo.
        T&C [4.1207]
            5.12

[HELEN, in TRIVET, the wife of Arsemius and daughter of Sallustius,
    the emperor's brother; i.e., she is really Constance's cousin.
        MLT 981, 982]

HELEN, the daughter of Jupiter and Leda and wife of MENELAUS. Her
    abduction by PARIS was the main reason for the Trojan war.
        BD 331
        PF 291
        Bo 4.m7.7
        T&C 1.62, 455, 677
            2.1447, 1556, 1576, 1604, 1625, 1641, 1667,
                1687, 1703, 1714
            3.204, 222, 225, 410
            4.1347
            5.890
        LGW 254(208)

MLT 170
MerchT 1754

ST. HELEN, c. 247-c. 327, the wife of Constantius I Calorus and
mother of Constantine the Great. She is the legendary dis-
coverer of the true Cross.
PardT 951

HELIE see ELI.

HELOISE, died 1164, the lover and wife of ABELARD who, after the
birth of a son, married against her wishes. She then entered
the convent of Argenteuil where she became abbess; Abelard
was emasculated by her uncle Fulbert; RR 8760-8818.
WBT p677

HEMONYDES see MAEON.

HERCULES (Ercules), the most famous of Greek heroes, the son of
Alcmene and Jupiter, noted for his strength, courage, and com-
passion. After strangling serpents while in his cradle and
after his instruction by the greatest experts he killed a lion
on Mt. Cithaeron and there chose a short but glorious life
offered to him by Virtue. He returned to Thebes and relieved
the city of an enforced tribute. CREON in gratitude gave him
his daughter MEGARA. After some years Juno sent a fit of
madness upon Hercules and he killed Megara and his children
thinking they were enemies. The oracle bid him to go to Tiryns
and serve Eurystheus; thereby Hercules would atone for his
crime and moreover win immortality. According to the generally
accepted list, he performed twelve labors: he (1) choked the
NEMEAN LION, (2) beheaded the Lernean HYDRA, (3) caught the
ERYMANTHIAN BOAR and incidentally killed the CENTAURS PHOLUS
and CHIRON, (4) ran down the Ceryneian hind, (5) shot the man-
eating STYMPHALIAN birds or HARPIES, (6) cleaned the Augean
stables, (7) captured the Cretan bull of MINOS, (8) killed the
horses of DIOMEDES, (9) obtained the girdle of the Amazon worn
by HIPPOLYTA, (10) secured the oxen of Geryon and killed CACUS
who tried to steal them, (11) after killing BUSIRIS, gathered
the apples of the HESPERIDES by killing LADON, the dragon that
guarded the tree, and (12) descended to Hades and bound CERBERUS.
Subsequently, he married DEJANIRA by outwrestling ACHELOUS.
After killing NESSUS Hercules embarked on the expedition of
the ARGONAUTS. He then rescued ALCESTIS, the wife of ADMETUS,
from Death. After serving Omphale for a year to atone for
having killed one of IOLE's brothers he led an expedition
against LAOMEDON, king of Troy. Finally, Hercules attacked
Oechalia and carried off Iole. Dejanira to win him back,
followed the advice of NESSUS and sent Hercules a robe smeared
with the Centaur's blood. To escape the suffering, Hercules
had himself carried to Mt. Oeta and placed on a pyre. He gave

Iole to his son Hyllus and persuaded Poias, father of
PHILOCTETES to light the pyre. He was carried to heaven and
married to HEBE. See Hoffman 186-92; _Meta_. 9.1-272, _Hero_. 9.
  BD 1058
  HF 402, 1413
  PF 288
  Bo 2.p6.68
   4.p6.20; m7.28, 40, 41, 47, 48, 50, 53, 56
  T&C 4.32 = astrological
  LGW 515(503), 1454, 1480, 1501, 1514, 1519, 1524,
   1544
  KnT 1943
  MLT 200
  MkT 2095(3285), 2135(3325)
  WBT p725

HEREMIANUS (Hermanno), one of the sons of ZENOBIA and ODENATUS;
 De Clar. Mulier. 98.
  MkT 2345(3535)

HERENUS see FURIES.

HEREOS, the "lover's malady," usually refers to the mad desire of
 a lover for the object of his affection; _Robin_ 673 and Lowes.
  KnT 1374

HERMENGILD, the wife of the constable of Northumbria, befriended
 Constance; she was murdered by her husband who placed the
 blame on Constance; TRIVET.
  MLT 533, 535, 539, 562, 595, 597, 600, 625, 627

HERMES BALLENUS see BELINOUS.

HERMES TRISMEGISTUS, a Greek name applied to the Egyptian god
 Thoth. A large number of fourth cent. writings were attributed
 to Hermes; "popular" Hermetism dealt with astrology and other
 occult sciences: _Robin_ 672.
  CYT 1434

HERMIONE, daughter of MENELAUS and HELEN, given in marriage against
 her will by Agamemnon to Achilles's son PYRRHUS, in fulfillment
 of a promise made at Troy. Her letter, _Hero_. 8, is to her
 lover Orestes, AGAMEMNON's son and her own cousin.
  MLT 166

HERO, the lover of LEANDER. She was a priestess of Venus at Sestos
 and to be with her Leander swam the Hellespont each night from
 Abydos. One night he was drowned and she threw herself into
 the sea; _Hero_. 19.
  LGW 263(217)
  MLT 169

HEROD, Herod Antipas, reigned 4 B.C.-39 A.D., the murderer of
    John the Baptist and judge of Christ; Matthew 2 and 14, Mark
    6.14-29. The ranting Herod is associated with his characteriza-
    tion in the cycle plays "The Magi," "Herod," and "The Slaughter
    of the Innocents."
        MillT 3384
        PrT 574(1764)
        PardT 488

<HERODOTUS, c. 480-c. 425 B.C., the Greek historian generally
    regarded as the "father of history"; or, diversely, as the
    "father of lies."
    Histories
        ?1.8   WBT p782-3   + Adv. Jov.
        1.86, 87   Bo 2.p2.58>

HEROIDES see OVID.

HERSE, the object of Mercury's lust. He tried to enlist the help
    of her sister AGLAUROS; Meta. 2.708-832.
        T&C 3.729

he seith,
        Mel 1460(2650) = ST. PAUL

HESPERUS, the evening star, son or brother of Atlas.
        Bo 1.m5.11
           2.m8.7
           4.m6.15

HEZEKIAH (Ezechias), son and successor to Ahaz of Judah; Isaiah
    38.15.
        ParsT 983

HIPPOCRATES (Ipocras), one of the most famous Greek physicians,
    was born c. 460 B.C. in the island of Cos.
        BD 572
        GP 431

HIPPOLYTA (Ypolita), queen of the Amazons, lover of THESEUS and
    mother of HIPPOLYTUS; Theb. 12.519ff. and Tes.
        A&A 36
        KnT 868, 881, 971, 1685, 2578

[HIPPOLYTUS, the son of Hippolyta and Theseus. He rejected the
    illicit advances of PHAEDRA; her accusation led his father
    to invoke a pledge of Neptune and Hippolytus was thrown into
    the sea from his chariot; De Gen. Deor. 11.29 and "CEFFI."
    Cf. Meta. 552-9, Hero. 4.
        LGW 2099]

HIPPOMEDON, one of the seven against Thebes; he was drowned in the
   battle. See Theb. 9.315-591; the account is not in Filo.
      A&A 58
      T&C 5.1502

HOGGE OF WARE see COOK.

<HOLCOT or Holkot, Robert, an English Dominican who fl. during the
   first half of the 14th cent. He was at Oxford 1326-34 and
   held chairs at Oxford and at Cambridge; Holcot died c. 1349.
   He was the author of   Moralitates; commentaries on Wisdom,
   Ecclestiasticus, the Twelve Lesser Prophets; a large number of
   sermons. Sypherd 74-6 and Smalley EFA 133-202.
   Liber Sapientiae (Basle, 1586)
         Lec. 102   HF 41
              103   21, 36>

HOLOFERNES (Oloferno), Nebuchadnezzar's general killed by JUDITH;
   Judith.
         MLT 940
         Mel 1099(2289)
         MkT 2556(3746), 2567(3757)
         MerchT 1368

HOMER (Omer), ninth cent. B.C. Greek epic poet, author of the
   Iliad and the Odyssey. Homer was known to the Middle Ages in
   piecemeal translations and selections; Homer was universally
   revered but his works were generally unknown.
         HF 1466, 1477
         Bo 5. [p2.48]; m2.1, 2
         T&C 1.146
             5.1792
         FranklT 1443
      <Iliad
         1.363   quoted in Boethius but not in
                                      Bo 1.p4.4
          .605   Bo 5.m2.3
         3.277   5.p2.48
         12.176   4.p6.331
         21.441-57   T&C 4.120-6
      Odyssey
         12.323   Bo 5.p2.48>

HONESTY (Honestee), one of the attendants at the hearse of Pity,
   was amused by the plight of the Lover.
         Pity 40

HOPE, in Rom one of the solaces promised by the God of Love to the
   Lover; in KnT one of the circumstances of Love depicted on the
   wall of the temple of Venus.
         Rom 2803, 4439, 4463, 4564
         KnT 1925

<HORACE, Quintus Horatius Flaccus, 65-8 B.C., primarily known as
a satiric poet, was the friend of Virgil and protégé of
Maecenas. See Hamm 91, Louns 2.261-4, Shannon 359-60.
Sermonum
    2.5.59   Bo 5.p3.134
Epistularum
    1.6.37   Mel 1562(2752)   + ALBERTANUS
    .18.9   LGW 166   + Policraticus
    6.67-8   Mel 1071(2261)
Ars Poetica
    1-5   T&C 2.1037-43   + Policraticus
    70-1   2.22-5   + Metalogicon
                                                    + Convivio
    ?304-5   1.631ff.
    335ff.   Rom 2349ff.
    355-6   T&C 2.1030-6
    394ff.   MerchT 1715-7
                              MancT 116>

HORASTE, a person fabricated by Pandarus in order to attribute
jealousy to Troilus; i.e., Pandarus tells Criseyde that Troilus
doubts his chances as her lover. The name is Chaucer's invention; cf. GUIDO.
    T&C 3.797, 806

HORN, King Horn, the hero of the earliest of the English romances
written c. 1225 based on Thomas' AN Horn and Rimenild (c. 1170-
80); Wells [1-5].
    Thop 898(2088)

HOSPITALLERS, the Hospitalers of St. John of Jerusalem, an order
of military monks founded in 1119 to minister to the poor
pilgrims to the Holy Land.
    Rom 6693

HOST, Herry Bailly, the innkeeper of the "Tabard" and judge of
the Canterbury Tales.
    GP 747, 751, 823, 827
    MillT p3114, 3128, 3134
    RvT p3899, 4343
    [CkT p4358]
    MLT i1, 39
        e1163, 1172, 1174, 1184
    ShipT 435(1625)
    Thop p693(1883), 707(1896)
        920(2110)
    MkT p1891(3081)
    NPT p2780(3970), 2808(3998), 2816(4006),
        e3447(4637)
    WBT p850
    FrT p1286, 1298
        1335

```
        SumT 1762
        ClT p7, 22
             1212b
        MerchT p1233, 1240
              e2419, 2420
        SqT e695, 703
        PardT i287
             941, 943, 958, 964
        CYT p594, 615, 628, 652, 663, 697
        MancT p4, 21, 28, 56, 94
        ParsT p13, 65, 67
```

HOUSE OF FAME, the destination of Chaucer and the eagle; Sypherd
    103-55, 173-81.
        HF 663, 821, 882, 1023, 1027, 1070, 1105

HOUSE OF FAME, mentioned in the list of Chaucer's works.
    LGW 417(405)

HUBERD, the name of the FRIAR.

SIR HUGH, a name given to one of the priests whose incontinence
    became known to the summoner through his wenches.
        FrT 1356

HUGH OF LINCOLN, murdered by Jews in 1255; see the ballad of
    Sir Hugh in Child 3.233ff. Cf. Skeat 5.181-2.
        PrT 684(1874)

HUGOLINO OF PISA, made himself master of Pisa in 1288 but in 1299
    he was seized by the irate Pisans and thrown into prison to-
    gether with his two sons and grandsons where they all starved.
    In Inf. 33 Hugolino is in the lowest circle because he was,
    in effect, a traitor to his country; Inf. 33.1-90.
        MkT 2407(3597)

HYDRA (Idre, Idra), the Lernean hydra, the offspring of Typhon
    and Echidna, overcome by HERCULES; Meta. 9.69ff.
        Bo 4.p6.19; m7.42
        [MkT 2105(3295)]

<HYGINUS, Gaius Julius, c. 64 B.C.-17 A.D., was a Spanish freeman
    of Augustus and a friend of Ovid. He wrote a commentary on
    Virgil, Fabulae, and De Astronomica. It is highly unlikely
    that Chaucer knew, directly or indirectly, Hyginus; Hamm 92,
    Louns 2.287, Skeat 1.464 and 3.333-4.
    Fabulae
         9   T&C 1.699-700   + Meta.
         14 & 15   LGW 1368ff.
         29   T&C 3.1428
         51   LGW 510   + De Gen. Deor.
         89   T&C 4.120-6>

HYMEN (Ymeneus), the god of marriage and fruitfulness, son of
    Dionysus and Aphrodite; Servius in Aen. 1.651, Hero. Meta.,
    RR 22004(Michel).
        T&C 3.1258
        LGW 2250
        MerchT 1730

HYPERMNESTRA (Ypermystra), one of the daughters of DANAUS forced
    to marry one of the sons of AEGYPTUS. She spared her husband
    LYNCEUS; Hero. 14 and "CEFFI."
        LGW 268(222), 2575, 2594, 2604, 2632, 2647, 2663
        MLT 175

HYPOCRISY, one of the necessaries of False Semblance.
        Rom 6112, 6779

HYPSIPYLE (Isiphile), the daughter of Thoas, king of Lemnos.
    When the jealous women of Lemnos decided to kill all the men
    she spared her father. When the Argonauts passed through she
    fell in love with and bore twin sons to JASON. After his
    desertion Hypsipyle was driven from the island because it was
    discovered that she had spared her father. She was captured
    by pirates and sold to LYCURGUS of Nemea, to whose son OPHELTES
    she became nurse. When the Seven marched against Thebes she
    left the child and he was devoured by a dragon. The seven
    champions gave him a splendid funeral and founded the Nemean
    games in his honor. Hypsipyle was saved from the anger of
    Lycurgus and finally rescued by her sons who arrived and
    recognized her; Hero. 6, Theb. 4.739ff., VALERIUS FLACCUS, GUIDO.
        HF 400
        LGW 266(220), 1395, 1467, 1469
        MLT 167

I

<IAMBLICUS, died c. 330 B.C., was a Syrian mystic and a pupil of
    Porphyry. He was also the author of an explanation of
    Pythagoreanism which was known as the Vita Pythagorae.
    De Vita Pythagorae
        18.86   Bo 1.p4.260>

IARBAS, the son of Jupiter and an African nymph, was ruler of
    Libya and a suitor of DIDO. He was told by Rumor of the love
    of Dido and AENEAS and his jealous prayer to Jupiter caused
    his father to send Mercury to tell Aeneas to be on his way;
    Aen. 4.196 and Servius.
        LGW 1245

ICARUS, the son of DAEDALUS, was killed when he flew too near the
    sun on the artificial wings constructed by his father for their

escape from Crete; Meta. 8.18ff., Ecl. Theod. 101-3, Inf.
17.109-14, Amorosa Visione 35, RR 5226-7.
    HF 920

IDLENESS (Ydelnesse), in Rom the porter at the door to the garden
of Mirth; in KnT the porter in the picture on the wall in the
temple of Venus.
    Rom 593, 629, 631, 643, 696, 1273, 3225, 3233,
        4526, 4564
    KnT 1940

IDRE see HYDRA.

INCARNATION, used for dating.
    Rom 7096

INFORTUNE, Misfortune, mentioned in Reason's discourse to the Lover
about friendship.
    Rom 5493, 5551

INNOCENT, Innocent III, pope 1198-1216, studied theology at Paris
and canon and civil law at Bologna. While a cardinal deacon
he wrote De Contemptu Mundi sive De Miseria Humanae Conditionis
between 1191-98; Hamm 92, Louns 2.329-36, Lewis.
    LGW (415)
    Mel 1568(2758)
De Contemptu Mundi (PL 217.701ff.)
    general   *LGW (416)
    [1.16   Mel 1568(2758)]
    <1.2   KnT 1303-12   + Ecclesiastes + Bo
      .22   MLT 1132-8   + Ecclestiasticus
                                             + Job
      .23   421ff.   + Ecclestiasticus
                                             + Proverbs + Bo
    2.1   MkT 2009(3199)?
     .17   PardT 505ff., 537ff.
     .19   MLT 771-7
     .21   925-31>

IOLE, the daughter of Eurytus, was loved by HERCULES. Hercules
murdered her brother Iphitus, for which he became the slave of
Omphale for a year. He finally carried off Iole and DEJANIRA
took NESSUS's advice and sent him the poisoned robe. Iole
was given to Hercules' son, Hyllus. See Hero. 9.6, 133;
Meta. 9.140, 278; "CEFFI."
    HF 403

IPOCRAS see HIPPOCRATES.

IPOMEDON see HIPPOMEDON.

IRE, one of the Seven Deadly Sins; in Rom one of the senators
in the palace of Age; in T&C one of the vices fled by Troilus
after he fell in love.
Rom 4997
T&C 3.1805

ISAAC (Yssak), son of ABRAHAM and SARAH, was the father of JACOB
and ESAU; Genesis 22 and 27.
Mel 1098(2288)
ABC 169

ISAIAH (Ysaye), 738-690 B.C., son of Amoz, was the greatest of
the Hebrew major prophets. Through a series of political
crises he remained the prophet of Faith; BIBLE.
HF 514
ParsT 198, 209, 210, 281

ISCARIOT (Scariot) see JUDAS ISCARIOT.

ISIDORE OF SEVILLE (St. Ysidre), c. 560-636, became archbishop of
Seville in 600. His Etymologiae sive Origines was the most
important encyclopedia used during the Middle Ages; Manitius
1.52-70, Pratt.
ParsT 89, 551
[?Sententiarum (PL 83.615)
2.3   ParsT 89]
Etymologiae (ed. Lindsay)
<8.11.81-3   BD 512
9.7.29   WBT p257-62>
[17.7   ParsT 551]

ISIPHILE see HYPSIPYLE.

ISIS (Isidis), the greatest of the Egyptian goddesses, was the
sister and wife of Osiris and mother of Horus. The reference
here, however, is to the famous incident in which Herostratus
set fire to the temple of Diana at Ephesus. The confusion has
not been satisfactorily explained. Skeat 3.283 suggests a
misreading of Ovid's Ex Ponto 1.1.52.
HF 1844

ISOLDE (Isoude, Isaude), the Fair, was the wife of Mark of Cornwall
but the lover of TRISTRAM.
HF 1796
PF 290
LGW 254(208)

ISOPE see AESOP.

ITHACUS see ULYSSES.

it is written (writen),
          Rom 5409   = BOETHIUS
          Mel 1463(2653)   = PUBLILIUS SYRUS
               1846(3036)   =   "   "
               1850(3040)   = DECREES

IULUS see ASCANIUS.

ST. IVES (Yve), is either Ivo of Chartres or Yves, the patron saint
     of Brittany. Ivo of Chartres, c. 1040-1116, bishop of
     Chartres, was of a noble family near Beauvais. He studied
     at Paris and Bec under Lanfranc. Yves, 1253-1303, was a
     lawyer and judge who studied at Paris and Orléans. Canonized
     in 1347, he became the patron saint of Brittany and of lawyers.
     Cline favors Ivo of Chartres.
          ShipT 227(1417)
          SumT 1943

IXION, a Thessalian who married Dia, murdered his father-in-law.
     Ixion was purified by Jupiter but he tried to win the affection
     of Juno. In order to deceive him Jupiter formed Nephele and by
     her Ixion sired the CENTAURS. For his crimes he was bound on
     a wheel that turned forever; Georg. 3.38 and 4.484, Meta. 4.461.
          Bo 3.m12.37
          T&C 5.212

J

JACK (Jakke), a common name, or nickname for John, often used with
     contempt.
          MillT 3708
          FrT 1357

JACK STRAW, the name or nickname of one of the leaders in the
     Peasant's Revolt of 1381.
          NPT 3394(4584)

JACOB, son of ISAAC and REBECCA and twin brother of Esau, by
     artifice obtained his brother's birthright: Esau sold the
     birthright and Jacob, with Rebecca's advice, deceived his
     father into giving him his blessing. Jacob married Leah and
     RACHEL by whom he was the father of JOSEPH. Genesis 24.28-34
     and 27.
          Mel 1098(2288)
          WBT p56
          MerchT 1362
          ParsT 443

JACOBIN see DOMINICANS.

JACOBUS JANUENSIS, Jacobus de Voragine, c. 1230–c. 1298, became
    archbishop of Genoa in 1292. He is the author of <u>Legenda</u>
    <u>Aurea</u>, a collection of saints' lives which was extremely
    popular.
        SecNT p[82], post84
    <u>Legenda</u> <u>Aurea</u> (ed. Grässe, Leipzig, 1850)
        general   SecNT p post 84
        [general   LGW 1689]
        <5   SumT 1980
        47   ABC 163
        56   MLT 500
        77   SecNT 177
        130   CYT 1185
        222   FrT 1613>

ST. JAMES (Jame), St. James the Great, the son of Zebedee and
    brother of JOHN, was one of the most important of the apostles.
    He suffered martyrdom under Herod Agrippa and according to
    popular, persistent legend, after his death his body was
    miraculously transported to Compostela. He is the patron
    saint of Spain. The reference in GP is to the shrine; the
    others are oaths taken in the name of the saint.
        HF 885
        GP 466
        RvT 4264
        ShipT 355(1545)
        WBT p312
        FrT 1443

ST. JAMES (Jame), St. James the Less, the son of Alpheus of
    Cleophas, was martyred in 62. Traditionally, he was the
    brother or cousin of Jesus.
        Mel 1119(2309), 1517(2707), 1676(2866) = Seneca,
            1869(3059)
        ClT 1154
        ParsT 348

JANICLE, the father of GRISELDA.
        ClT 208, 304, 404, 632

JANKIN,
        (1) a derisive name for a priest
        MLT e1172
        (2) the Wife of Bath's fifth husband
        WBT p303, 383, 548, 595, 628, 713
        (3) the squire who proposed the method of dividing Thomas's
            gift
        SumT [2243], 2288, 2293

JANUARY (Januarie), the old knight; the name is Chaucer's
        MerchT 1393, 1478, 1566, 1579, 1586, 1695, 1724,

MerchT 1750, 1788, 1801, 1805, 1821, 1859, 1886,
        1895, 1906, 1920, 1946, 1956, 2008, 2013, 2023,
        2042, 2054, 2056, 2065, 2069, 2102, 2107, 2118,
        2134, 2156, 2186, 2214, 2218, 2320, 2355, 2412,
        2417

JANUARY (Januarius), the first month of the modern calendar.
    FranklT 1252   = Janus
    Astr 1.10.3, 12

JANUS, the two-faced god of doorways, later became the god of
    beginnings.
    T&C 2.77

JASON, son of Aeson of Iolcos, undertook the quest of the Golden
    Fleece because his uncle, Pelias, who had usurped the throne,
    was told to beware the appearance of a lad wearing one sandal.
    At Lemnos Jason married HYPSIPYLE. At Colchis Jason, with the
    magical help of MEDEA, performed the tasks imposed by AEETES.
    Jason and Medea returned to Colchis where Medea exacted
    vengeance on Pelias but this made it necessary for Jason and
    Medea to flee to Corinth where Jason abandoned her for Glauce,
    the daughter of CREON. See Meta. 7, Hero. 6 and 12, VALERIUS
    FLACCUS, and GUIDO Book 1.
        BD 330, 727
        HF 400, 401
        LGW 266(220), 1368, 1383, 1394, 1402, 1410, 1415,
            1419, 1420, 1440, 1451, 1454, 1472, 1480, 1491,
            1499, 1501, 1513, 1524, 1544, 1548, 1559, 1570,
            1576, 1580, 1585, 1589, 1601, 1603, 1611, 1620,
            1636, 1651, 1654, 1663, 1667
        MLT 174
        SqT 548, 549

JEALOUSY (Jealousie), the personification of suspicious rivalry.
    In Rom Jealousy builds a castle and immures Fair Welcome and
    the Rose against the Lover; PF and KnT are due to Tes. 7.59.
        Rom 3820, 3828, 3858, 3868, 3909, 3960, 3964, 3980,
            3997, 4020, 4048, 4059, 4146, 4203, 4277, 4285,
            4301, 4311, 4381, 4391, 4483, 4554, 7563
        PF 252
        KnT 1928
        Ven 33, 43, 53

<JEAN DE MEUN, or Meung or Clopinel, c. 1240-c. 1305, was educated
    at the Sorbonne and spent the rest of his life in Paris. He
    was a defender of GUILLAUME DE ST. AMOUR and a critic of the
    mendicants. Between 1268 and 1285 he continued and finished
    the RR (lines 4137-21780). The Testament is one of his last
    poems. For conclusive evidence that Chaucer also used Jean's
    translation of BOETHIUS see Lowes and Dédeck-Héry.

Testament (in RR 4[ed. Méon, Paris, 1814])
    461ff.   WBT p483
    1734ff.   RvT p3883ff.]

<JEHAN DE TUIM, the author of a 12th cent. romance dealing with
the deeds of Julius Caesar; Root in S&A describes it as a
13th cent. prose paraphrase of the Pharsalia. See Lowes
Chaucer 81, 87 and S&A 642.
Li Hystore de Julius Cesar (ed. Settegast, Halle, 1881)
    general   HF 482
                  MkT 2671(3861)-2726(3916)
    8ff., 244f.   MLT 400>

JEPHTHAH (Jepte), one of the judges of Israel, whose promise to
sacrifice the first person out of his house if God would give
him victory over the Ammonites led to the death of his daughter.
His daughter, who is nameless, mourned her virginity but not
her death. Judges 11.1-12.7; see Hoffman.
    PhysT 240

JEREMIAH (Jeremye), son of Hilkiah, was the last of the great
pre-exilic prophets. He fl. c. 626 B.C. in Jerusalem. See
BIBLE.
    PardT 635
    ParsT ante75, 76, 189, 592, [680]

ST. JEROME, c. 340-420, learned grammar from Donatus and rhetoric
from Victorinus. His search for the ascetic life led him
throughout most of the Empire; he finally settled in Bethlehem.
His asceticism and orthodoxy are reflected in most of his
works, Contra Jovinian being no exception. The Vulgate, com-
missioned by DAMASUS, was done about 404. EB. The Epistola
adversus Jovinianum dates from c. 388; texts in PL 23 and S&A.
The use of the Epistola is treated generally in Louns 2.292-7;
for the form in which Chaucer knew it and the extent to which
he knew it, see Pratt and Correale. For the possible importance
of glosses from the Epistola in WBTp, see Silvia.
    LGW (281), (284)
    Mel 1595(2785)
    WBT p674
    ParsT 159, 174, 345, 657, 904, 933, 1047
Epistola adversus Jovinianum
    general   *LGW 281
       "   *WBT p675
       "   *SumT 1929
    [1.40   SumT 1930
    .49   ParsT 904]
    <1.3, 5   WBT p28   + Genesis + Matthew
    .7   p145   + John
    .9   p46   + I Corinthians
    .10   p47   + I Corinthians

Epistola adversus Jovinianum (cont.)
     .11   ParsT 861
    1.12   WBT p61, 155
     .14   p11, 54   + Genesis
     .15   p33
     .28   p362-70,
                          371ff., 376,
                        378   + Proverbs
     .30   MerchT 2138-48
     .34   WBT p107ff.   + RR
     .36   p115ff.   + RR
   .40-6   FranklT 1355-1456
     .43   NPT 3363(4553)
     .46   MerchT 2277-90
     .47   1294,
                      1601-4 + RR + Miroir
                 MancT 148ff.   + THEOPHRASTUS
     .48   WBT p492, ?670ff.,
                      727-45,
                      782-3   + HERODOTUS
  ?2.3   FrT 1653-62
                   SumT 1937
     .6   WBT p107ff.   + RR
     .8   PardT 505ff.
    .10   549
    .11   FormAge 33ff. + Policraticus
    .22   WBT p91>
Epistola ad Eustachium de Virginitate
   [22.7   ParsT 345]
   <22.20   WBT p71-2>
<Contra Hierosolymitanum
    §8   ParSt 788>
<Epistolae
   61.3   ParsT 788>

JESUS CHRIST, according to Christianity, the Son of God and Lord
   and Savior of the World.
   CHRIST
      Rom 445, 6547, 6564, 7010, 7122, 7174, 7225, 7226,
        7494
      HF 271, 492
      T&C 5.1860
      LGW 1879
      GP 481, 527, 739
      MillT 3308, 3478, 3504, 3508, [3512], 3766, 3782
      RvT 4084, 4263
      CkT p4227, 4349
      MLT p106
         237, 258, 277, 283, 369, 429, 450, [451], [459],
        501, 511, 549, 561, 567, 570, 574, 636, 686,
        693, 721, 760, 766, 811, 825, 902, 924, 950,

```
JESUS CHRIST (cont.)
    MLT 1041, 1123
    PrT 492(1682), 510(1705), 538(1728), 550(1740),
        556(1746), [581(1771)], [584(1774)], 597(1787),
        618(1808), 656(1846), 678(1868)
    WBT p10, 107, 139
        1117
    FrT 1347, 1647, 1662
    SumT 1732, 1762, 1867, 1871, 1884, 1935, 1946, 1949,
        1977
    MerchT 1384, 1512, 1652, 2171, 2282
    PhysT 81
    PardT p340
        501, 532, 593, 652, 658, 898, 946
    SecNT p70
        123, [138], 171, 295, 343, 417, 454, 553
    CYT 1002, 1072, 1122, 1467
    ParsT p40
        413, 462, 526, 558, 559, 590, 591, 593, 596,
        598, 604, 623, 642, 643, 652, 661, 665, 666,
        667, 674, 697, 700, 703, 704, 708, 760, 767,
        791, 801, 811, 817, 820, 843, 878, 879, 882,
        884, 902, 922, 925, 929, 970, 990, 1001, 1052,
        1067, 1070, 1073
    Ret 1084, 1087
    ABC 28, 99, 161
    Buk 1
CHRIST JESUS
    FrT 1590
FATHER'S SON
    SecNT 326
GOD'S SON
    SecNT 325, 330, 345, 417
JESUS (Jesu)
    T&C 5.1868
    MillT 3464, 3711, 3717
    MLT 538, 690
    PrT 603(1793)
    WBT p15, 365
        1181, 1261
    FrT 1654
    SecNT 359
    CYT 967
    ParsT p48
        273, 285, 286, 287, 289, 598
JESUS CHRIST
    Rom 7186
    [T&C 5.1842, 1845, 1846, 1847]
    GP 698
    MillT 3483
    MLT 318, 565, 993, 1160
    PrT 652(1842)
```

JESUS CHRIST (cont.)
    Thop 944(2134)
    Mel 987(2177)
    WBT p/17
        1258
    FrT 1561
    SumT 1821
    PardT 916
    SecNT 191
    ParsT 79, 94, 110, 115=St. John the Baptist, 208,
        273, 275, 282, 284, 314, 358, 360, 384, 385,
        429, 504, 528, 597, 625, 638, 663, 668, 679,
        702, 745, 746, 768, 776, 790, 808, 811, 842,
        889, 906, 933, 944, 948, 959, 994, 997, 1002,
        1007, 1015, 1023, 1035, 1039, 1040, 1048, 1053,
        1054, 1072, 1076
    [ABC 57, 58, 59, 60, 61]
LORD
    BD 544, 651, 690, 1042
    ShipT 178(1368)
    FrT 1590
    PardT 473
    SecNT 191
LORD CHRIST
    MLT 811
    WBT p469
    ParsT 256
LORD JESUS (Jesu)
    WBT p146
    SumT 1904, 1921
LORD JESUS CHRIST
    Mel 1032(2222), 1074(2264), 1075(2265)
    ParsT 79, 94, 110, 116, 124, 162, 246, 255, 267, 269,
        270, 272, 315, 382, 447, 502, 526, 588, 689,
        950, 996
    Ret 1081, 1089
SAVIOR
    Rom 6434
SON
    PrT p466(1656)
    ABC 125, 172

JESUS FILIUS SIRACH, Jesus, son of Eleazar, son of Sirach, was a
    sage lover of the Law and the priesthood who wrote, between
    200 and 175 B.C., what is known as the Ecclesiasticus; see
    BIBLE.
    [MillT 3529:att. Solomon]
    [MLT p113]
    Mel 995(2185)=Proverbs, 1045(2235), 1059(2249),
        1141(2331), 1671(2861):att. Solomon
    MerchT 2250
    [ParsT 640, 712]

the Jew PardT 364 possibly JACOB.

JOAB, the son of Zeruiah, David's sister, played an important part
    in the successes of David; II Samuel (= II Kings [Vulg.]) 2.28,
    18.16, 20.22.
        HF 1245
        MerchT 1719

JOB, one of the most tenacious of Old Testament heroes, was
    considered the OT counterpart of the Greek tragic hero because
    of his patient reaction to a complete reversal of Fortune.
    He is, of course, strengthened and rewarded through the test
    of his faith; cf. BIBLE.
        Mel 999(2189)
        WBT p436
        FrT 1491
        ClT 932
        ParsT 134, 176, 178, 181, 211, 217, 223

JOCE see JODOCUS.

JOHN, a common name,
    (1)   the name of the cuckolded carpenter
        MillT 3369, 3501, 3513, 3577, 3639, 3662
            [3142, 3189, 3221, 3300, 3364, 3400, 3423,
            3448, 3474, 3490, 3496, 3500, 3522, 3537,
            3601, 3614, 3640, 3644, 3651, 3662, 3816,
            3843, 3914]
    (2)   the name of one of the students who ruined the miller
        RvT 4013, 4018, 4020, 4025, 4026, 4037, 4040,
            4044, 4071, 4084, 4091, 4108, 4109, 4114,
            4127, 4160, 4169, 4177, 4180, 4188, 4198,
            4199, 4228, 4259, 4262, 4284, 4292, 4295,
            4316
    (3)   the name given the friar who was rewarded by Thomas
        SumT 2171
            [1711, 1713, 1732, 1771, 1802, 1855, 1954,
            2127, 2137, 2144, 2152, 2157, 2166, 2168,
            2190, 2219, 2248, 2275]

DON JOHN (Daun John), a polite but often derisive reference to
    (1)   the monk who defrauded the merchant
        ShipT [25(1215)], [34(1224)], [36(1226)], 43(1233),
            58(1248), 68(1258), 89(1279), 98(1288), [124(1314)],
            [148(1338)], 158(1348), 187(1377), [195(1385)],
            211(1411), 255(1445), 282(1472), 294(1484),
            296(1486), 298(1488), 308(1498), 312(1502),
            314(1504), 319(1509), 322(1512), 337(1527),
            342(1532), 349(1539), 387(1577), 402(1592),
            [438(1628)], [440(1630)]
    (2)   the name by which the Host addresses the MONK
        MkT p1929(3119)

    (3)   Sir John, the NUN'S PRIEST
         NPT p2810(4000), 2820(4010)

ST. JOHN, the Apostle, was the son of Zebedee and brother of JAMES.
    Although now questioned, he was considered to have been the
    author of the Epistles and the Apocalypse; cf. BIBLE.
         Rom 7167, 7178, 7183, 7204
         BD 1319
         HF 1385
         PF 451
         MLT 118
            1019
         PrT 582(1772)
         Thop 951(2141)
         WBT p164
         FrT 1647
         SumT 1800, 2171, 2252
         SqT 596
         PardT 752
         ParsT 216, 349, 565, 687, 841, 933
         Mars 9

ST. JOHN CHRYSOSTOM, 345-407, was Patriarch of Constantinople
    398-404.
         ParsT 109

ST. JOHN OF DAMASCUS, Chrysorrhoas, died c. 752. His works have
    nothing whatever to do with medicine; the reference is there-
    fore, uncertain. See Robin 662.
         GP 433

ST. JOHN THE BAPTIST, the patron saint of missionaries, baptized
    Jesus in the river Jordan. He denounced the sins of his con-
    temporaries and was thrown into prison, and later beheaded,
    because he opposed HEROD ANTIPAS's act of making away with his
    brother to secure his brother's wife Herodias.
         Rom 6998
         PardT 491

JOHN OF GADDESDEN, b. 1280, attended Merton College Oxford and
    later became physician to Edward II. He was a reputable
    physician but extremely interested in making money; Bowden 202.
    His Rosa Medicinae, written c. 1305-7, dealt with herbalism.
         GP 434

<JOHN OF GAUNT, Duke of Lancaster, 1340-1399, fourth son of
    Edward III and Philippa. He married BLANCHE OF LANCASTER in
    1359. He was with his brother Edward in Aquitaine and Spain
    1366-67. At the death of Blanche in 1369 he married Constance,
    daughter of Pedro of Castile, and became embroiled in supporting
    his claim to the throne of Spain. Constance died in 1394 and

John married Catherine Swynford (Philippa Chaucer's sister) and
thereby legitimated the Beauforts. The exile of his son Henry
led to his death in 1399.
>   BD 1319
          ?253, 445, 457
knight
          BD 452, 529, 1178>

<JOHN OF SALISBURY, Joannis Saresberiensis, c. 1115-1180, was
    educated on the continent and studied especially with Robert
    of Melun, Gilbert de la Porree, and William of Conches. In
    1150 he became secretary to Theobald, archbishop of Canterbury
    and in 1161 to his successor Thomas a Becket. John became
    bishop of Chartres in 1176. Both the Policraticus and the
    Metalogicon were submitted to Becket in 1159. Hamm 93, Louns
    2.362-4, and Fleming.
Policraticus (ed. Webb, London, 1909)

1.5	BD 663	+ RR
	PardT 591ff.,	+ SENECA
	603	
2.15	HF 1ff.	
.18	T&C 2.1037-43	
.29	GP 438	
3.8	MLT 784	+ Inf.
.14	MancT 226	+ AUGUSTINE + CICERO
		+ Gesta Rom.
5.10	RvT 4134	+ RR
7.21	Rom 6135ff.	
8.6	FormAge 33ff.	+ Adv. Jov.
.11	WBT p766	
	Buk 14	
.13	LGW 166	+ HORACE

Metalogicon (PF 199)

1.16	T&C 2.22-5	+ Convivio
3.3	" >	

<JOHN OF WALES, a Minorite educated at Oxford where he served as
    regent at Greyfriars 1257-8. He spent some time on the con-
    tinent: it is known that he preached in Paris in 1270 and
    again in 1282. In 1282 he also served as envoy from Archbishop
    Pecham to Llewelyn. John died perhaps in 1285. See Smalley
    EFA 51.5. For the use of the Communiloquium see Pratt4: the
    ascriptions are still subject to question.
Communiloquium sive summa collationum (Strassburg, 1489).

1.3.3	PardT 480-7,	
	560-1	
.3.11	SumT 2043-88	+ SENECA
.4.4	2017-42	+ SENECA
.10.7	PardT 467-9	
	591-602	
2.4.2	WBTp 637-65	+ VALERIUS + Ecclus.
		+ RR

Communiloquium sive summa collationum (cont.)
.7.3	SumT 2111-3
.8.2	2086-7
3.1.2	WBTp 457-68
.2.6	RvTp 3888-95 + SENECA
.3.1, 2, and 3	WBT 1109-76
.3.2	1168-70
	1175-6
.3.3	1165-7, 1172-4
.3.4	WBTp 784-5
.4.2	WBT 1177-1202
4.3.7	PardT 558-9, 573-8
5.1.7	492-7, 583-7 + INNOCENT
	+ ALBERTANUS
7.3.4	RvTp 3882-5>

JOLLITY (Jolitee), one of the figures around the bier of Pity.
    Pity 39

JONAH (Jonas), a vindictive prophet, who, when he attempted to run
    away from his commission, was cast overboard and swallowed by
    a great fish and sent on his way to Nineveh. To his surprise
    the wicked city listened and repented and God spared it; cf.
    BIBLE. Jonah is Chaucer's substitution for TRIVET's Noah.
        MLT 486

JONATHAN (Jonathas), the eldest son of Saul who, together with his
    father, freed Israel from the Philistines. Jonathan's name is
    most familiar for the firm friendship he enjoyed with DAVID;
    I Samuel 13ff.
        LGW 251(205)

<JORDANES, fl. c. 550, wrote his De Origine Actibusque Getarum in
    Constantinople in 551, under the reign of Justinian I. De Ori-
    gine Actibusque Getarum (ed. Mommsen, Berlin, 1882)
        49   PardT 579>

ST. JOSEPH, husband of MARY and father of Jesus.
        ParsT 286

JOSEPH, the son of JACOB and RACHEL, was envied by his brothers
    and sold into Egypt where he succeeded by interpreting
    Pharoah's dreams. During a famine he provided for his family.
    He later led his people in the conquest of Palestine; Genesis
    30.
        BD 280
        NPT 3131(4320)
        ParsT 443, 880

<JOSEPH OF EXETER, Josephus Iscanus, fl. 1190, was a companion
    of Baldwin, archbishop of Canterbury, to the Holy Land in 1188.

He returned to England when the archbishop died in 1190.
Joseph's De Bello Trojano, c. 1184, is based on DARES; see
Root, and Riddenough.
De Bello Trojano (ed. Dresemius, London, 1825)

1.505ff.	PF 176-82
4.61-4	T&C 5.827-40
.124-7	.799-805
.156-62	.806-26
?6.402ff.	BD 1069>

JOSEPHUS, Flavius, 37-c. 95, a Jewish statesman and soldier, the
author of Early History of the Jews to 66 A.D. and History of
the Jewish Wars from the capture of Jerusalem in 170 B.C. by
ANTIOCHUS Epiphanes to its capture (which he witnessed) by
Titus in 70 A.D.
    HF 1433

JOVE see JUPITER.

JOVINIAN see ST. JEROME.

[JUAN RUIZ see PAMPHILUS.]

JUDAS ISCARIOT or SCARIOT, the son of Simon; the twelfth apostle
and the traitor. He was motivated by avarice; the realization
of the enormity of his deed caused him to commit suicide;
Matthew 27.3-8 and Acts 1.18.
    NPT 3227(4417) = Scariot
    FrT 1350
    CYT 1003, 1007
    ParsT 502, 616, 696, 1015

JUDAS MACCABEUS, one of the sons of Mattathias the Hasmonaean,
brother of John, Simon, Eleazar and Jonathan; i.e. one of a
family of Jewish heroes which delivered the Jews from the
persecutions of the Syrian king ANTIOCHUS Epiphanes and established a long line of priest-kings which lasted until
supplanted by HEROD in 40 B.C.; cf. BIBLE. Judas was one of
the Nine Worthies.
    Mel 1658(2848), [1660(2850)]

JUDICUM = Judges see BIBLE.

JUDITH, the Bethulian, the Jewish heroine who brought about the
death of HOLOFERNES, the general of NEBUCHADNEZZAR, and
thereby a rout of the Assyrians; see Judith.
    MLT 939
    Mel 1099(2289)
    MkT 2571(3761)
    MerchT 1366

ST. JUDOCUS (Joce), a Breton saint who died in 669. Apparently
   his hermitage became a famous monastery, in the diocese of
   Amiens, and was called St. Josse-sur-mer; Skeat 5.303.
      WBT p483

ST. JULIAN, the patron saint of hospitality and accommodation, is
   said to have died c. 313.
      HF 1023
      GP 340

JULIUS CAESAR see CAESAR.

JULY, the seventh month of the modern calendar.
      Astr 1.10.4, 12, 14, 17

JUNE, the sixth month of the modern calendar.
      Astr 1.10.4, 14

JUNO, daughter of Saturn, sister and wife of Jupiter, and the
   guardian deity of women.
         BD 109, 129, 132, 136, 187, 243, 267
         HF 198, 461
         A&A 51
         T&C 4.1116, 1538, 1594
             5.601
         LGW 2249
         KnT 1329, 1543, 1555, 1559

JUPITER (Juppiter), or JOVE, a son of Saturn, brother and husband
   of JUNO, the chief god among the Romans. The references in
   CYT and Astr are astrological. For the possible use of Jupiter
   as a Supreme Being see the ambivalent references under GOD.
   JUPITER
         HF 199, 215, 464, 591, 609, 642, 955
         Bo 2.p2.74
         T&C 2.233
             4.669, 1683
         LGW 1338, 1806, 2585
         KnT 2442, 2786, 2792, 3035, 3069
         MkT 2744(3934), 2752(3942)
         SecNT 364, 413
         CYT 828
         FormAge 56
         Astr 2.12.24, 28; 40.51, 72
   JOVE
         HF 219, 586, 597, 630, 661, 1041, 2007
         T&C 1.878
             2.1607
             3.3, 15, 150, 625, 722, 1015, 1016, 1428
             4.335, 644, 1079, 1149, 1192, 1337
             5.2, 207, 957, 1446, 1525, 1544, 1853

JOVE (cont.)
    LGW 525(513)
    KnT 2222
    MerchT 2224
GOD
    T&C 4.1086

JUSTINIAN I, the Great, 483-565, Roman emperor at Constantinople 527-65. In 529 Justinian instituted the commission responsible for the Corpus Juris Civilis (published in 553) which consisted of the Institutiones, Digesta (or Pandects), Codex, and Novellae.
    Rom 6615
    <Digesta

1.17.35	Mel 1783(2973)
.17.36	1541(2731)
45.1.26	1229(2419)>

    Codex

<8.4.1	Mel 1380(2570)>
[11.25(26)	Rom 6615]

JUSTINUS, as the name suggests, JANUARY's brother who advises against the marriage to MAY.
    MerchT 1477, 1519, 1655, 1689

JUVENAL, c. 60-140, the great Roman satirist. He was most active 98-128; i.e., during the reigns of Trajan and Hadrian. Hamm 94, Louns 2.260.
    [Bo 2.p5.181]
    T&C 4.197
    WBT 1192
    Saturae (ed. Ramsey, London, 1917)

<2.161	T&C 5.971	
6.440ff.	Bo 4.m5.11ff.	+ PLINY + TACITUS
9.54ff.	GP 626>	+ PLINY
[10.2-4	T&C 4.197-201	
.21	Bo 2.p5.179ff.	+ Convivio
	WBT 1192ff.	
.22	Bo 2.p5.181]	

K

KAY, the son of Ector and foster brother of ARTHUR. He was a knight of the Round Table and seneschal or steward to Arthur. His reputation for surliness and discourtesy is evident in most of the Arthurian romances.
    Rom 2206, 2211

KENELM, Cenhelm, the son of KENULPHUS, king of Mercia, became heir in 821 at the age of seven. His aunt, Quenedreda, arranged his

murder, of which Kenelm had a premonition in a dream.
>   NPT 3110(4300), 3112(4302)

KENULPHUS, Cenwulf, king of Mercia 796-821.
>   NPT 3111(4301)

KIND, the personification of nature; that is, of natural inclination
>   or behavior appropriate to species.
>   Rom 1699, 4865
>   T&C 2.1374
>   4.1096
>   ComA 56

BOOK OF KINGS, the first and second books of Kings in the Old
>   Testament; in the Vulgate III and IV Kings because I and II
>   Samuel are considered I and II Kings. See BIBLE.
>   Mel 1668(2858)
>   [MerchT 2300]
>   ParsT 897, [900]

KING OF ARABY AND INDE, perhaps the legendary Prester John, 12th
>   cent. Christian ruler of Asia; S&A.
>   SqT 110

KNIGHT, the most important of the secular pilgrims.
>   GP 42, 43, 72, 837, 845
>   MillT p3109, 3119, 3127
>   NPT p2767(3957)
>   PardT 960

KORAN (Alkoran), the sacred scripture of Islam, the word of Allah
>   dictated through Gabriel to MUHAMMAD. The Koran (Alkoran from
>   Al-Qūran) was translated into Latin by Robert of Chester and
>   Hermann the Dalmatian for Peter the Venerable in 1143 in
>   Toledo.
>   MLT 332

L

LABAN, father of Leah and RACHEL and uncle of JACOB whom Jacob
>   served 14 years; Genesis 29.
>   ParsT 443

LABOR, one of the courtiers of Age.
>   Rom 4994

LACHESIS see FATES.

<LACTANTIUS, born c.250, was a professor of rhetoric at Nicomedia
>   and later tutor to Crispus, son of Constantine; he was known

as the "Christian Cicero." The De Ira Dei refutes the notion
that God is impassive and incapable of wrath.
De Ira Dei
     13   Bo 1.p4.199>

book of xxv. Ladies, i.e. the LGW.
     Ret 1086

[LADON, the dragon which guarded the garden of the Hesperides,
    slain by HERCULES during the labor of the apples of the
    Hesperides.
     MkT 2101(3291)]

LAIUS, legendary king of Thebes, son of Labdacus and father of
    OEDIPUS.
     T&C 2.101

LAMECH (Lameth), a descendant of Cain, had two wives, Adah and
    Zillah, and three sons, Jabal, Jubal, and TUBAL; Genesis 4.17-24
    and 5, and Adv. Jov. 1.14.
     BD 1162
     A&A 150
     WBT p54
     SqT 550

LANCELOT, the most prominent of Arthurian heroes and lover of
    Guinevere.
     SqT 287

BOOK OF LANCELOT DE LAKE, is probably a reference to one of the
    French Vulgate romances but could be a reference to the
    stanzaic Le Morte Arthur.
     NPT 3212(4402)

LAODAMIA (Ladomya, Laudomia), the wife of PROTESILAUS who took her
    own life after her husband who was killed at Troy was allowed
    to return to her for three hours. She sent him a letter at
    Aulis warning him of the prophecy that the first Greek ashore
    would die; Hero. 13.2, 36, 70 and Amores 2.18.36.
     LGW 263(217)
     MLT 171
     FranklT 1445

LAOMEDON (Lamedon), king of Troy and father of PRIAM, duped APOLLO
    and Neptune into building the walls of the city. Neptune sent
    a sea-monster against the city; in order to avert the danger
    it was necessary for Laomedon to sacrifice his daughter Hesione
    but HERCULES undertook to slay the monster in return for
    Laomedon's famous horses. Laomedon defrauded Hercules; Hercules
    raised an army, captured the city, and gave Hesione to Telamon.
    See Meta. 11.194ff.; Hero. 17.58, 206; Amores 3.6.54; BENOIT

25920ff.; De Gen. Deor. 6.6; Myth. III 174.
>   BD 329
>   T&C 4.124

LAPIDARY (Lapidaire), probably a reference to Marbodus of Rennes Lapidarius or De Gemmis, an 11th cent. compilation, chiefly from Pliny and Solinus, on the efficacy and symbolic properties of precious stones. It was known to Chaucer probably through one of the French translations or through Spec. Nat. 8. Skeat 3.274.
>   HF 1352

LARGESS, Bounty, one of the dancers about the God of Love.
>   Rom 1150, 1157, 1161, 1187, 1197, 5853

LATINUS, king of Latium and father of LAVINIA; Aen. 7.45ff.
>   HF 453

LATONA see DIANA.

LATUMEUS (Latumyus), in MAP 4.3 Pacuvius, the owner of the marvelous tree on which his wives persisted in hanging themselves.
>   WBT p757

LAUDE, one of the two trumpets of AEOLUS. Aeolus with the trumpets is perhaps due to ALBRICUS but the name is Chaucer's; Louns 2.382.
>   HF 1673

LAVINIA (Lavyne), daughter of LATINUS, was betrothed to Turnus but was given in marriage to AENEAS; Aen. 7.359. The form of the name may be due to French or Italian: RR 20831 or Purg. 17.37; Robin 781.
>   BD 331
>   HF 458
>   LGW 257(211), 1331

for the lawes seyn; the old law,
>   Mel 1229(2419), 1541(2731), 1783(2973) = Digesta see
>   JUSTINIAN
>   1583(2773)
>   ParsT 837 = Exodus, Leviticus, Deuteronomy

LAZARUS, of Bethany, the brother of MARTHA and MARY, was raised from the dead; John 11.35.
>   Mel 987(2177)

LEANDER, of Abydos, swam the Hellespont nightly to be with HERO, priestess of Venus at Sestos. One night he drowned and Hero threw herself into the sea; Hero. 19.
>   MLT 169

LECHERY (Leccherie), one of the Seven Deadly Sins, assailed by
    Jealousy as carnality.
        Rom 3911, 3914

LEGENDA AUREA see JACOBUS JANUENSIS.

our legende see JACOBUS JANUENSIS.

LEMUEL, king of Massa, taught by his mother to forsake women and
    wine and find a capable wife; Proverbs 31.4ff.
        PardT 585, 586

LENNE, Nicholas of Lynne, a Carmelite friar and lecturer in theology
    at Oxford who enjoyed a considerable reputation as an
    astronomer during the reign of Edward III, was the author of
    a treatise on the astrolabe and a 76-year calendar in 1387;
    Robin 868.
        Astr 86

LEO see LION.

ST. LEONARD, a Frank at the court of Clovis in the sixth cent.
    He founded the monastery of Noblac and is the patron saint of
    prisoners; cf. Skeat 3.249.
        HF 117

LESYNGES, Deceits, one of the figures painted on the wall of the
    temple of Venus; Tes. 7.56.
        KnT 1927

LEWIS, the recipient of the treatise. His identity is disputed;
    Robin 867.
        Astr 1, [28], 50
            1.6.3

LIBRA, the seventh sign of the zodiac; cf. Wood 272-97.
        Astr 1.8.4; 17.16, 24, 27
            2.6.15; 12.12; 20.6; 22.2; 25.16, 31, 39, 46,
                52; 28.18, 37; 31.6

LIFE OF ST. CECILE, probably a reference to SecNT.
        LGW 426(416)

GIOVANNI DA LIGNANO (Lynyan), c. 1310-1383, scientist, professor
    of canon law at Bologna, and papal emissary; Skeat 5.342-3
    and, for a thorough account of Giovanni's life and reputation,
    see Cook.
        ClT p34

LIGURGES see LYCURGUS.

LIMOTE (Elymas), the sorcerer who tried to dissuade the proconsul
    Paulus (on Cyprus) from listening to Barnabas and Saul. He
    was blinded for his disbelief; Acts 13.8. Cf. Skeat 3.273.
        HF 1274

BOOK OF THE LION (Leoun), probably a redaction of MACHAUT's
    Dit dou Lyon.
        Ret 1087

the lion (lyoun, leoun), the NEMEAN LION, the first labor of
    HERCULES in Bo and the first in MkT.

LION, Leo, the fifth sign of the zodiac; a northern constellation
    east of Cancer.
        T&C 4.1592
            5.1019, 1190
        SqT 265
        FranklT 1058   = Leo
        Astr 1.8.3   =
            2.6.17; 25.40; 28.37 =

LIVIA (Lyma), daughter of Claudius Drusus, sister of Germanicus,
    and wife of Drusus the son of Tiberius. In league with Sejanus
    she caused her husband to be poisoned; Sejanus proposed to
    Livia but Tiberius put the proposal aside; cf. Louns 2.369
    for the suggestion that the reference is from MAP 4.3.
        WBT p747, 750

LIVY (Titus, Titus Livius), 59 B.C.-17 A.D., spent his mature
    years in Rome where he enjoyed the friendship and patronage of
    Augustus. His great history of Rome, Ab Urbe Condita, 142 books
    in decads. was begun between 27 and 25 B.C. See RR 5589ff.,
    8605-12.
        BD 1084
        LGW (280), 1683, 1873
        PhysT 1
    Ab Urbe Condita
        <1. 3-4   PF 283ff.>
        [.57-9   LGW 1680-1885
          .58   1839-49
        3   BD 1084
                                    PhysT]
        <45.8   Bo 2.p2.65>

LOLLARD (Loller), a contemptuous reference to a follower of Wyclif.
        MLT e1173, 1177

LOLLIUS, Chaucer's authority for T&C. Various attempts have been
    made to account for the name and to use it to prove that
    Chaucer was actually using the name to acknowledge Boccaccio.
    The most extended treatment is that of Kittredge; the most

convincing is that of Pratt who maintains that Lollius became
an authority because Chaucer misunderstood Horace Epist. 1.2.1-2
as it appears in Policraticus 7.9. The hypotheses of Hornstein
and Epstein are untenable.
    HF 1468
    T&C 1.[133], [159], 394, [495]
        2.[18], [31=story], [49]
        3.[502, 575, 1196, 1325, 1817]
        5.[1037=story, 1051=story, 1088, 1094=story,
          1651=story], 1653

LONGIUS, or Longinus, the centurion who supposedly pierced the side
    of Christ; perhaps Leg. Aurea 47.
        ABC 163

LORD see GOD and JESUS CHRIST.

LOT, son of Haran and nephew of ABRAHAM, migrated from Haran to
    Canaan and escaped the fate of Sodom and Gomorrah because he
    had been warned. His wife, however, was turned to a pillar of
    salt because she glanced back. Lot migrated to Zoar and then
    to the mountains east of the Dead Sea where his daughters
    planned and executed incest; Genesis 19.30-8.
        PardT 485

GOD OF LOVE, LOVE, CUPID, are all names for the same divinity.
    Chaucer seems to usually follow RR or Boccaccio by using the
    God of Love. In Roman myth, Cupid or Love is the son of VENUS
    and is not particularly important in the pantheon. See Fleming
    191ff.
    LOVE
        Rom 22, 33, 1470, 1523, 1771, 1775, 1827, 1874,
            2083, 2113, 2176, 2236, 2351, 2597, 2685, 2721,
            2767, 3085, 3103, 3181, 3295, 3310, 3311, 3327,
            3339, 3373, 3411, 3491, 3521, 3533, 3648, 3732,
            3779, 3783, 3786, 3884, 4126, 4345, 4350, 4353,
            4438, 4500, 4524, 4561, 4569, 4573, 4586, 4587,
            4592, 4604, 4631, 4703, 4771, 4777, 5093, 5126,
            5136, 5142, 5172, 5175, 5193, 5278, 5358, 5811,
            5816, 6058, 6115, 6118, 6220, 6474, 6797, 7297,
            7328, 7337
        BD 766, 835
        HF 625, 645, 675
        PF 4, 8, 159
        Bo 4.m6.19
        T&C 1.16, 27, 31, 34, 42, 46, 48, 234, 237, 255,
            303, 304, 308, 319, 518, 909, 912, 998
            2.522, [523, 526, 533], 827, [829, 837], 860
            3.1254, 1261, 1328, 1552, 1610, 1744, 1745,
            1746, 1748, 1757, 1762, 1764, 1766, 1794,
            1804
            4.162, 288, 1189, 1306

LOVE (cont.)
    LGW 280(183), 282(185), 327, 476(466), 508(496),
        537(525)
    MerchT 2127
    Pity 7
    Lady 15, 33, 36, 38
    Ven 25, 37, 49, 57, 66
    Scog 30, 49
    MercB 27, 32, 34, 37
GOD OF LOVE
    Rom 878, 885, 918, 1003, 1330, 1450, 1715, 1858,
        1878, 1888, 1927, 2145, 2735, 2951, 2963, 3232,
        3245, 3289, 3558, 3703, 3792, 5108
    HF 1489
    T&C 1.15, 206, [330, 350], 421, [422, 424, 430],
            932, [936], 967
        2.848
        5.143, 167
    LGW 213(142), 226(158), 302(228), 311(237), [342(318)],
        (327), 442(432), 457(447), 492(482), 498(486)
    KnT 1785, 1802
    FranklT 765
CUPID
    Rom 1616, 3702
    HF 137, 617, 668
    PF 212, 652
    T&C 3.186, 461, 1808
        5.207, 582, [589, 590, 591], 1590
    LGW 1140
    KnT 1623, 1963
    Scog 22
GOD
    T&C 1.1006
        2.526
    LGW 342(318)
    KnT 1788
LORD
    T&C 1.330, 350, 422, 424, 430, 936
        2.523, 533, 829, 837
        3.1345, 1373, 1380

his love see TIMANDRA.
    FranklT 1440

ST. LOY see ST. ELIGIUS.

LUCAN, Marcus Annaeus Lucanus, 39-65 A.D., was the grandson of
    Seneca the rhetorician and nephew of SENECA the philosopher.
    His favor with NERO quickly turned to disgrace because Nero
    was jealous of his poetic ability. Lucan joined the conspiracy
    of Piso and although he begged for forgiveness he was ordered

to commit suicide. See Hamm 98, Louns 2.253-4, Shannon 333-9.
          HF 1499
          Bo 4.p6.232
          T&C 5.1792
          MLT 401
          MkT 2719(3909)
Pharsalia
          [1.128   Bo 4.p6.232]
          <2.326ff.   LGW 249ff.
          3.440ff.   PF 176-82
          4.358-62   MLT 400-1   + JEHAN DE TUIM
          .590-660   Bo 4.m7.51
                                    ?MkT 2108(3298)
          5.328-34   MLT 400   + JEHAN DE TUIM
                                    MkT 2719(3909-
                                         20(10)
          8.494-5   T&C 2.167-8
          9   HF 482
          .1-14   T&C 5.1807-27>

LUCIFER, the morning star, the planet Venus.
          Bo 1.m5.16
             3.m1.9
             4.m6.17
          T&C 3.1417

LUCIFER, the counterpart of SATAN. Isaiah 14.12 is actually a
    reference to a king of Babylon but the name was applied to
    Satan in the New Testament, viz. Luke 10.18; Skeat 5.227-8.
          MkT 1999(3189), 2004(3194)
          ParsT 788

LUCILIA (Lucye), the wife of Lucretius the poet. The story is
    apocryphal; MAP 4.3 and see Louns 2.369-70.
          WBT p747, 752

LUCINA see DIANA.

LUCRETIA, the wife of L. Tarquinius Collatinus; she was violated
    by Sextus (son of Tarquinius Superbus) and having revealed
    this to her husband she took her own life; LIVY, Fasti 2.685-852,
    RR 8605-12. See Shannon 220ff. and La Hood.
          BD 1082
          A&A 82
          LGW 257(211), 1686, 1691, 1786, 1872
          MLT 163
          FranklT 1405

ST. LUKE, author of the third gospel and Acts, was a physician and
    therefore a Roman citizen. He is associated with Antioch and
    is patron of physicians and painters; cf. BIBLE.

        Thop 951(2141)
        ParsT 700, 701, 702-3

<LULL, Raimon (Raymond Lully), c. 1235-1315, Catalan author, mystic,
    and missionary; see Folch-Pi.
    ?Felix
        6.4   CYT>

LUNA, the Moon, the association of the planet with the metal silver
    was apparently common; Skeat 5.426-7.
        CYT 826, 1440

LUST, Concupiscence, one of the attributes of love.
        PF 219
        Pity 39

LYBEAUX DISCONU, a 14th cent. romance Libeaus Desconus about
    Guinglain, the bastard son of Gawain and the adventures which
    led to his election to the Round Table; Wells [38].
        Thop 900(2090)

LYCURGUS (Ligurges), a legendary king of the Edones in Thrace who
    persecuted Dionysus and was struck blind or driven mad so he
    killed his son Dryas. He became the father of PHYLLIS on the
    authority of Hero. 2.111, "CEFFI," De Gen. Deor. 11.25. In KnT,
    Lycurgus as the father of OPHELTES is the result of confusion
    between Lycurgus, son of Pheres, king of Nemea, Theb. 5.733,
    and the above-mentioned Lycurgus in Theb. 4.386, 7.180; cf. Tes.
    6.14.
        LGW 2425
        KnT 2129, 2644

LYMA see LIVIA.

LYNCEUS (Lyno), the son of AEGYPTUS and husband of HYPERMNESTRA;
    Hero. 14 and "CEFFI." The form is probably due to the Italian
    translation.
        LGW 2569, 2604, 2608, 2676, 2711, 2716

[LYRA, Arion's harp, the constellation in the northern hemisphere.
    HF 1005]

M

MABEL (Mabely), a common name derisively applied to the old woman.
        FrT 1626

MACABEES see BIBLE.

<MACHAUT, Guillaume de, c. 1300-1377, was secretary to John of
    Luxembourg, king of Bohemia, who was killed at Crécy in 1346
    whereupon Machaut served John the Good of France. See Hamm 78,
    Louns 2.212-5, Stilwell, Severs, and especially Wimsatt.

Dit de la Marguerite (ed. Tarbé)
    pp. 123, 125   LGW 123
        124   50–2
        126–7   86–7
Dit dou Vergier (SATF)
    141–50   BD 6–15
    155–8   805ff.
Confort d'Ami
    1899–1900   HF 534
Lay de Confort
    10–3   BD 617–709
    164–6   844–5
Dit dou Lyon
    57–61   BD 39–43
    207–12   1108–11
    325ff.   388–97
    1368ff.   1024ff.
    2040–76   T&C 4.1584
                   FranklT 773–5
Jugement dou Roy de Navarre
    34–6   LGW 127
    ?   562
    109–12   BD 23–9, 42
    301–2   534
    1743   T&C 1.449
    2741ff.   HF 405–26
1st Complainte
    1.24   BD 16–21
38th Balade Notée
    passim   BD 1054–74
8th Motet
    5–9, 16–8   BD 617–709
9th Motet
    passim   BD 617–709
Dit de la Fonteinne Amoureuse
    591–2   BD 155–6
    632   184
    807–10   242–69
Remede de Fortune
    23–60   BD 759ff.
    54–6   948–51
    64–5   1088ff.
    71–2   833–45
    89–94   1088ff.
    95–9   833–45
    102–3   833–45
    107ff.   1054–74
    123–4   985–7
    135ff.   1088ff.
    139–40   1285–6
    167–74   966–74

Remede de Fortune (cont.)

197–9	BD 833–45
217–38	919–37
295–302	1088ff.
357–66	1146–50
401–3	1155–7
681–2	1181–2
696	1216
751–2	1250–1
918	617–709
1049–62	T&C 4.1–11
1052–6	BD 617–709
1138	617–709
1162	617–709
1167–8	617–703
1190–1	617–709
1198	600
1467–9	39–43
1629–30	904–6
1636–51	T&C 1.813–9
1662	1.813–9
1671–83	BD 1195–8
	T&C 1.897–900
2531–8	1.848ff.
4074–5	BD 1273

Roy de Behaingne

13–4	BD 291ff.
56ff.	502–4
70ff.	526–66
75–101	526–66
125–33	805ff.
148–53	1035–40
156–8	1035–40
166–76	1270
177–87	599–616
193–200	442
196–7	583
253–6	749–52
261–73	759ff.
281ff.	805ff.
286ff.	817ff.
297–330	848–74
321–2	871–2
356–8	904–6
361–3	939–47
364–83	952–60
397–403	907–11
411–4	912–3
421–5	1054–74
453–6	1183–91
461–2	1195–8

Roy de Behaingne (cont.)

466	BD 1192
467-76	1203-18
504-5	1219
509-12	1236-8
541-8	1239-44
580-1	918
582	907-11
610	1258-67
641	1270
642-3	1275-8
670	1270
656-8	1226-8
684-91	T&C 4.1-11
1072-4	BD 617-709
1078-80	617-709
1204ff.	388-97>

MACROBIUS, Ambrosius Theodosius, fl. 395-423, Roman writer and
philosopher whose commentary on the Somnium Scipionis in
CICERO's De republica was greatly admired during the Middle
Ages; indeed, he was often considered the author of the
Somnium. See Hamm 98-9, Louns 2.276-8, Lowes, CM&A 135-6.
    Rom 7
    BD 284
    PF 111
    NPT 3123(4313)
Comm. in Somnium Scipionis
    [general   Rom 7
                                BD 284
                                PF 111
                                NPT 3123(4313]
    <1.3   HF 7-11, 18>

MADRIAN, perhaps a blunder for Hadrian or Adrian. Adrian and his
wife Natalia were third cent. Greek martyrs; Adrian became the
patron of Flemish brewers. See Byers and Haskell; cf. Skeat
5.224.
    MkT p1892(3082)

MAEON (Hemonydes), son of Haemon, was one of the fifty sent by
ETEOCLES to ambush TYDEUS. Tydeus killed 49 and sent Maeon
back to Eteocles; not in Filo., but see Theb. 3.40ff.
    T&C 5.1492

the Magdalene see ST. MARY MAGDALENE.

MAHOMET, Muhammad, the founder of Islam, was born c. 570 and died
in 632. In 622 he undertook the hijira to Madinah. See Hitti
611-22. Obviously used derisively.
    MLT 224, 336, 340

MALYNE, the wife of miller Simkin; the name is another form of
    Malkin, a pet name for Matilda: Skeat 5.126.
        RvT 4236

MALKIN, a pet name for Matilda.
        MLT i30
        NPT 3384(4574)

MALLE, the sheep belonging to the "povre wydwe."
        NPT 2831(4021)

free man see ANAXARCHUS.
        Bo 2.p6.52, 57

old man see ST. PAUL.
        SecNT 201

the wise man,
        MLT p118   ?
        Mel 1473(2663)   = CAECILIUS BALBUS
            1612(2802)   ?
            1635(2825)   = Ecclesiasticus
            1691(2881)   = MARTINUS DUMIENSIS
        ParsT 569   = Proverbs
              640   = Ecclesiasticus
              664   = Proverbs
              712   = Ecclesiasticus
              875   ?

MANCIPLE, a servant who purchased provisions for an inn of court;
    Bowden 255-8.
        GP 544, 567, 586
        MancT p25, 47, 56, 69, 76, 91, 103
        ParsT p1

<MANDEVILLE, Sir John, c. 1300-1372, author of an account of
    fantastic travels in the Near and Far East. Mandeville was
    supposedly born at St. Albans and embarked on his journey in
    1322, the account of which is dated 1357; see Bennett.
    ?Travels (EETS OS 153[1919 for 1916] ed. P. Hamelius).
        1 (p. 165)   SqT 69-72>

MANES, the departed spirits of the slain Trojans; generally, the
    spirits of the dead, regarded as hostile and thus euphemistically
    addressed as "the kindly ones"; cf. Root, Clogan.
        T&C 5.892

MANNER, conduct or deportment, a quality worthless without Pity.
        Pity 78

<MAP or Mappe or Mappes, Walter, died c. 1208/9, was educated in
    Paris probably 1150-60. By 1162 he was attached to the court
    of Henry II and received several preferments; Map attended the
    Lateran council in 1179. See Hamm 99, Louns 2.367-70, S&A.>
    De Nugis Curialium, 4.3: Epistola Valerii ad Rufinum de Non
    Ducenda Uxore.
        LGW (280)
        WBT p[669], 671, [672, 714ff., 747, 757]
        <MerchT 1523-9>

MARBODUS see LAPIDARY

MARCH, the third month of the modern calendar, traditionally the
    final month of winter. March was the beginning of the legal
    year in England.
        T&C 2.765
        GP 2
        WBT p546
        SumT 1782
        SqT 47

MARCIA see MARSYAS.

MARCIA CATO (Catoun), supposedly the wife of Cato Uticensis, but
    the reference in Adv. Jov. 1.46 is really to the daughter of
    Cato. Cato gave his wife to his friend who returned her;
    Louns 2.294 and Skeat 3.298-9. Cf. Pharsalia 2.326ff., VINSAUF
    1780, Inf. 4.128, Purg. 1.78ff.
        LGW 252(206)

MARCIEN see MARS.

MARCUS TULLIUS see CICERO.

MARDOCHEE see MORDECAI.

MARK ANTONY, Marcus Antonius, c. 82-30 B.C., the loyal friend of
    CAESAR, was triumvir with OCTAVIAN and Lepidus, and lover of
    CLEOPATRA, who brought about his ruin; De Casibus 6.15,
    De Clar. Mulier. 86.
        LGW 588, 625, 629, 652, 657, 684, 701
        KnT 2032

ST. MARK, author of the second Gospel, associated with ST. PAUL
    and St. Barnabas on their missionary journey through Cyprus.
    He was also in Rome with St. Paul and St. Peter; see BIBLE.
        Thop 951(2141)
        WBT p145

MARS (Marcien, Marte), after JUPITER the most important god in the
    .Roman pantheon, was the god of war and the lover of VENUS. See

particularly <u>Theb</u>. 7.34-73 and <u>Tes</u>. 7.29-37; for his
astrological importance see Wood 66-78, 103-60, 221-8. The
references in Mars are mythological and astrological; for a
thorough explication see Wood, Chap. III.
  HF 1446
  A&A 1, 31, 50, 355
  T&C 2.435, 593, 630, 988
    3.22, 437, 724
    4.25
    5.306, 1853
  LGW 533(521), 2063, 2109, 2244
  KnT 975, 1559, 1682, 1708, 1747, 1907, 1969, 1972,
    1974, 1982, 2021, 2024, 2035, 2041, 2050, 2159,
    2248, 2367, 2369, 2372, [2373, 2402, 2419],
    2431, 2434, 2441, 2473, 2480, 2581, 2669, 2815
  Mars 25, [29], 45, 53, 75, 77, 78, 90, 92, 106, 123,
    148
Astrological references:
  T&C 3.716
  LGW 2589, 2593
  MLT 301, 305
  WBT p610, 612, 613, 619
  SqT 50
  CYT 827
  Astr 2.4.35; 12.24, 28

MARSYAS (Marcia),a satyr who picked up the flute that Pallus Athene had
  invented and challenged APOLLO. It was agreed that the victor
  should treat the vanquished as he wished; when Apollo won he
  flayed Marsyas alive. See <u>Meta</u>. 6.382-400, <u>Parad</u>. 1.20, <u>Tes</u>.
  11.62. The feminine form is due to the Italian.
    HF 1229

MARTE(S) <u>see</u> MARS.

MARTIANUS CAPELLA (Marcien), fl. during the first half of the
  fifth cent., was born in Madaura and spent most of his life
  in Carthage. The <u>De Nuptiis</u> was composed to introduce his son,
  Martianus, to the seven liberal arts; <u>Hamm</u> 99, <u>Louns</u> 2.356-8,
  Raby 1.100-4.
    HF 985
    MerchT 1732
  <u>De Nuptiis Mercurii et Philogiae</u>
    [general   HF 985
           MerchT 1734]
    <1.12   T&C 5.8> + VALERIUS FLACCUS

ST. MARTIN, c. 316-400, was born of heathen parents but was converted in Rome and became bishop of Tours in 371. He is the
  patron saint of drinking and jovial meeting, as well as of
  reformed drunkards.
    ShipT 148(1338)

MARTINUS DUMIENSIS, about whom little is known, was the bishop of
   Dumium in Gallicia and Braga. He died c. 580. Following
   VINCENT OF BEAUVAIS, Spec. Morale, his works were often
   attributed to SENECA because he was one of Martinus's favorite
   authorities. Texts in PL 72.
         Mel 1071(2261):att. SENECA, 1147(2337):att. SENECA,
            [1171(2361)], 1437(2627):att. SENECA, 1531(2721):
            att. SENECA, [1691(2881)], 1775(2965):att. SENECA
   Formula Honestae Vitae
         [?   Mel 1171(2361)]
         <3   1071(2261)>
   De Moribus
         [3   Mel 1691(2881)]
         <?   1147(2337)
         4   1775(2965)
         5   1437(2627)
         6   1531(2721)>

MARY, the Blessed Virgin Mary, the mother of Jesus.
         [Rom 7108]
         HF 573
         [T&C 5.1869]
         [GP 695]
         MLT 641, 841, 920
            [950, 977]
         ShipT 402
         PrT [p467(1655), 474(1664), 477(1667), 481(1671)]
            [506(1696), 508(1698), 510(1700), 532(1722),
            538(1728), 543(1733), 550(1740), 556(1746),
            597(1787), 654(1844), 656(1846), 664(1854),
            678(1868)]
            689(1879)
         Thop 784(1974)
         FrT 1604
         [SumT 1762, 2202]
         MerchT 1337, 1899, [2334], 2418
         PardT i308
            685
         SecNT p ante 29=Mariam, [29-84 passim]
         CYT 1062
            [1089, 1243, 1354]
         [ParsT 558]
         [Ret 1089]
         [ABC passim]
         [Astr 108]

MARY MAGDALENE, mentioned in the Gospels; in Luke she went with
   Jesus on the last journey to Jerusalem, witnessed the
   Crucifixion, followed the body of Jesus to the tomb and
   returned to prepare spices. John 20 gives the account of the
   empty tomb and Mary's interview with the risen Christ. Mary

Magdalene has been confused with (1) the fallen woman who in Simon's house anointed Christ's feet [Luke 7.37] and (2) with Mary of Bethany, sister of Lazarus and Martha.
>   ParsT 502, 504, 996

ST. MARY OF EGYPT (Egypcien Marie), fifth cent., according to legend, after a youth of debauchery, lived alone in the wilderness beyond Jordan for the last 47 years of her life. Skeat 5.156 cites Leg. Aurea 56 and notes that she was often confused with MARY MAGDALENE.
>   MLT 500

MASSINISSA (Massynisse), c. 238-149 B.C., king of Massylian or eastern Numidia, was host to SCIPIO AFRICANUS MINOR during the third Punic war in 150. Massinissa had fought for both Scipios in Spain in 212; in 204 SCIPIO AFRICANUS MAJOR had helped Massinissa defeat Syphax, prince of western Numidia. The associations are narrated in the Somnium Scipionis.
>   PF 37

ST. MATTHEW (Mathew), son of Alpheus, was a tax-collector who became one of the disciples and the author of the first Gospel (before 70 A.D.).
>   Rom [445], [6636], 6887
>   Thop 951(2141)
>   [WBT p79]
>   PardT 634
>   ParsT 588, [661-2], 842, 845, 1036

MAUDELAYNE, the Shipman's barge.
>   GP 410

[MAUNY, SIR OLIVER, an Armorican or Breton knight who took part, with BERTRAND DU GUESCLIN, in the murder of PETER OF SPAIN; Skeat 5.238-40.
>   MkT 2385(3575)]

MAURICE, the son of Constance and Alla.
>   MLT 723, 1063, 1086, 1121, 1127

ST. MAURUS (Maure), d. 565, was a disciple of ST. BENEDICT and a legendary introducer of the Benedictine rule and life into Gaul.
>   GP 173

<MAXIMIANUS, fl. sixth cent., a young friend of Boethius who decided to revive the Roman elegy and was, according to Raby, the "last of the Roman poets." The ascription is made by Kittredge. Cf. Raby 1.124-6.
>   Elegiae
>   1.1-4, 223-8   PardT 727-33>

MAXIMUS, the prefect who was converted by CECILIA and then
    martyred.
        SecNT 368, 372, 377, 400

MAY, the lascivious young wife of JANUARY.
        MerchT 1693, 1748, 1774, 1782, 1822, 1851, 1849, 1871,
            1882, 1886, 1888, 1895, 1914, 1932, 1936, 1955,
            1977, 1995, 2002, 2050, 2054, 2092, 2100, 2116,
            2137, 2157, 2185, 2218, 2321, 2328

MAY, the fifth month of the modern calendar, a month celebrating
    rebirth and the defeat of winter and age: it was the month
    or season of lovers.
        Rom 49, 51, 55, 74, 86, 581, 2277, 3222, 3978,
            4748
        BD 291
        PF 130
        T&C 2.50, 56, 112, 1098
            3.353, 1062
            5.425, 844
        LGW 36(36), 45(45), 108(89), [(128)], 176, 613
        GP 92
        KnT 1034, 1037, 1042, 1047, 1462, 1500, 1510, 1511,
            1675, 2484
        MLT 16
        WBT p546

        SqT 281
        FranklT 906, 907, 928
        Astr 1.10.4, 13
            2.45.28

MEDEA, daughter of AEETES of Colchis, helped JASON achieve the
    Golden Fleece by magically enabling him to perform certain
    tasks. Jason and Medea returned to Iolcos where she took
    vengeance on Pelias (Jason's uncle) by restoring Aeson's
    youth and convincing Pelias's daughters to boil him. Pelias's
    son Acastus drove Jason and Medea away and they settled in
    Corinth. Jason fell in love with Glauce, daughter of CREON,
    and ordered Medea away. Medea contrived the deaths of Glauce,
    Creon, and her own children by Jason; she escaped to Athens
    to king AEGEUS. Medea's attempt to poison THESEUS was
    thwarted because Aegeus recognized his son's arms. Medea
    returned to Colchis with her son Medus and restored her father
    to the throne which had been usurped by Perses; Meta. 7.350-412,
    Hero. 6, 12, 17, BENOÎT, GUIDO.
        BD 330, 726
        HF 401, 1271
        LGW 1395, 1599, 1629, 1652, 1663
        KnT 1944
        MLT 172

MEED (Mede), Bribery, one of Cupid's companions in the park of
Venus; <u>Tes</u>. 7.56.
    PF 228

MEGAERA (Megera), one of the FURIES.

MELANCHOLY (Malencholy), one of the "senators of the palace" of
Old Age.
    Rom 4998

MELEAGER (Meleagre), the son of Oeneus of Calydon. The FATES
appeared at his birth and declared that he would survive as
long as a brand on the fire remained unburned. Meleager's
mother, Althea, snatched it out of the fire and hid it away.
When Oeneus forgot to sacrifice to DIANA the goddess sent the
boar which became the object of the hunt organized by Meleager.
Since ATALANTA's spear first wounded the boar Meleager awarded
her the head; when Althea's brothers tried to take it from
her Meleager killed them. In a blind rage Althea threw the
brand into the fire; <u>Meta</u>. 8.260-546, <u>De Gen</u>. <u>Deor</u>. 9.15, 19.
    T&C 5.1474, 1482, 1515
    KnT 2071

MELIBEE (Melibeus), a rich and powerful but somewhat imprudent
young man. His name is explained in line 1410(2600).
    Mel 967(2157), 973(2163), 986(2176), 1001(2191),
        1004(2194), 1008(2198), 1011(2201), 1019(2209),
        1026(2216), 1049(2239), 1050(2240), 1055(2245),
        1112(2302), 1232(2422), 1261(2451), 1279(2469),
        1333(2523), 1410(2600), 1427(2617), 1444(2634),
        1463(2653), 1518(2708), 1540(2730), 1672(2862),
        1681(2871), 1697(2887), 1710(2901), 1724(2914),
        1732(2922), 1745(2935), 1768(2958), 1770(2960),
        1773(2963), 1785(2975), 1787(2977), 1790(2980),
        1791(2981), 1801(2991), 1804(2994), 1805(2995),
        1806(2996), 1808(2998), 1809(2999), 1827(3017),
        1830(3020), 1832(3022), 1834(3024), 1870(3060)
    MkT p1889(3079), 1896(3086)

for men seyn,
    Mel 1466(2656) = PUBLILIUS SYRUS

MENELAUS, king of Sparta, son of Atreus, brother of AGAMEMNON,
and husband of HELEN.
    Bo 4.m7.7

MERCHANT, the representative of a rich and powerful class in
14th cent. England; Bowden 146-53.
    GP 270
    MerchT p1215
           e2425

MERCURY, identified with Hermes, was the messenger and herald of
the gods. He was the particular divinity of merchants and
mercantilism; he was also the patron of scholars and artists.
He was born on Mt. Cyllene in Arcadia. Mercury the planet is
the smallest of the major planets and the nearest to the sun;
astrologically his influence was neutral. For MerchT 1734 <u>see</u>
MARTIANUS CAPELLA; cf. Hoffman 62-3, Seznec, and Wood.
    HF 429
    Bo 4.m3.17
    T&C 3.729
        5.321
    LGW 1297
    KnT 1385
    WBT p697
    Mars 113=Cilenios, 144=Cilenius
Astrological references:
    T&C 5.1827
    WBT p699, 703, 705
    SqT 672
    CYT 827, 1438
    Astr 2.12.25, 32

MERCY, caused by Pity to rule Courtesy and therefore overcome
Danger.
    LGW 162

MESSAGERYE, the personification of the sending of messages to
advance love, was one of Cupid's companions in the park of
Venus; <u>Tes</u>. 7.56.
    PF 228

MESSENUS <u>see</u> MISENUS.

METAMORPHOSES <u>see</u> OVID.

METELLIUS, according to VALERIUS MAXIMUS 6.3, beat his wife to
death because she drank excessively.
    WBT p460

MICAH (Michias), one of the minor prophets, was a younger
contemporary of ISAIAH; cf. <u>BIBLE</u>.
    ParsT 201

MICHAELMASS (Michelmesse), the feast of St. Michael the Archangel
on 29 September.
    Scot 19

MIDAS (Myda), a semi-legendary king of Phrygia, who, because he
was hospitable to Silenus (the companion of Dionysus) when he
had lost his way, received his wish that all he touched might
turn to gold. He revoked the wish by bathing in the river

Pactolus; <u>Meta</u>. 11.100ff., <u>Purg</u>. 20.106-8, 116-7. The story
of Midas is not in <u>Filo</u>.
    T&C 3.1389
    WBT 951, 953

MILKY WAY <u>see</u> GALAXY.

MILLER, Robin by name, reveals the general traits of the trade as
    well as a physiognomy which suits his particular nature;
    Bowden 246-9.
        GP 542, 545
        MillT p3120, 3129=Robin, 3136, 3150, 3167, 3182
        RvT p3913, 4324

MINERVA (Minerve) <u>see</u> PALLAS.

MINOS, son of Zeus and Europa, was tyrant king of Crete who imposed
    an annual tribute on Athens because the Athenians had killed
    his son ANDROGEUS because he had won the Panathenaic games.
    Minos also caused DAEDALUS to construct the Labyrinth to hide
    the MINOTAUR, the offspring of PASIPHAE and the Cretan bull
    sent by Neptune to seduce her because Minos had refused to
    sacrifice to him. Minos and Pasiphae were the parents of
    ARIADNE and PHAEDRA; Ariadne helped THESEUS escape from the
    Labyrinth. Minos died while following Daedalus. As reflected
    in <u>De Gen</u>. <u>Deor</u>. 11.26 some mythographers regarded Minos as
    a just king who was selected to become a judge in the lower
    world; cf. <u>Meta</u>. 7.456-8, 8.6-151, "CEFFI," <u>De Gen</u>. <u>Deor</u>.
    11.26, 28, 29.
        T&C 4.1188
        LGW 1886, 1894, 1900, 1906, 1911, 1915, 1922, 1924,
            1928, 1936, 1938, 1949, 1964, 2042

MINOTAUR, the offspring of PASIPHAE and the Cretan bull; cf. MINOS.

        LGW [1928], 2104, 2142, 2145
        KnT 980

MIRRA <u>see</u> MYRRHA.

MIRTH, the lord of the love garden.
        Rom 601, 607, 614, 617, 627, 633, 703, 725, 733,
            734, 780, 817, 852, 3234

MISENUS (Messenus), trumpeter to HECTOR and AENEAS, challenged the
    gods to a contest in music. For his impiety he was dragged
    into the sea and drowned; <u>Aen</u>. 3.239, 6.162ff.
        HF 1243

MNESTHEUS (Monesteo), in <u>Filo</u>. 4.3 one of the Trojan captives. In
    <u>Aen</u>. 5.116ff. he is eponymous founder of the Memmius and the

commander of the winning ship in the race during the funeral
games for Anchises. The form is Italian.
>   T&C 4.51

moder,
>   T&C 4.1207 = HECUBA

moder of Romulus
>   PF 292 = SILVIA

MONDAY, the second day of the week.
>   KnT 2486
>   MillT 3430, 3516, 3633, 3659

MONESTEO see MNESTHEUS.

MONK, the most important of the ecclesiastical pilgrims;
Bowden 107-16.
>   GP 165, 175
>   MillT p3118
>   MkT p1924(3114), 1965(3155)
>   NPT p2781(3971), 2788(3978), 2792(3982)   + daun Piers,
>   2806(3996)

a monster,
>   LGW 1928 = MINOTAUR

MORDECAI (Mardochee), the uncle of ESTHER, who saved his people
from the plots of Haman through his wise counsel to his niece.
>   MerchT 1373

MORPHEUS, one of the sons of Somnus the god of sleep. Morpheus
appears in human shapes while Phobetor and Phantasus assume
the forms of animals and inanimate objects; Meta. 11.635ff.
and FROISSART, Paradys d'Amours 28ff.
>   BD 136, 167, 242, 265
>   [HF 69, 74, 77]

MOSES (Moyses), the hero under whose leadership the Israelites
left Egypt and made their way to the Promised Land; BIBLE.
>   Rom 6889
>   PrT 468(1658)
>   SumT 1885
>   SqT 250
>   ParsT 195, 355
>   ABC 89, 93

MUSES, daughters of Mnemosyne, were the goddesses of literature
and the arts. The original seats of their worship were Pieria
and Mt. Helicon.
>   HF 1401
>   Bo 1.m1.4, 8; p1.43, 58, 72; m11.44

[T&C 3.1809]
MLT p92
MerchT 1735

MUSIC, the personification of one of the subjects of the quadrivium.
Bo 2.p1.44; p3.10

MYRRHA (Mirra), daughter of Cinyras, king of Cyprus, was the mother
by her father of ADONIS. She was smitten with unnatural love
by Venus because she refused to honor the goddess. When
Cinyras discovered the crime he sought to kill her but she was
changed into a myrtle from which Adonis was born; Meta.
10.311ff.
T&C 4.1139

N

NABAL, a wealthy citizen of Carmel, was the husband of ABIGAIL;
his refusal to provender David's troops would have provoked
an attack had not Abigail taken supplies herself. When she
returned and told her husband what she had done "his heart
died within him" and ten days later he died. I Samuel 25;
see Landrum, p. 89.
Mel 1100(2290)
MerchT 1370

NABUGODONOSOR see NEBUCHADNEZZAR.

NARCISSUS was the son of the river god Cephisus and the nymph
Leiriope. He repulsed ECHO and later became enamored of his
own image seen in a pool. His attempts to approach the
beautiful creature increased his passion which finally con-
sumed him; Meta. 3.407-510, RR 1439ff. (=Rom 1469ff.).
Rom 1468, 1469, 1491, 1501, 1505, 1525, 1545, 1602
BD 735
KnT 1941
FranklT 952

NASO see OVID.

NATURE, the personification of the physical world and all therein.
Rom 1463, 3207, 4871, 4907
BD 467, 871, 908, 1195
HF 490, 1366, 2039
A&A 80
PF 303, 317, 325, 368, 372, 377, 379, 447, 467,
519, 531, 617, 629, 639, 655, 659, 667, 676
Bo 3.m2.3
T&C 4.251
LGW 975
PhysT 9, 11, 29, 31

PardT 1295
Ven 14
ComA 53, 58
MercB 21

NEBUCHADNEZZAR (Nabugodonosor), 604-561 B.C., the king of Assyria
    who rebuilt Babylon and conquered the Jews and carried them
    into captivity; Daniel 1-4.
        HF 515
        MkT 2145(3335), 2562(3752)
        ParsT 126

NEMBROT see NIMROD.

NEMEAN LION, an invulnerable monster, the offspring of Typhon and
    Echidna. HERCULES choked the monster and clothed himself with
    its skin.
        [Bo 4.m7.31
        MkT 2098(3288)]

NEOPTOLEMUS see PYRRHUS.

ST. NEOT (Note), died c. 877, is associated with king Alfred and
    the foundation of Oxford. New College, founded by William of
    Wykeham in 1386, appropriated St. Neot as patron; see Cline.
        MillT 3771

NEPTUNE (Neptunus), the god of the sea and other waters, brother
    of JUPITER and husband of Amphitrite; cf. LAOMEDON.
        T&C 2.443
            4.120
        LGW 2421
        FranklT 1047

NERO, the cruel and egocentric son of Ahenobarbus and Agrippina,
    was emperor 53-68. Although he showed great promise as a
    student of SENECA his selfishness soon got the upper hand.
    His reign was marred by the murders of Agrippina and Octavia,
    the revolt in Britain, the great fire in Rome, and the con-
    spiracy of Piso which led to the ordered suicides of LUCAN,
    SENECA, and PETRONIUS. See SUETONIUS, RR 6185ff., 6414ff.,
    Spec. Hist.
        Bo 2.m6.3, 13, 19, 23, 29
            3.m4.1, 6, 10; p5.47, 55
        KnT 2032
        MkT 2463(3653), 2504(3694), 2511(3701), 2518(3708),
            2520(3710), 2537(3727)
        NPT 3370(4560), 3373(4563)

NESSUS, the Centaur who attempted to violate DEJANIRA after bearing
    her across the Evenus and was killed with a poisoned arrow by

HERCULES. Nessus advised Dejanira to keep some of his blood
to be used to win Hercules back should the need arise.
    MkT [2099(3289)], 2128(3318)

the wicked nest,
    MkT 2386(3576) = MAUNY

NEW THOUGHT, one of the arrows "of other gise" held by Sweet-
Looking for Love. It was used to corrupt or pervert love.
    Rom 982

NICANOR (Nichanore),
    (1) one of the generals chosen by Lysias to bring about the
         destruction of the Jews; he was defeated by JUDAS MACCABEUS.
         I Maccabees 3 and II Maccabees 8.
         MkT 2591(3781)
    (2) an officer of Alexander the Great at the capture of Thebes
         in 336 B.C.; Adv. Jov. 1.41.
         FranklT 1432

NICERATES, the son of Nicias, was put to death by the Thirty Tyrants
imposed upon Athens by the menace of the Spartan Lysander in
404 B.C. His wife thereupon took her own life; Adv. Jov. 1.44.
    FranklT 1437

NICERATE'S WIFE, see NICERATES.

NICHOLAS, the student at Oxford whose particular skill in astrology
enables him to cuckold John the carpenter.
    MillT 3199, 3272, 3285, 3288, 3298, 3303, 3386, 3396,
          3397, 3401, 3403, 3409, 3413, 3420, 3424, 3426,
          3437, 3444, 3462, 3472, 3477, 3487, 3492, 3499,
          3513, 3526, 3538, 3579=Nicholay, 3638=Nicholay,
          3648=Nicholay, 3653, 3721, 3742, 3798, 3806,
          3810, 3824, 3832, 3853
    RvT p3856

ST. NICHOLAS, bishop of Myra, was persecuted by Diocletian but
released by Constantine. In 1087 he was translated to Bari
in Apulia. He is the protector of children, scholars, merchants,
and sailors.
    PrT 514(1704)

[NICOCREON, the tyrant of Cyprus in the time of Alexander the Great.
The story is told that he had ANAXARCHUS OF ABDERA pounded
alive in a mortar; Cic. Tusc. 2.22.52, Diogenes Laertius 9.59,
VALERIUS MAXIMUS 3.3.
    Bo 2.p6.51, 56, 58, 59]

<NICOLE DE MARGIVAL, the supposed author of La Panthère d'Amours,
the date of which is uncertain; Sypherd 3, 49, 51, 62, 73, 83,
118, 126, 131, and Bennett 105.

La Panthère d'Amours
  beginning   HF 501ff.
  50-1   112-3
  155-64   1569ff.
  797ff.   120ff.
  1961-70   1130
  2008ff.   2016ff.>

[NIGELLUS WIREKER, a precentor in Canterbury during the time of
    Richard I, author of the Speculum Stultorum; Louns 2.338-41.
      NPT 3313(4502)]
    Speculum Stultorum (ed. Wright)
      1.55   NPT 3312(4502) = Daun Burnell the
                                           Ass

NIGHT, the offspring of Darkness and Chaos, was the parent of the
    FURIES; Aen. 12.845-7, Meta. 4.451-2, De Gen. Deor. 3.6-9.
      T&C 4.22

NIMROD (Nembrot), son of Cush, according to medieval tradition the
    builder of the tower of Babel; Genesis 10.8-12.
      FormAge 58

NINUS, the eponymous founder of Nineveh who, during the siege of
    Bactria, met and took SEMIRAMIS, the wife of one of his
    officers. They had a son named Ninyas. After the death of
    Ninus, Semiramis erected a temple-tomb in his honor near
    Babylon. See Meta. 4.55-166 and Ovide Moralisé.
      LGW 785

NIOBE, daughter of Tantalus, wife of AMPHION and mother of seven
    sons and seven daughters. Niobe boasted of her superiority
    to Leto (who had only twins by Zeus; i.e. Artemis and APOLLO)
    so Apollo and Artemis killed her sons and daughters. Niobe
    wept and was turned into a column of stone; Meta. 6.267-312.
      T&C 1.699, 759

NISUS was the king of Megara whose daughter, SCYLLA, enamored of
    MINOS, cut off the lock of purple hair on which the safety of
    the kingdom depended; Meta. 8.6-151 and cf. Meech.
      T&C 5.1110
      LGW 1904, 1908

NOAH (Noe, Nowellis), the son of Lamech designated by God to save
    all creatures during the Flood; Genesis 5 and 9.
      MillT 3518, 3534, 3539, 3560, 3582, 3616, 3818, 3834
      ParsT 766

NONIUS, a person whose position in high office is extremely
    offensive to CATULLUS. In Carmina 52 Nonius is a foul disease.
      Bo 3.p4.12, 15

NOTUS see AUSTER.

hire norice see BARCE.

NOVEMBER, the eleventh month of the modern calendar.
        Astr 1.10.5, 15

NOWELLIS see NOAH.

NUN,
        GP 118 = PRIORESS
            163 = SECOND NUN

NUN'S PRIEST, the confessor who accompanied the PRIORESS; Bowden 104.
        [GP 164]
        NPT p2809(3999)
            e3447(4637)

O

OCTAVIA, the sister of Octavian (CAESAR AUGUSTUS) and second wife
    of MARK ANTONY whom Antony married to ensure Octavian's good
    will. Antony deserted her for CLEOPATRA when he left for the
    Parthian wars in 36 B.C.
        [LGW 592]

OCTAVIAN see CAESAR AUGUSTUS.

OCTOBER, the tenth month of the modern calendar.
        Astr 1.10.5, 15

OCTOVYAN see CAESAR AUGUSTUS.

ODENATHUS (Odenake), ruler of Polmyra in the second half of the
    third cent. B.C., was the husband of ZENOBIA. He took the
    side of the Romans against the Persians and defeated them after
    the sack of Antioch. He also took the part of GALLIENUS, son
    and successor of VALERIAN, and helped restore Roman rule in the
    East. Ready to start against the Goths, Odenathus was
    assassinated by his son Herodes and his nephew Maeonius.
    After his death Zenobia governed Palmyra on behalf of her
    young son Athenodorus. See De Clar. Mulier. 98 and De Casibus
    8.6
        MkT 2272(3462), 2291(3481), 2295(3485), 2318(3508),
            2327(3517)

OEDIPUS (Edippus), son of Laius and Jocasta, murdered his father,
    solved the riddle of the sphinx, became ruler of Thebes, and
    by his mother became the father of ETEOCLES, POLYNICES, Ismene,
    and ANTIGONE. When his crimes were discovered he blinded

himself and began a life of exile. He pronounced a curse on
his sons and when they killed each other rather than share the
rule of the city CREON, Jocasta's brother, became king; Theb.
1.46-8, Tes. 10.96.
    T&C 2.102
        4.300

OENONE, a nymph loved by PARIS before his adventure with HELEN.
    Paris deserted her, but when injured by the arrow of
    PHILOCTETES he sought her aid but too late; perhaps Filo.
    1.219ff. but both references are specifically to Hero. 5.
        HF 399
        T&C 1.654

OETES see AËETES.

OLD TESTAMENT.
        Rom 6891

OLIFANT, Sir Elephant, i.e. a proper name, according to Skeat 5.191,
    for a giant.
        Thop 808(1998)

OLIVER, son of Regnier, Duke of Genoa, was one of the great heroes
    of the Charlemagne legend who perished with ROLAND at
    Roncesvalles. He stood by Roland even though he had misgivings
    about Roland's persistence.
        BD 1123
        MkT 2387(3577), 2389(3579)

OLOFERNO see HOLOFERNES.

OMER see HOMER.

OPHELTES (Archemorus), infant son of LYCURGUS, was killed by a
    dragon when abandoned by his nurse HYPSIPYLE who had gone to
    lead the seven against Thebes to a spring. The Nemean games
    were instituted at his funeral; Theb. 5.505ff. and Roman de
    Thèbes 2621-30.
        [T&C 5.1499]

OPILIO, brother of Cyprian, also mentioned in CASSIODORUS, Epistolae
    5.41, 8.16.
        Bo 1.p4.115

the four orders: DOMINICANS, FRANCISCANS, CARMELITES, and
    AUGUSTINIANS.
        GP 210

ORIGEN (Origenes), 185-254, of Alexandria, was one of the Greek
    fathers of the Church. He wrote many exegeses on the Bible,

compiled the Hexapla, and was the supposed author of the
De Maria Magdalena.
>   LGW 428(418)

the original,
        LGW 1558 = Hero. 6

ORION see ARION.

<OROSIUS, of Tarragona, fl. 415, was the author (at the request of
St. Augustine) of the Historiae adversum Paganos.
Historiae adversum Paganos.
        4.23   NPT 3363(4553)>

ORPHEUS, a legendary poet supposedly the son of Calliope and so
marvellous a player that even the beasts were spellbound. His
wife EURYDICE, while running from Aristaeus, stepped on a
snake, was bitten, and died. Orpheus went to Hades to recover
her and convinced PROSERPINE to let her go on the condition
that Orpheus not look back; Orpheus forgot the condition and
Eurydice vanished forever; Georg. 4.454-527 and Meta. 10.1-85
and 11.
        BD 569
        HF 1203
        Bo 3.m12.[4], [17], 46, 56, 58
        T&C 4.791
        MerchT 1716

OSWALD see REEVE.

OTES DE GRANSON (Graunson), a knight of Savoy loyal to the king
of England, fought with the English (according to FROISSART).
In 1391 he was charged with complicity in the death of
Amadeus VII of Savoy and in 1393 his estates were confiscated
and he was pensioned by Richard II. In 1397 he was killed
in a judicial duel; Robin 862 and Braddy.
        Ven 82

OVID, Publius Ovidius Naso, 43 B.C.-17 A.D., was of equestrian rank
and was educated at Rome in rhetoric and perhaps law but gave
himself over to poetry. His work brought him acceptance in
court circles and won him the friendship of Horace and
Propertius. In 8 A.D. he was banished to Tomis where he died
without ever returning to Rome; see Wilkinson and Otis, and
for his influence on Chaucer see Shannon, Hoffman, and Meech.
The real nature of Ovid's influence can be assessed only after
a great deal more work. The poetry of his youth was amatory
and includes Amores, Heroidem Epistolae, Medicamina Formae,
Ars Amatoria, and Remedia Amoris; his early mature poems are
the Metamorphoses and the Fasti; Tristia, Ibis, and Epistulae
ex Ponto are later.

BD 568
HF 379, 1487
T&C 5.1792
LGW (305), 725=Naso, 928=Naso, [1139, 1228, 1352],
     1367, 1465, 1678, 1683, 2220=Naso
MLT 154
Mel 976(2166), 1325(2515), 1414(2604)
[MkT 2127(3317)]
WBT p680
     952, 982
MerchT 2125

Amores

[1.8.104	Mel 1414(2604)]
<1.1.21-6	PF 10-3
.6.65-6	T&C 3.1417
.13.9	3.1450-60
.15-34	3.1433-5
.33, 39-42,	
45-6	3.1450-60
.14.33-4	3.1807-10 + Ars Amat. + Aen.
.15.10	4.1548-53
.34	Bo 3.m10.12
2.1	PF 10-3
.4.9-48	T&C 4.407-12
.11.55-6	3.1417
.19.3	A&A 201-3
3.1	PF 10-3
.4.17, 25-6	A&A 201-3>

Heroides

general	LGW (305)
	MLT 154
6	LGW 1467, [1558]
7	HF 379
10	LGW 2220
12	1678
[6	LGW 1368-1579
7	924-1367
9	MkT 2095(3285) + Meta. + De Clar.
	Mulier.
12	LGW 1580-1679, 2220]
<1.12	T&C 4.1645
.33-4	4.1548-53
2.1ff.	HF 388ff.
	LGW 2496ff. + "CEFFI"
.45-7	2411ff.
.49	A&A 247-55
.63-6	"
.75-6	LGW 2400, 2446ff.
3.1ff.	HF 388ff.
.3	T&C 2.1027
.139-41	A&A 284-9
.144	273-7

Heroïdes (cont.)

<5.1ff.	HF 388ff.
.29–30	T&C 4.1548–53
.149–53	1.659–65
6.1ff.	HF 388ff.
.122	KnT 2085 + <u>Meta</u> + <u>Ars Amat.</u> + <u>Fasti</u>
7.1ff.	HF 379
.1–6	325–37
.1–8	LGW 1352
.3ff.	A&A 346
.29–30	HF 345–59
.45–6	
.61–4	
.97–106	
.133–8	LGW 1323
.145	T&C 4.1548–53
8.97	1.58–60
9.1ff.	HF 388ff.
.61	Bo 4.m7.30
.67–70	MkT 2098(3288)ff.
.87	Bo 4.m7.55
10.1ff.	HF 388ff.
.3	LGW 2198
.5–6	HF 416–20
.7–12	LGW 2185–9
.9–10	HF 416–20
.21–3	LGW 2190–3
.25–32	2195–7
.35–6	HF 416–20
	LGW 2200–6
.41–2	
.47	HF 416–20
.51–8	LGW 2208–13
.59ff.	HF 416–20
	LGW 2163
.63–4	2214–6
.67	1895 + <u>Aen.</u> + <u>Filo.</u>
.71–2	HF 412–3
	LGW 2146–9
.71–4	HF 421–4
.83ff.	LGW 2163
.86	HF 416–20
.103	412–3
	LGW 2146–9
.129	HF 416–20
.137–8	A&A 201
.137–40	207
.139	214
.140	208–9
.151	HF 416–20

Heroïdes (cont.)
   11.55   KnT 2085   + Meta. + Ars Amat.
                                            + Fasti
     .103ff.   T&C 4.22ff.
   12.1ff.   HF 388ff.
     .3-6   A&A 342-8
     .11ff.   LGW 1670
     .12   1371-6
     .35   1609-10
     .53-4   1661
     91-2   1371-6
     .175-8   A&A 229-34
   13.1ff.   FranklT 1445
     .53-4   T&C 4.1548-53
     .97   1.58, 60   + Aen.
   14.1ff.   LGW 2563ff.   + "CEFFI"
   15(16).17-8   T&C 5.904-10, 916-7
     .41-2
     .123ff.   A&A 328-34
     .181-2   T&C 4.120-6
   16(17).1ff.   2.659ff.
     .17-8   2.480, 727-8
     .39-40   2.786-8, 793
     .41, 47-8   5.1067-8
     .111-4   2.409-27
     .136-7   2.758-9
     .143-4   2.1213-4
     .149-51   5.1611-3
     .191-2   HF 269-70
     .207-12   T&C 5.1057-64
     .234   Rom 4443ff.
   17(18).111ff. T&C 3.1464-70
     .112   3.1417>
<Ars Amatoria
   1.9   PF 10-3
    .17   HF 1206
    .68   T&C 4.32
    .99   WBT p552
    .229-44   p464ff.
               ?PhysT 65
    .243-4   59
    .261-2   T&C 3.731
    .295ff.   WBT p733
    .361-2   T&C 5.790-1
    .467ff.   2.1023
    .513-24   Rom 2255-84
    .595ff.   2311-2
    .669   MillT 3725
    .729, 733   Rom 2684
   2.9-10   T&C 1.969
    .11-3   3.1634
    .101-4   HF 1272

<u>Metamorphoses</u> (cont.)

< .394ff.	FranklT 951-2	
.407ff.	KnT 1941	
4.55-166	LGW 706-923	
.64	T&C 2.538-9	
.171ff.	KnT 2388-90	+ <u>Ars</u> <u>Amat.</u> + <u>RR</u>
.171-2	T&C 3.1450-60	
.171-89	Mars <u>passim</u>	
.416	KnT 1329	+ <u>Theb.</u> + <u>Inf.</u>
		+ <u>Tes.</u>
4.416-542	T&C 5.601-2	
.416-562	4.1538-40	
.450	Bo 3.m12.31	
.451-2	T&C 4.22-4	
.457	Bo 3.m12.42	
	T&C 1.786	
.458	Bo 3.m12.38	
	T&C 3.593	
.461	Bo 3.m12.37	
	T&C 5.212	
5.302	MLT 192	
.304	KnT 2085	+ <u>Hero.</u> + <u>Ars</u> <u>Amat.</u>
		+ <u>Fasti</u>
.533ff.	PF 343	
.533-50	T&C 5.319	
.539ff.	LGW 2253ff.	
6.177-9, 224ff.,		
271ff.	MerchT 1715-7	
.382ff.	HF 1229	
.392-4	T&C 4.1543-5	
.402ff.	MerchT 1716	
.412-674	T&C 2.64-71	
.424ff.	LGW 2244ff.	
.430	2252	
.432	T&C 5.319	
	LGW 2253ff.	
.542-50	2330-4	
7.43-5, 84-90	LGW 1371-6	
.162ff.	HF 1271-4	
.432	T&C 5.319-20	
.443	LGW 1904	
.456ff.	1896ff.	
.461-6	1923	
.472-89	2155	
8.6-151	PF 283ff.	
	LGW 1900-21	
.11-151	T&C 5.1110	+ <u>Aen.</u> + OVIDE
		MORALISE
.155ff.	LGW 1928	
.158ff.	HF 1920	
.171	LGW 1932	+ <u>Servius</u> <u>in</u> <u>Aen.</u>

Metamorphoses (cont.)

<.172-3	HF 412-3	+ Hero.
	LGW 2146-9	
.175-6	HF 416-20	
.183ff.	BD 569ff.	
	HF 919	
	LGW 2010ff.	
.260-546	T&C 5.1464-84	
.270-444	5.1464-79	
.275	5.999	+ Theb.
.298ff.	KnT 2071-2	
C.394	T&C 5.655	+ Aen.
.445-525	5.1482-3	
.481ff.	4.22ff.	
9.190ff.	Bo 4.m7.28ff.	
.294-5	KnT 2085	+ Hero. + Ars Amat.
		+ Fasti
.453ff.	PF 283ff.	
.698	KnT 2085	
10.1ff.	HF 1203	
.1-85	Bo 3.m12.4	
	T&C 4.789-91	
	MerchT 1716	
.40ff.	BD 569ff.	
.41	Bo 3.m12.38	
.42	T&C 5.212	+ Aen.
.43	1.786	
.44	BD 589	
.90ff.	PF 176-82	
.155-61	HF 529ff.	
.159-60	589	
.242ff.	PhysT 14ff.	+ RR
.298-502	T&C 4.1138-9	
.453	5.319	
	LGW 2253ff.	
.503-739	T&C 3.720	
.507	KnT 2085	+ Hero. + Ars Amat.
		+ Fasti
.519ff.	2224	
.715	T&C 3.720-1	
11.1ff.	HF 1203	
.1-66	MerchT 1716	
.56-8	HF 2043-80	
.61-6	T&C 4.789-91	
.100-93	3.1373-9	
.174ff.	WBT 951	
.194-210	T&C 4.120-6	+ Servius in Aen.
		+ Filo.
.410ff.	BD 48	
.480-557	68ff.	
.514-5	72	

Metamorphoses (cont.)

<.586	152
.591	163-4
.592	153-65 + Theb.
.592ff.	HF 66ff.
.594-6	BD 170-1
.608-9	HF 1954
.613-5	1946
12.27ff.	Bo 4.m7.13
.39-40	HF 845-6
.39-63	712, 1925ff.
.43	1116
.53	2034-5
.54-5	2108-9
.112	SqT 156, 236
.536	Bo 4.m7.29
13.171-2	T&C 4.927
	SqT 156, 236
.324	T&C 4.1548-53
.730-4	PF 283ff.
14.1ff.	HF 1272
.18ff.	PF 283ff.
.75	T&C 5.644
.816	HF 589
15.234ff.	Rom 387
.392ff.	BD 982
.427	MerchT 1716
.630-1	SqT 1077
.791	T&C 5.319-20
	LGW 2253ff.
.863	T&C 4.25>

Fasti

[2.685-852	LGW 1683, 1721]
<1.125-7	T&C 2.77
.415	PF 253
.415ff.	?MerchT 2034
.457	HF 1002
.543ff.	Bo 4.m7.54
2.79-118	HF 1205
.153ff.	KnT 2056ff.
.156	PF 283ff.
.243-66	HF 1004
.419	T&C 4.25
.449	KnT 2085 + Hero. + Ars Amat.
	+ Meta.
.475-6	T&C 4.25
.721	LGW 1694
.731	1703
.751-2	1729
.810	1812-26
.813-4	1829-31

Fasti (cont.)
    < .841-3   1870-2
    3.9-45   PF 288
    .255   KnT 2085
    .461-516   LGW 2223-4
    5.385-6   HF 1206
    6.285-6   ?MerchT 2265>
<Tristia
    1.9.5   MLT p120
                                 ?Mel 1558(2748):
                                   att. PAMPHILIUS
    3.3.73-6   T&C 4.323-9   + Tes.
    .5.31-2   LGW 503
                                 KnT 1761
    .11.39   Bo 2.p6.66   + Ecl.
    4.2.25-6   SqT 220-3
    5.2.15   156, 236
    ?.14.35-42>   FranklT 1442-7: Hoffman
<Ibis
    482   Bo 3.m12.22-3>
<Ex Ponto
    1.6.37   Rom 2755
    2.7.41-2   T&C 1.712-4
    .9.11   Rom 3539
    ?3.1.105-13   FranklT 1442-7: Hoffman
    4.10.13   HF 1272
    .16.51-2   T&C 1.712-4>

<OVIDE MORALISÉ, an early 14th cent. compilation which was fairly
  typical of the moralizations of classical texts. It was used
  in PETRUS BERCHORIUS's Ovidius Moralizatus. See Meech,
  Steadman, Lowes, Stillwell, Seznec 174-9, Smalley SBMA 261-4,
  Liebeschutz, Wilkins.
  Ovide Moralisé (ed. de Boer, 2 vols. [Amsterdam, 1915-20]):
  STILLWELL
    1.71-97   LGW 2228
    2.1548-55,
      1739-42,
      1489-99   Mars passim
    .2121-2622   MancT 309-62
    ?.2130-2548   : Hoffman
    .4977-87   FranklT 764-6
    11.3427-30   BD 136-52
    ? .3427-30,
    .3450-5   201-5: Wimsatt
    .3450-5   160-5
  Ovide Moralisé (BN MS fr. 373): MEECH
    168b   LGW 1919-20
    171c-172b   1922-47
    172b   1943-9
    172b-c   LGW 1952-9, 1960-6

Ovide Moralise (BN MS fr. 373) (cont.)

172b–173d	HF 405–26 + MACHAUT Roy de Navarre
172c, 173a–b	LGW 1985–2024
173b	2003–18, 2029–73,
	2080–2101
173d	2223–4

Ovide Moralisé, Philomena (ed. de Boer, Paris, 1909): LOWES

6–10	LGW 2244–8
15–7	2249–50
20–3	2253
24–6	2254
28–31	2251–2
49–51	2259
52–5	2260–2
55–64	2263–7
69–72	2270
106–21	2272–8
170–2	2291
188–93	2250–3
684–5	2305
725–7	2307
738–41, 745	2310, 2312–3
844–52	2330–4
1120–33	2361–5
1147–53	2354–5
1193–6	2361–2
1202–5	2369–70
1234	2371>

P

PAIN, one of the "senators" at the court of Age.
> Rom 4997

PALAMON, the knight of Venus who ultimately wins Emily. His name
is from Boccaccio, although it appears in Theb. and Roman de
Thèbes also.
> Knt 1014, 1031, 1063, 1070, 1092, 1115, 1123, 1128,
> 1234, 1275, 1334, 1341, 1348, 1450, 1452, 1455,
> 1467, 1479, 1516, 1561, 1574, 1590, 1620, 1627,
> 1636, 1655, 1698, 1714, 1734, 1791, 1870, 2094,
> 2117, 2128, 2210, 2212, 2261, 2271, 2314, 2471,
> 2584, 2629, 2633, 2639, 2643, 2647, 2652, 2742,
> 2763, 2783, 2794, 2797, 2817, 2858, 2882, 2909,
> 2976, 3077, 3090, 3098, 3101, 3107

PALAMON AND ARCITE, probably an allusion to the KnT; Robin 669.
> LGW 420(408)

PALINURUS, the pilot of AENEAS's ship and the whole Trojan fleet,
was seen by Aeneas when he descended to the underworld. As the
fleet was sailing from Sicily to Italy, the god of sleep overcame Palinurus and threw him into the sea; Palinurus reached
Italy but was murdered by the natives. See Aen. 6.337-83.
        HF 443

PALLADION, the image of Pallas Athene said to have fallen to
earth in answer to the prayer of Ilus, the founder of Troy.
The Palladion was carried off by Odysseus and Diomedes and
the destruction of the city was determined; Aen. 2.162-70,
GUIDO m3b2, BENOÎT 25406-8, and Filo. 1.17-8.
        T&C 1.153

PALLAS, surname of the Greek goddess Athene and hence of the Roman
goddess Minerva. She was the goddess of war, wisdom, and
handicrafts; Meta. 5.263.
        BD 1072=Minerva
        T&C 1.153, 161, 164
            2.232=Minerva, 425, 1062=Minerva
            3.730
            5.308, 977, 999
        LGW 932=Minerva

PAMPHILUS, the hero of the Liber de Amore. The work, attributed
to the 13th cent. poet Pamphilus Maurlianus, consists of a
dialogue, or rather a series of dialogues, primarily between
Pamphilus and GALATEA. Chaucer may have known the work through
the Liber de Buen Amor of Juan Ruiz; Garbaty. Cf. Louns 2.370-2.
        Mel 1556(2746), 1558(2748), 1561(2751)
        FranklT 1110

Liber de Amore
        [general   FranklT 1110
        53-4   Mel 1556(2746).]
        <1   T&C 1.209
        3-4   1.381, 581
        13-5   1.512, 530-2
        25-7   1.237, 243-4
        29-30   1.430-4
        39   1.172
        43-4   1.487
        45-6   1.580-1
        49   1.127
        55-6   3.77-84
        73   1.792-812
                                        2.1501-2
        135-8   3.484-90
        155-62   3.77-84
        169-71   2.736-41
        187-8   2.786-93
        217-9   2.477-81, 731-5

Liber de Amore (cont.)

253-6	2.367-8, 785-6, 804
265-6	1.776
267-70	1.837-40
281-2	Rom 4286ff.
	T&C 3.694-5
289	1.864-8
<293-4	2.367-8, 785-6, 804
297-8	3.484-90
299	1.498-501
308-10	1.974-5
	2.239-49
	3.250-8
329-30	2.975
339-50	2.157-61, 204-10
345	2.204-7
357-62	2.155-61, 190-207, 316-33
365-8	2.586-8
379-80	2.1284-8
381-4	2.386-9
387	3.400-3
395	2.746-9
396-400	2.586-8
407-8	1.246-52
	2.848-54
411	"
413-20	2.367-71, 785-6
	3.295-308, 456-62, 582-8
417	Rom 3878
423-4	T&C 3.559-60, 582-95
425	Rom 4286ff.
429-30	T&C 3.120-1
451-6	3.1086-92
463-70	1.701-7, 792-8
499-500	4.960-1085
502	4.600-1
506-10	2.498-504, 1021-2
545-8	2.1497-1505
	3.736-7, 1098, 1126
551-2	1.582
	2.326
	3.113-5
555	2.330-50, 1149-52, 1240-6, 1736
	3.771-7, 876-82
573-6	2.694-812
578-80	2.351-7
645-6	2.109-12, 221-4, 393-9
647-8	3.559-60, 582-95
652	3.743
653-6	3.785-91
669-74	3.1135-41

Liber de Amore (cont.)
    679-80   3.1184-90, 1202-8
    701-3   3.108, 1288-1302
    725-8   3.1555-63
    729-30   3.1563-70
    738
    757-60   >

PAN, son of Mercury and Penelope, was the god of flocks and
    shepherds; as "god of kind" Kittredge cites Servius in Ecl.
    2.31, Etym. 8.11.81-3, Spec. Doct. 17.10, Myth. I.126, Myth.
    II.48, Myth. III.8.1-2, in Robin 775.
        BD 512

PANDARUS (Pandar, Pandare), uncle of Criseyde and friend of Troilus,
    acted as go-between; Meech and Robin 816.
        T&C 1.548, 582, 588, 610, 618, 624, 658, 725, 727,
            736, 761, 771, 778, 822, 829, 841, 868, 876,
            939, 1009, 1015, 1023, 1030, 1037, 1045,
            1051, 1058, 1070
        2.57, 67, 85, 93, 106, 120, 155, 169, 190, 208,
            220, 254, 429, 490, 505, 937, 939, 953, 974,
            989, 1046, 1051, 1093, 1109, 1142, 1180, 1185,
            1193, 1207, 1226, 1252, 1260, 1075, 1285,
            1296, 1308, 1313, 1318, 1329, 1341, 1344,
            1352, 1355, 1399, 1406, 1415, 1431, 1459,
            1479, 1492, 1531, 1539, 1547, 1561, 1588,
            1600, 1612, 1625, 1640, 1676, 1679, 1681,
            1688, 1710, 1723, 1727
        3.59, 68, 115, 148, 183, 208, 227, 235, 346,
            358, 484, 512, 548, 603, 629, 654, 680, 694,
            708, 736, 747, 762, 841, 932, 960, 974, 1077,
            1094, 1105, 1135, 1188, 1555, 1571, 1582, 1585,
            1592, 1616, 1644, 1656, 1662, 1664, 1678, 1738
        4.344, 353, 366, 368, 376, 379, 445, 452, 461,
            463, 521, 578, 582, 638, 641, 806, 822, 828,
            849, 872, 913, 946, 1085, 1086
        5.280, 281, 295, 323, 430, 477, 484, 498, 505,
            521, 554, 557, 682, 1111, 1120, 1121, 1128,
            1147, 1157, 1160, 1170, 1244, 1245, 1253, 1268,
            1275, 1291, 1668, 1709, 1723

PANDION, king of Athens and father of PHILOMELA and PROCNE.
    LGW 2247, 2279, 2295

[PANTHEA, the wife of HABRADATES.]

COUNTESS AND EARL OF PANYK, the sister and brother-in-law of WALTER
    of Saluzzo. Magoun identifies Panyk with Panico, near Bologna.
    COUNTESS OF PANYK
        ClT 590

EARL OF PANYK
    ClT 764, 939

PAPINIANUS, Aemilius, a Roman jurist who flourished under Marcus
    Aurelius and Septimus Severus. After the death of Severus,
    Caracalla murdered his brother Geta and asked Papinianus to
    defend his action; Papinianus refused and Caracalla (MARCUS
    AURELIUS ANTONINUS) had him put to death.
        Bo 3.p5.50, 51

PARABLES OF SOLOMON = Proverbs.
        Rom 6530, [6543]
        WBT p679

PARCAE (Parcas) see FATES.

PARDONER, one of the most explicitly described but least admirable
    of the pilgrims. The pardoners had papal authority to hear
    confession and pardon sin; Bowden 274-86.
        GP 543, 669, 675
        WBT p163, 185
        PardT p318
            956, 963, 965, 966

PARIS, son of PRIAM and HECUBA, brother of HECTOR, TROILUS,
    CASSANDRA. He fell in love with and deserted OENONE; he
    abducted HELEN and thereby brought about the Trojan war. Paris
    was wounded by the arrow of PHILOCTETES and died while seeking
    Oenone; Hero. 5, 15(16), 16(17).
        BD 331
        HF 398
        PF 290
        T&C 1.63, 653
            2.1449
            4.608
        MerchT 1754
        SqT 548

PARLEMENT OF FOULES, one of the works in the list of ascriptions
    to Chaucer.
        LGW 419(407)

PARMENIDES, of Elea, born c. 539 B.C., was a contemporary of
    Heraclitus and founder of the ELEATICS.
        Bo 3.p12.193

PARSON, the idealized parish priest; Bowden 230-8.
        GP 478
        MLT e1166=Sir Parish Priest, 1170
        ParsT p30

PARTHENOPAEUS (Parthenope), the son of MELEAGER and ATALANTA,
    was one of the seven against Thebes who fought on the side of
    POLYNICES; Aen. 6.480, Theb. 4.248, 9.812-907
        A&A 58
        T&C 5.1503

PASIPHAE (Phasipha), wife of MINOS, mother of ARIADNE and PHAEDRA;
    her illicit passion for the Cretan bull resulted in the birth
    of the MINOTAUR; Adv. Jov. 1.48.
        WBT p733

PATIENCE, one of the figures on the portal of the temple of Venus,
    was the personification of the quality which required the lover
    to wait for the acceptance of his suit.
        PF 242

ST. PAUL the Apostle was the greatest theologian and missionary of
    the early Church. He was beheaded in Rome in 66. As Saul of
    Tarsus he had persecuted Christians until his conversion by
    Jesus. Cf. BIBLE.
        Rom 6661, 6679, 6776
        Mel 989(2179), [1130(2320)], 1291(2481), [1406(2596)],
            1440(2630), [1460(2650), 1509(2699), 1515(2700),
            1634(2824), 1840(3030)]
        NPT 3441(4631)
        WBT p[49, 64], 73, [79, 160, 341]
        FrT 1647
        SumT 1819, [1881]
        PardT 521, 523, [529]
        SecNT [201]
        ParsT p32
                162, 322, 342, 343, 598, 619, 630, 651, 725,
                739, 748, 819, 820, 867, 879, 895, 929, 1054

[PAUL THE HERMIT, St. Paul of Thebes, was confused with ST. PAUL
    the Apostle. During the persecutions of Decius, Paul fled east
    of the Nile and became "the first hermit." He died in 342.
        PardT p443]

PAULUS, Lucius Aemilius, surnamed Macedonicus, c. 229-160 B.C.,
    served as consul in 168 and ended the Macedonian war at Pydna
    in the same year. He captured Perseus III and showed him in
    the triumph at Rome.
        Bo 2.p2.64

<PAULUS DIACONUS, c. 720-?800, one of Charlemagne's court poets,
    entered Monte Cassino before 782 and there completed De
    Gestis Romanorum; Raby 1. 197-9.
    De Gestis Romanorum
        15   PardT 579>

PAULYN <u>see</u> DECIUS PAULINUS.

PEACE (Pees), Harmony, one of the portal figures; perhaps
<u>Tes</u>. 7.61-2.
PF 240

PEGASUS (Pegasee), the winged horse of the MUSES, who sprang from
the blood of Medusa when she was beheaded. With a blow of his
hoof he caused the fountain of the Muses (Hippocrene) to
spring from Mt. Helicon. Pegasus was caught by Bellerophon
at Pirene and used to slay the Chimaera; but when Bellerophon
attempted to fly to heaven he was thrown and Pegasus became
a constellation; <u>Meta</u>. 4.785, 5.262ff., <u>Fasti</u> 3.458.
SqT 207 .

PELEUS (Pelleus), son of Aeacus, went to Phthia to be purified for
murder; Hippolyte, the wife of Acastus, fell in love with him
and when he repulsed her she denounced him to her husband.
Acastus abandoned Peleus on Mt. Pelion after removing the
marvelous knife given to Peleus by Vulcan. However, CHIRON
restored the knife and Peleus survived. It was fated that
THETIS should have a son more powerful than Jupiter; thus
Thetis was married to Peleus in order that their son ACHILLES
would not be immortal; <u>Meta</u>. 11. See <u>Shannon</u> 208ff.
LGW 1397, 1400, 1409, 1439

PENELOPE, daughter of Icarius and Periboea, was the wife of
ULYSSES, celebrated for her constancy and chastity; <u>Hero</u>. 1,
<u>Adv</u>. <u>Jov</u>. 1.45, <u>RR</u> 8605-12.
BD 1081
A&A 82
T&C 5.1778
LGW 252(206)
MLT 175
FranklT 1443

PENEUS (Penneus), a river-god, the father of Cyrene and Daphne;
<u>Meta</u>. 1.569ff., <u>Myth</u>. III 8.4.44.
KnT 2064

[PENNAFORTE, Raymond of, a 13th cent. Dominican who became
general of the order in 1238. His <u>Summa</u> <u>Casum</u> <u>Poenitentiae</u>
and collection of the <u>Decretals</u> of Gregory IX were prescribed
as canon law texts; <u>S&A</u> and Petersen.
ParsT 85, 159:att. JEROME, 321-86, 960-81
<u>Summa</u> <u>Casum</u> <u>Poenitentiae</u>, "De Poenitentiis et Remissionibus"
94^v-96^r ParsT 75-127
96^v-97^r 128-315
97^v-101^r 316-21, 957-1027]

PEPIN, III, the Short, the son of Charles Martel and father of
   CHARLEMAGNE, was the greatest of the major domos for the
   Merovingians.   In 751 he took the title of king.   He died
   in 768.
         Rom 1458

PERCIVAL (Percyvell), one of the purest of the Arthurian knights;
   Wells [39].
         Thop 916(2106)

KYNG OF PERCYENS, Perseus III, see PAULUS.

PERKIN REVELOUR, the suitably named hero of the CkT; the name is
   unexplained.
         CkT 4371, 4387

<PERSIUS, Flaccus, Aulus, 34-62, was of equestrian family and was
   educated in Rome in literature and rhetoric.   He was also a
   student of the Stoic Cornutus to whom Persius addressed the
   Fifth Satire.   The allusion is extremely conjectural.
   Saturae
         prologue 1-3   FranklT 721>

PEROTHEUS see PIRITHOUS.

PERTELOTE, the heroine of the tale.   In Le Roman de Renart she is
   Pinte or Pintain; Skeat 5.250, Hinckley 129.
         NPT 2870(4060), 2885(4075), 2888(4078), 3105(4295),
               3122(4312), 3158(4348), 3177(4367), 3200(4390),
               3268(4458), 3362(4552)

ST. PETER the Apostle, also called Simon, was the son of John the
   Bethsaida; he was led to Jesus by his brother Andrew and
   became the most important of the disciples.   He was crucified
   in Rome in 66.   Cf. BIBLE.
         Rom 7166, 1794, 7198
         HF 1034, 2000
         GP 697
         MillT 3486
         ShT 214(1404)
         Mel 1501(2691)
         WBT p446
         FrT 1332
         SumT 1819
         CYT p665
         ParsT 142, 287, 597, 783, 930, 988, 994

ST. PETER'S SISTER, an uncertain allusion, is perhaps a substitution
   for St. Peter's daughter, St. Petronilla; Skeat 5.106.
         MillT 3486

PETER OF CYPRUS, Peter I, Pierre de Lusignan, was the last great
king of Cyprus. He visited England 1362-3, captured Attalia
in 1361, Alexandria in 1365, and reduced Lyas in 1367; he was
assassinated in Rome in 1369. Braddy, PMLA 50, suggests that
Chaucer was familiar with Peter through MACHAUT's Prise
d'Alexandrie.
    MkT 2391(3581)

PETER OF SPAIN, Pedro the Cruel, king of Castile and Leon 1350-69,
was murdered by his brother Eurique who was assisted by BERTRAN
DU GUESCLIN and SIR OLIVER MAUNY. Peter's daughter Constance
was married to John of Gaunt in 1371.
    MkT 2375(3565)

PETRARCH, Francesco Petrarca, 1304-74, Italian scholar, poet, and
humanist, was a Florentine by birth but moved to Avignon in
1313 and to Vaucluse in 1337. In 1339 he began the first
drafts of the Africa and in 1341 he received the laureate wreath
in Rome. There followed a period of journeys to and from
Vaucluse but he finally settled in Arqua in 1369 and remained
there until his death. See CCS 144-5, S&A, and Severs.
Boccaccio is actually the source in MkT; the parallels in ClT
are so close the reader is referred to S&A.
    MkT 2325(3515)
    ClT p31
        [1141], 1147
[Epistolae Seniles
     17.3   ClT passim]
<Sonneto
     23   T&C 3.1464-70
     42   2.50-5, 64-71
     88   1.400-20>
<Canzone
     8   T&C 2.1-3>

<PETRONIUS Arbiter, Gaius, consul and governor of Bithynia, became
elegantiae arbiter to Nero; he was later exiled to Cumae, and
an ominous order from Nero caused him to commit suicide in 65.
In addition to the fragmentary Saturae et Liber Priapeorum he
was the author of the Satyricon; Robin 794 but Skeat 1.513
suggests Fasti 1.415.
Saturae et Liber Priapeorum (Berlin, 1904)
    No. 25   PF 256>

PETRUS ALFONSUS (Piers Alfonce), a converted Spanish Jew, was born
in Aragon in 1062 and converted in 1106. The De Disciplina
Clericalis is a collection of moral tales; Skeat 5.205.
        Mel 1053(2243), [1144(2334)], 1189(2379), 1218(2408),
            1309(2499), 1561(2751):att. PAMPHILUS,
            1566(2756)

[De Disciplina Clericalis (ed. Hilka and Soderhjelm,
Heidelberg, 1911)
    Exodus 2(p.6ff.)   Mel 1144(2334)
                                  1189(2379)
                                  1566(2756)
        4(p.10)   1218(2408)
                                  1561(2751)
      17(p.27)   1309(2499)
      24(p.37)   1053(2243)]

<PETRUS BERCHORIUS, Pierre Bersuire, c. 1290-1362, became a
Benedictine in Poitou before 1317 and spent the years 1328-42
in Avignon where he became the friend of Petrarch. In 1342
Berchorius returned to Paris and remained there until his
death. The Ovidius Moralizatus is the 15th book of Berchorius's
Reductorium Morale. The Ovidius is based on Ovid's Meta, but
contains material from Fulgentius, Rabanus Maurus, Myth. III,
Africa 3.128-264, the Ovid Moralisé, and Ridevall's Fulgentius
Metaforalis; Wilkins, Steadman, Seznec, Clogan, Smalley SMBA
261-4, Quinn, and Liebeschütz.
Ovidius Moralizatus (ed. Badius, Paris, 1509, 1511)
    1.5   HF 131-9
                          KnT 1387-8, 1955-66, 2041-8>

[PETRUS DE RIGA, Canon of Rheims, in the 12th cent. The Aurora is
an allegorical interpretation of the Bible; Louns 2.334-6,
Skeat 1.492-3, Young, Robertson.]
Aurora (PL 212.17-46)
    general   BD 1169

Phaedo see PLATO.

PHAEDRA (Phedra), daughter of MINOS and wife of THESEUS, fell in
love with HIPPOLYTUS (the bastard son of Theseus and Hippolyta);
when he rejected her she hanged herself and in a letter denounced him as her seducer. Theseus invoked Neptune and
Hippolytus's horses were frightened as he was driving by the
sea and he was dragged to death; Hero. 4, Ovide Moralise,
MACHAUT Jugement dou Roy de Navarre.
    HF 419
    LGW 1970, 1978, 1985

<PHAEDRUS, a freedman in the household of Augustus, was the author
of a collection of fables based on Aesop. The reference is
probably to Gesta Roman. 174; Robin 715, Skeat 5.360-1.
Fabulae (ed. Mai, Rome, 1831)
    4.18   MerchT 1786>

PHAETHON (Pheton) asked to drive the chariot of his father the Sun.
He proved unequal to the task: the horses ran wild and almost
burned up the earth so Jupiter intervened with a thunderbolt;

Meta. 1.750-9, 2.1-332.
    HF 942
    T&C 5.664

PHANIA (Phanie), Croesus's daughter. Apparently from RR 6489ff.
    but the story is in Myth. I.196 and Myth. II.190. Cf.Gelbach,
    Wimsatt.
        MkT [2747(3937)], 2758(3948)

PHARAOH (Pharao, Pharoo), the king of Egypt whose dream was
    interpreted by JOSEPH; Genesis 41.
        BD 282
        HF 516
        NPT 3133(4323)
        ParsT 443

PHARISEES, a Jewish sect polemicized in the Gospels (viz. Matthew
    23.15; Mark 7.6) as religious hypocrites.
        Rom 6893

PHEBUSEO, a character invented by Chaucer, was one of the prisoners
    taken by the Greeks; Robin 827, Skeat 2.485, Root.
        T&C 4.54

PHIDON (Phidoun), an Athenian whose daughters were forced to dance
    naked but preserved their modesty and virginity by throwing
    themselves into a well; Adv. Jov. 1.41. Skeat refers to the
    excesses committed in Athens during the reign of the Thirty
    Tyrants.
        FranklT 1369

PHILIP OF MACEDON, c. 382-336 B.C., king of Macedon and father of
    ALEXANDER THE GREAT.
        MkT 2656(3846)

PHILISTINES, the inhabitants of Philistia, whose gods were Dagon
    and Astarte and Baal-zebub. Gaza was one of the confederation
    of five cities; Judges 13.1-16.31.
        MkT 2048(3238)

PHILOCTETES (Philotetes), the pilot for the Argonauts. In VALERIUS
    FLACCUS he is the son of Poeas of Oeta: this identification
    would make him the Philoctetes who was responsible for the
    death of PARIS. See Argonautica, Book I, and GUIDO, Book I.
    The spelling is Guido's.
        LGW 1459

PHILOMELA, daughter of PANDION and sister of PROCNE who married
    TEREUS. Philomela was violated and had her tongue cut out by
    her brother-in-law; she depicted the events in needlework and
    sent them to her sister. Procne killed her son Itys and fed

him to Tereus. Tereus drew his sword to kill the two and they
were all changed into birds: Tereus into the hoopee, Philomela
into the nightingale, and Procne into the swallow; Meta. 6.42ff.
and Ovide Moralisé.
    LGW 2274, 2284, 2339

the philosopher, many a philosopher,
    LGW 381(365) = Aristotle?
    Mel 1063(2553) = PUBLILIUS SYRUS, 1191(2381), 1651(2841)
    ParsT 484, 536, 650, 658, 660, 670, 806
many a philosopher
    MLT p25 = ST. THOMAS AQUINAS?

PHILOSTRATE see ARCITE.

PHILOSOPHY, the personification of knowledge.
    HF 974
    Bo 1.p3.6, 17, 22; p4.[147], 273
        4.p1.1; p6.256

PHILOTETES see PHILOCTETES.

PHITONISSA see WITCH OF ENDOR.

PHITOUN see PYTHON.

PHLEGETHON (Flegetoun), the river of fire, in Hades; not in Filo.
    T&C 3.1600

PHOEBUS see APOLLO.

PHOLUS, the Centaur, the son of Silenus and the nymph Melia, who
entertained HERCULES on his way to fetch the ERYMANTHIAN BOAR.
The wine which Pholus opened brought the Centaurs, some of
whom Hercules killed and others he chased. When he returned
he discovered Pholus dead: Pholus had become curious about
the arrow; it fell and stuck in his foot and he died; Meta. 9
and 12.306, Hero. 9.
    [MkT 2099(3289)]

PHYLLIS, daughter of Sithon of Thrace, was the queen of Thrace
who sheltered and loved DEMOPHON: she was betrothed to Demophon
but when he did not return on schedule she killed herself;
Hero. 2, "CEFFI," De Gen. Deor. 11.25, RR 13174ff. Chaucer's
error, which makes her the daughter of Lycurgus, is due to
De Gen. Deor; Louns 2.232: but cf. Hero. 2.111 and "CEFFI."
    BD 728
    HF 390
    LGW 264(218), 2424, 2452, 2465, 2469, 2482, 2494,
        2497
    MLT 165

PHYSICS see ARISTOTLE.

PHYSIOLOGUS (Phisiologus), the Latin bestiary attributed to
    Theobaldus?, Physiologus de Naturis XII Animalium; Skeat 5.256,
    Robin 754.
        NPT 3271(4461)

PICTAGORAS see PYTHAGORAS.

PIERIDES, the daughters of Pierus who contended with the MUSES;
    they lost, of course, and were changed into magpies; Meta.
    5.302.
        MLT i92

PIERS see MONK.

PIGMALION see PYGMALION.

PILATE, the judge of Jesus; the reference here is to the character-
    ization of Pilate in some of the medieval cyclic mystery plays
    in which Pilate (and HEROD) are arrogant, boastful, and
    irascible.
        MillT p3124

<PINDAR, the Greek lyric poet, c. 522-474 B.C., whose odes celebrate
    victories in the Olympic, Pythian, and Nemean games. The
    ascription is doubtful.
    Nemeans
        10.61ff.   Bo 3.p8.39-40>

PIRAMUS see PYRAMUS.

PIRITHOUS (Perotheus), king of the Lapiths, husband of Hippodamia.
    The Lapiths defeated the Centaurs who started a brawl at the
    wedding feast. After the death of Hippodamia, THESEUS helped
    Pirithous try to abduct Persephone from Hades. Pirithous was
    torn to pieces by CERBERUS; Theseus was delivered by HERCULES;
    Meta. 8.302ff.; Tes. 3.47-51, RR 8186. See Hoffman 52-6.
        KnT 1191, 1202, 1205, 1227

PIRRUS see PYRRHUS.

PISCES, the 12th sign of the zodiac.
        WBT p704
        SqT 273
        Astr 1.8.4
            2.6.18; 17.25; 28.19, 37; 40.52, 55, 59, 73

PITY, the personification of the quality in a courtly mistress
    which motivates her to accept the suit of a lover.
        Rom 3501, 3543, 3575, 3603, 3865

LGW 161
Pity 1, 5, 10, 22, 43, 49, 50, 87, [92]
MercB 15, 20, 25

PLACEBO, SumT is from Psalm 114.9(Vulg.) which begins an anthem
for the dead; MerchT is the proverbial flatterer.
SumT 2075
MerchT 1476, 1478, 1520, 1571, 1617
ParsT 617

PLATO, the famous Greek philosopher, c. 427-348 B.C., Chaucer
surely knew him indirectly through Bo, De Civ. Dei 8.16, RR
7099ff., 15190ff. For CYT see S&A 686.
HF 759, 931
Bo 1.p3.25, 27; p4.27, 33
3.p9.191; m11.44; p12.2, 206
4.p2.258
5.p6.52, 60, 97
GP 741
CYT 1448, 1453, 1456, 1460, 1463
[Republic
5.473D   Bo 1.p4.26
6   .33
9end   .23
10   4.m2   ]
[Gorgias
passim   Bo 4.p2.ff.
507C   .258]
Timaeus
[1st part   Bo 3.m9]
27C   .p9.192
[29B   3.p12.205
GP 742
MancT 207-10]

[Phaedo
72E   Bo 3.m11.44ff.]
[Sophistes
244E   Bo 3.p12.193]
[De Legibus
10   Bo 4.p6.94]

[PLEIADES, the seven daughters of Atlas and Pleione pursued by
ARION. They were all turned into constellations; Fasti 5.83,
599-62.
HF 1007]

PLENTY, the personification of bounty.
Bo 2.m2.1

PLESAUNCE, the personification of cheerful disposition; Tes. 7.55.
PF 218

KnT 1925
Lady 26

PLEYNDAMOUR, the unidentified hero of an unidentified romance.
Thop 900(2090)

<PLINY the Elder, Gaius Plinius Secundus, 23 or 24-79, had a
    distinguished career as soldier and statesman and when at Rome
    enjoyed close relations with Vespasian. He perished in the
    eruption of Vesuvius. Pliny was an industrious reader and
    voluminous writer. The Naturalis Historia was dedicated to
    Titus in 77 and published for the most part posthumously.
    Naturalis Historia

2.9(12)	Bo 4.m5.11-2	+ TACITUS + JUVENAL
.10.7.48	T&C 5.1020	+ CLAUDIANUS
10.3	PF 333	
.23	342	
.24	T&C 3.1496	+ Spec. Nat.
.29	PF 345	
.36	GP 626	+ JUVENAL
12.18	Bo 3.m3.4-5>	

PLOWMAN, the brother and companion of the PARSON, apparently a
    small tenant farmer; Bowden 238-42.
        GP 529

PLUTO, god of the lower world, husband of PROSERPINA, brother of
    JUPITER and NEPTUNE. Cf. Spencer.
        HF 1511
        T&C 3.592
        KnT 2082, 2299, 2685
        MerchT 2038, 2227, 2311, 2354
        FranklT 1075

the poet seith, other poets,
        BD 54
        Mel 1496(2686)

POLIPHETE see POLYPHOETES.

POLITE(S), a son of PRIAM, killed by PYRRHUS; Aen. 2.526, 5.564.
    His capture in T&C is due to Filo. 4.3. The form is Italian.
        HF 160
        T&C 4.53

POLIXENA, POLIXENE see POLYXENA.

POLLUX and his brother CASTOR formed the constellation GEMINI,
    the third sign of the zodiac. The brothers were the sons of
    Tyndarus and Leda.
        HF 1006

POLYDAMAS, the son of Antenor, was a friend of HECTOR; <u>Meta</u>. 12.547,
   <u>Hero</u>. 5.94, BENOIT 12551-65, GUIDO 11^{al}, <u>Filo</u>. 4.3.
      T&C 4.51

POLYHYMNIA (Polymya), one of the MUSES, the muse of sacred song;
   she is not mentioned in <u>Tes</u>. 1.1-3. See HORACE <u>Carmina</u> 1.1.33,
   <u>Fasti</u> 5.9, <u>Parad</u>. 23.56-7, <u>Myth</u>. III.8.18.
      A&A 15

POLYMNESTOR (Polymestore), king of Thrace, husband of Ilione;
   <u>Meta</u>. 13.536, <u>Servius in Aen</u>. 3.6, 15, <u>Purg</u>. 20.114-5, <u>Filo</u>. 4.3,
   <u>Myth</u>. II.209.
      T&C 4.52

POLYNICES (Polymytes), one of the sons of OEDIPUS, cursed by his
   father. Eteocles and Polynices agreed to rule Thebes in
   alternate years but Eteocles refused to yield. Polynices, who
   had been at the court of ADRASTUS and married his daughter
   Argeia, returned to Thebes with an army raised by his father-
   in-law and headed by the seven against Thebes. In the battle
   the sons fulfilled the father's curse by killing each other;
   <u>Theb</u>. 5.738ff., <u>Filo</u>. 6.24.
      T&C 5.938, 1488, 1507

POLYPHEMUS (Poliphemus), a Cyclops, son of Neptune, who captured
   and devoured some of Odysseus's men before he was intoxicated
   and blinded by Odysseus; <u>Meta</u>. 3.618-9, 13.772, 14.167,
   ultimately from <u>Odyssey</u> 9.
      Bo 4.m7.20, 22, 25, 26

POLYPHOETES (Poliphete), Criseyde's vociferous opponent (according
   to Pandarus' allegations which are a fabrication used to con-
   vince Criseyde to seek Troilus' protection), seems to be
   Chaucer's invention although Hamilton 97n.3 suggests <u>Aen</u>. 6.484.
      T&C 2.1467, 1616, 1619

POLYXENA (Polixena, Polixene), daughter of PRIAM, was, according
   to <u>Meta</u>., sacrificed by PYRRHUS at the grave of his father,
   ACHILLES. See <u>Meta</u>. 13.448, <u>Aen</u>. 3.321, DARES 34, JOSEPH OF
   EXETER 6.402ff., GUIDO 13^v, BENOÎT 21838ff., <u>Inf</u>. 30.17,
   <u>Filo</u>. 1.42, 3.18.
      BD 1071
      T&C 1.455
          3.409
      LGW 258(212)

POMPEY (Pompe, Pompeye, Pompeus), Gnaeus Pompeius, Pompey the
   Great, 106-48 B.C., the great Roman general who formed the
   triumvirate with Caesar and Crassus in 60. He married Julia,
   Caesar's daughter, whose death in 54 estranged Caesar and
   Pompey. Caesar defeated Pompey at Pharsalia in 48; Caesar

pursued Pompey to Egypt only to discover that he had been
murdered. The error that Pompey was Caesar's father-in-law
may be due to SUETONIUS 27. See Phars. 8.609-10, SUETONIUS 27,
VALERIUS MAXIMUS 5.1.10, JEHAN DE TUIM 137-9, Spec. Hist.
6.35-42, De Casibus 6.9; cf. Shannon 335ff., S&A.
    HF 1502
    MLT 199
    MkT 2680(3870), 2684(3874), 2688(3878), 2693(3883)

THE POPE, an ecclesiastical title used to designate the head of the
Roman Catholic Church; a title which, during the Middle Ages,
was gradually reserved for the bishop of Rome, who acquired
primacy over the worship, teaching, discipline, administration,
and politics of the Church.
    Rom 6368, 6847
    MLT 992, 1122
    WBT p420
    ClT 741, 744, 746
    ParsT 772

POPE-HOLY, the personification of hypocrisy.
    Rom 415

PORTIA (Porcia), daughter of Cato Uticensis, wife of MARCUS BRUTUS,
was an ardent supporter of the republican cause and believed
in the actions of her husband. She committed suicide after
Brutus was forced to flee after the assassination of CAESAR.
Her death by swallowing coals is related in Plutarch's Brutus
53. See Adv. Jov. 1.46.
    FranklT 1448

POVERTY (Povert), a quality which diminishes love, was personified
on the wall outside the garden of Mirth.
    Rom 450, 5351

PRESENTUS (Pseustis), of doubtful identity, is probably Pseustis
in the Ecloga Theoduli, a common school text in the Liber
Catonianus. Pseustis, who relies on ancient mythology, is
ultimately defeated in debate by Alithia who uses scripture,
i.e. the Truth. According to Bennett 123 Chaucer associated
Pseustis "etymologically and archetypally" with Fraud.
    HF 1228

PRIAM (Priamus), the son of Laomedon and husband of HECUBA, was
king of Troy and father of HECTOR, PARIS, TROILUS, POLYDORUS,
CASSANDRA, POLYXENA, and DEIPHOBUS. He was slain by PYRRHUS.
For NPT Pratt suggests Nov. Poet. 363-8 [Faral 208].
    BD 328
    HF 159
    T&C 1.2
        3.791

         T&C 4.57, 139, 142, 194, [276, 552, 555, 558, 646],
              921, 1206, 1393
              5.284, 1226
         LGW 939
         NPT 3358(4548)

PRIAPUS, a phallic deity who was also a god of gardens; Fasti
    1.415ff., Tes. 7.60; cf. Hoffman[3] 154-6.
         PF 253
         MerchT 2034

PRIDE, one of the Seven Deadly Sins.
         Rom 975
         T&C 3.1805
         ParsT 554

PRINCES = Dukes of Lancaster, York, and Gloucester.
         Fort 73

PRINCESS, perhaps Isabel who married Edmund of York in 1372;
    Braddy 76-8 suggests GRANSON's Souhait de saint Valentin.
         Ven 73

PRIORESS, Madam Eglentine, the most delicate of the ecclesiastical
    pilgrims, received deferential treatment from all; Bowden
    92-104.
         GP 118, 121 = Madam Eglentine, 839
         ShipT 446(1636)

PROCNE (Proigne), sister of PHILOMELA and wife of Tereus.
         T&C 2.64
         LGW 2248, 2275, 2346, 2348, 2373, 2380

<PROPERTIUS, Sextus, c. 50-c. 16 B.C., the Roman elegiac poet whose
    four books of elegies record his infatuation with "Cynthia."
    Elegiae
         5.3.3-4   T&C 2.1027   + Hero. 3.3>

THE PROPHET,
         Mel 1630(2820)=Psalms 37.16, 1692(2882)=Psalms 34.14,
              1700(2890)
         ParsT 850

PROSERPINA (Proserpyna, Proserpyne), daughter of Ceres and Jupiter,
    wife of PLUTO who seized her as she was gathering flowers in
    Sicily and carried her away to the lower world; Meta. 5.391,
    Inf. 9.44. T&C is not in Filo.; see Spencer.
         HF 1511
         T&C 4.473
         MerchT 2039, 2229, 2264

PROTEUS, a sea-god who had the ability to change form; Meta.
    8.731, Ars Amat. 1.761, Fasti 1.367.
        Rom 6319

PROTESILAUS (Protheselaus), a son of Iphiclus, a native of Phylace
    in Thessaly, the husband of LAODAMIA, and the leader of the
    Thessalians against Troy, where he was the first man killed;
    Meta. 12.68, Hero. 13, Adv. Jov. 1.45.
        FranklT 1446

PROVERBS see BIBLE.
        [MLT 115, 118
        ParsT 569]

PRUDENCE, the personification of cautious and judicious conduct;
    T&C is perhaps from Purg. 29.130-2. The Mel usage is taken by
    ALBERTANUS 6 from CASSIODORUS Variarum 2.15.
        T&C 5.744
        Mel 967(2157), 974(2164), 976(2166), 979(2169),
            988(2178), 1001(2191), 1002(2192), 1004(2194),
            1051(2241), 1055(2245), 1064(2254), 1112(2302),
            1115(2305), 1232(2422), 1265(2455), 1283(2473),
            1335(2525), 1433(2623), 1447(2637), 1467(2657),
            1518(2708), 1526(2716), 1551(2741), 1672(2862),
            1687(2877), 1697(2887), 1706(2896), 1713(2903),
            1726(2916), 1733(2923), 1752(2942), 1769(2959),
            1779(2969), 1784(2974), 1791(2981), 1811(3001),
            1815(3005), 1832(3022), 1836(3026), 1870(3060)
        MkT p1890(3080), 1896(3086)

PSALMS see BIBLE.
        [Mel 1630(2820), 1692(2882)
        FrT 1656
        SumT 2075]

PSEUSTIS see PRESENTUS.

PTOLEMY (Tholome), probably Ptolemy XII Philopator, 51-47 B.C.,
    coregent with his sister CLEOPATRA; Ptolemy XIII, an even
    younger brother, reigned 47-44 and was murdered at Cleopatra's
    orders.
        LGW 580

PTOLEMY, Claudius Ptolemaeus, an Alexandrian mathematician of the
    second cent., author of the Mathematike Syntaxis, known by its
    Arabic title of Almagest ("great work"). He invented trigo-
    nometry and wrote on geography, optics, and the theory of
    music. The Syntaxis was translated into Arabic in 827; the
    first Latin translation from the Arabic was made by Gerard
    of Cremona in 1175.
        Bo 2.p7.33

```
          WBT p182, 324
          SumT 2289
     Megale Syntaxis=Almagest
          general                     MillT 3208
                                      WBT p183, 325
                                      Astr 62
          2 beg.                      Bo 2.p7.33
```

PUBLILIUS SYRUS, fl. first cent. B.C., a Syrian slave who was freed
   in Rome and became a writer of mimes. His sayings were known
   in the Middle Ages under Seneca.
       Mel att. Seneca: 1127(2317), 1185(2375), 1320(2510),
          1324(2514), 1437(2627), 1449(2639), 1450(2640),
          1455(2645), 1859(3049)
          att. Cicero: 1347(2537)
     [Sententiae

```
          64              Mel 1859(3049)
          116                 1320(2510)
          125                 1347(2537)
          172                 1455(2645)
          189                 1450(2640)
          255                 1324(2514)
          281                 1127(2317)
          320                 1449(2639)
          366                 1866(3056)
          380                 1320(2510)
          389                 1185(2375)
          483                 1488(2678)
          489                 1777(2967)
          542                 1320(2510)
          607                 1320(2510)]
          <32                 1135(2325)
           91                 1183(2373)
          172                 1466(2656)
          293                 1846(3036)
          324                 1063(2253)
          354                 1197(2387)
          362                 1231(2421)
          479                 1842(3032)
          528                 1439(2629)
          594                 1048(2238)
          645                 1463(2653)>
```

PUELLA, a figure in geomancy; Skeat 5.82-3, Robin 677.
     KnT 2045

PYGMALION (Pigmalion), a legendary king of Cyprus who fell in love
   with a beautiful statue; Venus gave the statue life and
   Pygmalion thus married the woman so created. Meta. 10.242ff.,
   RR 16177ff.
     PhysT 14

PYRAMUS (Piramus), a Babylonian in love with THISBE. They were
forbidden to marry so they exchanged vows through a wall and
agreed to flee and meet at Ninus's tomb. Thisbe was
frightened away by a lion; Pyramus arrived and discovered
Thisbe's bloodied robe and committed suicide. Thisbe returned,
discovered her dead lover, and took her own life; Meta. 4.55-
166 and Ovide Moralisé.
     PF 289
     LGW 724, 777, 794, 823, 855, 868, 880, 907, 916, 918
     MerchT 2128

PYROIS (Pirois), one of the four horses of the Sun; the others were
Eous, Aethon, and Phlegon. Meta. 2.153ff., VALERIUS FLACCUS
5.432.
     T&C 3.1703

PYRRHUS (Pirrus), Neoptolemus, son of ACHILLES and Deidamia, was
summoned to Troy after the death of his father. He went with
Odyssus to bring PHILOCTETES to the siege and he killed PRIAM.
He received ANDROMACHE and she accompanied him to his kingdom
in Epirus. He was killed at Delphi by Orestes. Aen. 2.333-4,
Hero. 8.3, DICTYS 4.15.
     HF 161
     MLT 288
     NPT 3357(4547)

PYTHAGORAS (Pithagores, Pittagoras, Pictagoras), was born c. 580
and died at the end of the sixth cent. B.C. He was known
mainly for his doctrine of the transmigration of souls and
for his theory of harmony.
     Rom 5649
     BD 667, 1167
     Bo 1.p4.260
The Golden Verses [Langlois suggests Chalcidius on Timaeus 136]
     Rom 5650

PYTHON (Phitoun), a dragon personifying the forces of darkness.
The first feat of APOLLO was to slay the Python and seize
Delphi for his abode. Meta. 1.438ff., CLAUDIAN In Ruf. 1.1,
Myth III.8.4-5.
     MancT 109, 128

PYTHONESS see WITCH OF ENDOR.

Q

<QUINTUS CURTIUS, a romantic historian who flourished under
Claudius or Vespasian; cf. GUALTIER DE CHATILLON and Spec.
Hist. 4.1.1ff.: S&A.

Historiam Alexandri Magni
       passim   MkT 2631(3821)-80(60)>

QUIRINUS, ROMULUS (Quyryne) see ROMULUS.

R

RACHEL, daughter of Laban and wife of JACOB; Genesis 29-35.
    Robin 735 suggests the possibility of Matthew 2.18 and its
    use in the Mass on the Feast of the Holy Innocents.
        PrT 627(1817)

RALPH (Rauf), a common name here applied to a priest.
        FrT 1357

RAM see ARIES.

RAPHAEL, the angel who, in human disguise and under the name of
    Azarias, accompanied TOBIAS in his adventurous journey and
    conquered the demon Asmodaeus; Tobias 6.17 (Vulg.), Enoch 20.
        ParsT 906

RAVEN, the constellation Corvus which adjoins Virgo on the south;
    Fasti 2.243-66.
        HF 1004

RAZES see RHAZES.

REASON (Resoun), the mother of Shame and one of the guardians of
    the Rose.
        Rom 3034, 3037, 3040, 3051, 3055, 3193, 3218, 3332,
            4542, 4543, 4620, 4685, 4785, 5135, 5149, 7543
        ?PF 632

REBEKAH (Rebekka, Rebekke), the wife of ISAAC. She was the mother
    of JACOB and Esau and suggested the deception whereby Jacob
    gained his brother's birthright and his father's blessing;
    Genesis 27.
        Mel 1098(2288)
        MerchT 1363, 1704

REEVE, Oswald, an influential manorial official; Bowden 249-54.
        GP 542, 587, 599, 615, 619
        MillT p3144, 3151=Oswald, 3183
        RvT p3860, 3909=Oswald
        CkT p4325

REGULUS, Marcus, consul in 267 and 256 B.C., was one of the com-
    manders in the first Punic war; overconfidence led to his defeat
    by Xanthippus. In 250 the Carthaginians, defeated at Palermo in

251, sent him to Rome to propose peace, making him swear to
return if the negotiations failed. He advised the Romans to
continue the war, returned to Carthage, and was put to a cruel
death; CICERO De Officiis 3.99.
    Bo 2.p6.69

RENARD (Reynard), the fox, the name of the hero of a popular
medieval beast epic known in England by the 13th cent.; RR
14027ff.
    LGW 2448

<RENAUD DU LOUEN, a Dominican friar of the convent of Poligny who
in 1336 adapted ALBERTANUS's Liber Consolationis et Consilii.
The use of Renaud's version is so literal that the reader is
referred to Severs'text in S&A. Severs argues that if Chaucer
had also used Albertanus for Mel, some of the faults of the
French text would have been corrected.>

REVELATIONS see BIBLE.
    [MLT 491-8]

RHAZES (Razis), Abu-Bakr Muhammad ibn-Zakarīyā al-Rāsi, 865-925,
probably the greatest of all the Muslim physicians. His
Kitāb al-Asrār, an alchemical treatise, was translated by
Gerard of Cremona (d. 1187) and is included in Roger Bacon's
works as De Spiritibus et Corporibus. Rhazes's al-Hāwi (the
comprehensive book) was translated in 1279, at the order of
Charles I of Anjou, as the Liber Continens. The Kitāb
al-Tibb al-Mansuri, Liber Almansoris, was also translated by
Gerard of Cremona. See Hitti 365-7 and Bowden 201.
    GP 432

RHEA SILVIA, Ilia, the daughter of Numitor, was a vestal virgin
who became by MARS the mother of Romulus and Remus and was
thrown into the river by order of her uncle Amulius, king of
Alba. The river-god took her to wife; LIVY 1.3-4, Fasti 3.9-45.
    [PF 292]

RHETORIC (Rethorice, Rethorik), the personification of the art of
persuasion.
    Bo 2.pl.43; p3.10

RHODOGONE (Rodogone), the daughter of DARIUS, killed her nurse
when she suggested a second marriage; Adv. Jov. 1.45.
    FranklT 1456

RICHARD, Richard I, Coeur de Lion, king of England 1189-99, was
the third son of Henry II and Eleanor of Aquitaine; he was a
favorite hero of troubadours and romancers because he was an
accomplished and versatile knight and lover. See VINSAUF
Poetria Nova (Faral 208).

NPT 3348(4538)
?[Sted 22]

RICHESSE, the personification of bounty. In Rom one of the
     companions of the god of Love; in PF [from Tes. 7.64] the
     porter of the temple of Venus; in KnT one of the figures on
     the wall in the temple of Venus.
          Rom 1033, 1044, 1071, 1085, 1107, 1126, 1129, 1139,
               1143, 5357, 5599, 5819, 5844, 5845, 5950, 5975,
               5998
          PF 261
          KnT 1926

RIGHT, Justice, prevailed over by Mercy because Pity caused Danger
     to relent.
          LGW 162

RIPHEUS (Ripheo), a Trojan warrior who was killed defending AENEAS
     before PRIAM's palace; Aen. 2.339, Filo. 4.3.
          T&C 4.53

ROBERT, Sir Robert, a common name applied to a priest.
          Rom 6337
          FrT 1356

ROBIN,
     (1)   a name for a common man or rustic
          Rom 6337, 7453
     (2)   the name of the hero of several 13th cent. pastourelles;
          Root.
          T&C 5.1174
     (3)   the name given the MILLER; cf. ROGER see COOK, and Pratt
          (16).
          MillT p3129
     (4)   the knave of John the Carpenter
          MillT 3466, 3555

ROGER see COOK.

ROGER, bishop of Pisa, Archbishop Ruggieri degli Ubaldini, the
     enemy of HUGOLINO who was, according to Chaucer, responsible
     for his imprisonment. In Inf. 33 he is represented as the
     leader of the Ghibellines and prompted them to rise against
     the tyrant.
          MkT 2416(3606)

ROLAND (Rowland), hero of the Chanson de Roland, was the most
     famous of CHARLEMAGNE's knights; his death at Roncesvalles.
     (778) was due to the treachery and jealousy of GANELON. He
     was accompanied by OLIVER and Turpin; cf. Parad. 18.
          BD 1123

another Roman see SOPHUS.

a romance,
        BD 48 = Meta.

ROMANCE OF THE ROSE, the English version of the Roman de la Rose.
        Rom 39, 2148, 2154, 2168, 2170
        BD 334
        LGW 329(255), (344), 441(431), 470(460)
        MerchT 2032

<ROMAN DE LA ROSE, the 21780-line allegorical romance, of which a
        part was probably translated by Chaucer, was the work of
        Guillaume de Lorris and Jean de Meun. De Lorris completed the
        first part, lines 1-4058, about 1230; the second part was com-
        pleted by de Meun c. 1270. De Lorris, about whom little is
        known, presents an extremely idealistic allegory; de Meun,
        c. 1240-2. 1305, was a student--perhaps master--at Paris who
        added rhetoric, satire, and eroticism to his extensive addition.
        The Roman has been edited by F. Michel in 2 vols. (Paris, 1864)
        and by Ernest Langlois for SATF in 5 vols. (Paris, 1914-24);
        Fansler, Fleming.

        Roman de la Rose (ed. Langlois unless otherwise noted)

1ff.	T&C 5.1277
7-10	BD 284ff.
(Rom 23-5)	HF 112-4
45-7	BD 291-2
45-66	T&C 2.50-6
47-54	3.351-4
53ff.	BD 410-5
57(Rom 61)ff.	LGW (113ff.)
67-73	SqT 52-5
74ff.	BD 318
78-80	T&C 3.351-4
88	BD 291-2
101	318
124-5	339-43 + MACHAUT
130-1	PF 122
163-4(Rom 175-6)	KnT 2087
309-11	BD 487-92
484-5	304-5
515-82(Rom 528ff.)	KnT 1940
(Rom 543-4)	BD 871-2
(Rom 582)	PF 261
661-70	190-6
667-8	BD 306-8
703-4	LGW 139-40
705	BD 304-5
876ff.(Rom 896-8)	GP 88
(Rom 878ff.)	KnT 1785ff.
1000	ClT p2-3
1034	LGW 352

1034-5(Rom 1050ff.)	NPT 3325-6(4514-6)
1361-82	BD 416-42
1367-9(Rom 1391-4)	419-22
1375-82	PF 190-6
1439ff.(Rom 1469ff.)	BD 735-7
1681-3	833-45
1876ff.	Scog 28
1881-2022	BD 759ff.
1996-7	1152-3
2009-10	T&C 5.460
2083(Rom 2181-2)	WBT 1158
2245-6(Rom 2367-8)	T&C 1.960-1 + SENECA + Bo
2277-8	2.811
2339-57	1.435-48
2358(Rom 2478)	1.449
2430-1(Rom 2560-1)	1.856
2535-8	5.551-3
2601-2(Rom 2740-2)	4.1305-6
2686-716	1.617-8
2965-6	5.445
	MerchT 1341
3403-4(Rom 3674ff.)	MillT 3725
3424-5	MerchT 1727
3936	GP 476
4229ff.	KnT 1785ff.
(Rom 4250)	HF 1224
4293ff.	T&C 1.411
4293-330	5.1375-9
4385ff.	NPT 3345(4535)
4401-24	WBT p115ff. + Adv. Jov.
4623-4(Rom 5123)	HF 1257-8
4640-1(Rom 5151-2)	T&C 4.432-4
4733-4	PF 574
?4747ff.(Rom 5285ff.)	Scog 47 + CICERO
4901-4(Rom 5479-82)	Fort 1-4 + Bo
4905ff.(Rom 5486ff.,	
5549ff.)	33
4949-52	9ff. + Bo
4953-6(Rom 5551-2)	WBT 1203-4 + Bo
4975-8(Rom 5579-81)	Fort 9ff.
5045-6(Rom 5671-2)	"
5071-118	PardT 407ff.
5113-4(Rom 5763-4)	"
5226-7	HF 919
(Rom 5510)	T&C 3.861
5541	KnT 2452
5589ff.	PhysT passim
5612ff.	168ff.
5635-58	255-76
5660-2	T&C 2.167-8
5744-5	2.716-8

5842ff.	1.834–56
5845–50	Fort 17ff.
5847–56	BD 717–9
5942ff.	LGW 127
6185ff.	MkT 2463(3653)ff.
6382–3	T&C 4.519–20
6414ff.	MkT 2463(3653)ff.
6489ff.	HF 105
6489–622	MkT 2727(3917)ff.
6579–92	WBT 1109ff.
6652ff.	BD 659ff.
	T&C 2.754
6691–20	BD 663
6738–40	HF 1329–35
6887–90	Fort 17ff.
7037	T&C 3.292–4
	MancT 329
7041–5	T&C 3.292–4
7055–7	"
7099	GP 742 + Bo
7410ff.	BD 963–5
	WBT p333–6 + Ars Amat. + CICERO
7518–20	RvT 4134 + Policraticus
7557–8	T&C 1.747–8
7761–6	MancT 175ff.
8003–4	T&C 3.329
8019–22	Fort 32
8023–6	T&C 4.386–92
8039–41	4.7–8
8261–4	3.1634 + Ars Amat.
8364–78	FormAge 6ff.
8373	11
8379–80	15–8
8381–4	9–10
8388–9	15–8
8393ff.	42–6
8411ff.	BD 402–3
	LGW 171ff.
8427ff.	BD 405–9
8445–8	FormAge 54
8516	WBT p624
8579–600	p248–75 + Adv. Jov.
8605ff.	A&A 82
8605–12	BD 1080–5
8667–82	WBT p282–92 + Adv. Jov.
8721–2	T&C 2.193
8838–8	HF 117–8
8907ff.	BD 628–9
9029–30	WBT p552 + Ars Amat.
9091–6	p407–10
9195ff.	p715ff. + MAP

9203ff.	WBT p.715ff.	+ MAP
9203–6	BD 738–9	
9424ff.	FranklT 764–6	
9449–54	792–6	
9522–34	FormAge 52–3	
9561–8	61–3	
9800–4	SumT 2001–3	+ Ars Amat.
9855–8	HF 1758–62	
9917	WBT p229	
9945ff.	929–30	
9980	p662	
10097–8	MerchT 2321–2	
100299–300	FrT 1568	
10633–4	T&C 3.1194	
10827ff.	LGW 338	
	KnT 2452	
11017ff.	WBT p229	
11216	NPT 3443(4634)	
11332	SumT 1760	
11366ff.(Rom 6491ff.)	GP 243ff.	
11375ff.	WBT p107ff.	+ Adv. Jov.
11535	T&C 2.784	
11565(Rom 6837)	PardT p403	
12093–4(Rom 7419–20)	KnT 2087	
12139–42(Rom 7467ff.)	HF 265–6	
12179–83	T&C 3.292–4	
12277–8	LGW (326)	
12504(Michel)	PardT p443ff.	
12759–60	T&C 1.969	
12781	GP 461	
12790–6	BD 416–42	
12802ff.	WBT p1–2	
12818ff.	KnT 2447–8	
12889–92	BD 759ff.	
12924–5	WBT p469–73	
12932ff.	"	
13174ff.	BD 726–34	
13213	HF 392	+ Hero.
13225–8	T&C 4.1548–53	
13263–4	KnT 1953–4	
13269–72	WBT p207–10	
13336	p618	
13452–63	p467–8	+ Ars Amat.
13552–8	p555–8	
13697–708	p516–24	
13828–30	p393	+ DESCHAMPS
13838ff.	KnT 2388–90	+ Ars Amat.
		+ Meta. + Tes.
13851–2	MerchT 1560–1	
13870	LGW 249ff.	
14015–6	T&C 4.1586	

	KnT 3042	
	SqT 593	
14027ff.	LGW 2448	
14027-30	MancT 160ff.	+ Policraticus
14039-52	175ff.	
14145	LGW 917-8	
14157ff.	KnT 2388-90	+ Ars Amat.
		+ Meta. + Tes.
14381-4	WBT p357-61	
14393-4	"	
14397ff.	HF 1271-4	
14399	1273	
14404-6	KnT 1944	
14472ff.	WBT p503-14	
15190ff.	GP 742	+ Bo
15195ff.	NPT 3260(4450)	
15621-2	LGW 655	
15663	KnT 1936-7	
15778-9	MerchT 1777	
15959ff.	GP 429	
15977ff.	BD 982	
16029-31	HF 1212-3	
16096-105	SqT 254	
16171	SumT 2289	
16177ff.	PhysT p14ff.	
16242	32-4	
?16347-64	WBT p534ff.	
16367-8	968	
16438-42	MerchT 1334-6	
16521-30	WBT 961	
16541-700	MkT 2091(3281)ff.	
16591ff.	SumT 1994ff.	+ Ecl.
16616	PF 140	
16677-88	MkT 2015(3215)ff.	
16677ff.	BD 738-9	
16689-90	KnT 1953-4	
16782	PF 379	
	PhysT 20	
16785-8	KnT 2987ff.	+ Bo
16961	PF 380-1	
17443-4	HF 1710-1	
?17563ff.	BD 1024ff.	
18006	HF 1571	
18031-60	SqT 228ff.	
18061ff.	KnT 2388-90	+ Ars Amat.
		+ Meta. + Tes.
18136-7	WBT p227-8	
18176	SqT 228ff.	
18181	HF 11	
18187	SqT 228ff.	
18208	HF 12	

18247ff.	HF 15-8
	SqT 228ff.
18298	T&C 2.1564
18342-9	HF 24-31
18357-60	33-5
18365-6	41-2
18394-402	36-40
18424	11
18509-12	T&C 5.365-8
18513	HF 55-6
18566	WBT 1187
18607-896	1109ff.
18619ff.	Gent 15ff. + Purg. + Convivio
18620-34	WBT 1118-24
18802-5	1170
18979-80	Fort 56
19220	WBT 950
19279-99	BD 709
19505ff.	PhysT 20
19507	PF 379
19731-2	MerchT 1862
19768ff.	T&C 5.3
20095ff.	FormAge 48-63 + Meta.
20279-636	PF 127ff.
20395ff.	204-10
20559ff.	"
20651ff.	127ff.
20655-6	204-10
20313	Gent 15ff. + Purg. + Convivio
20364-5	T&C 4.1208
20375-6	MerchT 1341
20702-3(Michel)	T&C 4.1546
20831	HF 458
20831-2	BD 331-2
20889-92	T&C 1.810-2
21086	LGW 338
21096	KnT 2236
21498	LGW 137
21551-2	T&C 1.927-8
21559ff.	1.638-44
21573ff.	1.637
21772-3	KnT 1929>

<ROMAN D'ÉNÉAS, a roman d'aventures based on the Aeneid; it was
produced in the northwest, probably Normandy, c. 1160-80;
Faral.

general	LGW 924ff.
8047ff.	T&C 2.611-44
8381ff.	" >

<ROMAN DE RENARD, a late 12th cent. version of the Reynard beast
   epic; Muscatine.
       general   Rom 6204, 6259-60
                                            GP 269>

<ROMAN DE THÈBES, c. 1150, a rhetorical redaction of STATIUS;
   ed. Constans for SATF, Paris, 1890.
       general   BD 326ff.
       175-224   T&C 2.101-2
       497-500   4.300-1
       ?2026   2.100
       3872   A&A 72
       4711-842   T&C 2.100-8
       5053   2.100, 104
       ?5079   2.100
       5190, etc.   KnT 938, 949ff.
       ?6630   Rom 1093
       9127ff.   KnT 2065   + Meta.
       9944ff.   949
       9946   952
       9994   950
       9997ff.   957
       10073ff.   989
       10131   T&C 5.1510
       21838ff.   BD 1069   + DARES + GUIDO
    ?specious B and C
       625ff. (9501ff.)   SATF 2.88   T&C 3.1428
    ?S
       451ff.   2.17   3.1600>

<ROMAN DE TROIE see BENOÎT DE ST. MAURE.>

<LE ROMAN DE TROYLE ET DE CRISEIDA, a redaction of Filo. by
   Beauvau, Seneschal of Anjou; its use was discovered and
   analyzed by Pratt. Although the biographical problem has not
   been solved, it is certain that Chaucer used Beauvau or an
   intermediate version. Pratt used the edition by L. Moland
   and C. d'Héricault in Nouvelles Françoises en Prose du XIVe
   Siècle, Paris, 1858.
       p. 121   T&C 1.57-60
         121-2   .68
         122   .80, 100, 109
         123   .107, 118-9, 120, 124, 131
         124   .162-6, 170, 181-2, 184
         125   .186, 194, 199
         126   .272
         129   .372, 378, 386
         130   .388
         131   .463-4
         132   .475-6, 481
         133   .506, 520

p. 134   1.534
135   .574, 548, 551, 571-2, 577
136   .583
137   .610
138   .675, 681-2
140   .877
141   .888-9
144   .1046
147   2.587, 281-2, 284
148   .303
149   .413
150   .507
151   .522
152   .540-1, 555-7
153   .601-2
154   .756
157   .1718-9
159   .1003-7, 1051-6
160   .1059
163   .1088, 1090, 1129-30
164   .1137, 1154
166   .1195
168   .1226
169   .1327, 1329
175   3.260-1, 280, 286
176   .276, 287, 353, 356
177   .373, 386-8, 414-5
178   .424
179   .425, 436-8
180   .602-3
182   .1317
183   .1385
184   .1415
185   .1450
186   .1522
187   .1542
189   .1619-20
191   .1696, 1711
192   .1716
193   .10, 13
197   .1777
198   .1781, 1805-6
199   4.48-9, 50, 56
200   .60, 65-6, 68, 71, 73-4, 78
201   .92-3, 106
203   .159, 162, 211
204   .1114-5, 1118, 219-20
204-5   .223
207   .253-5, 248, 265-6, 277, 285
208   .288, 302-4
211   .399, 400-1

p. 212	4.406
214	.485, 490, 493
215	.512–4
216	.533–4
217	.575–6, 577
218	.600–2, 619, 623
219	.673
220	.683, 689–90, 691, 694, 696
221	.715
222	.744–6
223	.813, 816–7
224	.855, 858, 860, 872–3
225	.881, 887–8, 888–9, 897, 899
226	.911–2, 922–3, 946
228	.1150–1, 1169
230	.1209, 1223–5, 1227
231	.1237–8, 1240–1, 1245
232	.1333, 1345
233	.1305, 1340
234	.1431, 1434, 1436
236	.1529, 1536
237	.1558–9, 1572
238	.1576–7, 1580
239	.1606
242	.1690, 1689
	5.16, 22, 20
243	.36, 42, 45
245	.78, 79, 83
246	.199
247	.211, 244
248	.229, 231
249	.323, 330
250	.358
251	.412, 430–1
253	.465, 470–1
254	.489, 500, 512
255	.531, 534, 563, 562
256	.567, 596, 603, 606
257	.618, 634
259	.662, 683
260	.688, 708, 718, 728
260–1	.731
261	.765
262	.775, 800, 849
263	.862–3, 870
264	.904, 906, 912, 913
265	.923, 930–1, 935
266	.953–4, 958, 959, 967
267	.978, 981
268	.802
269	.1117, 1126–9, 1138, 1140, 1139

p. 270	T&C 5.1146
272	.1206
273	.1220
275	.1256
276	.1268, 1269-70
281	.1320, 1346, 1353
282	.1356-7
287	.1411, 1422, 1438, 1439
295	.1574
296	.1577
297	.1651, 1653
297-8	.1667
298	.1667-8, 1675-6
300	.1702-3, 1724, 1725
302	.1802, 1806, 1828
304	.1786, 1789>

ROMULUS, one of the sons of MARS and RHEA SILVIA. Romulus and Remus were abandoned and fostered by a she-wolf; when they grew up they killed Amulius and restored their grandfather, Numitor. Romulus became king, killed his brother Remus, and instigated the war against the Sabines in order to provide wives for his followers. Quirinus, the Sabine name of Mars, was therefore associated with his son. See Aen. 1.274-92, LIVY 1.3-4, Meta. 14.816ff., 15.863, Fasti 2.475-6, 3.9-45, and Parad. 8.131-2.
> HF 589
> PF 292
> T&C 4.25 Quyryne

RONAN (Ronyan, Ronyon), Skeat 5.266-7 suggests the Celtic saint, bishop of Kilmaronen, who died in 737; Robin 728, following Hamilton, suggests the British saint who died in 432. St. Ninian, according to Bede 3.4, dedicated his church to St. Martin of Tours.
> PardT 1310, 320

ROSE, the object of the quest of the Lover, the personification of the gratification of desire.
> Rom 48, 1700, 1710, 1816, 3122, 3187, 3488, 3627,
> 3633, 3659, 3757, 3759, 3937, 4118, 4123, 4229,
> 4371, 4558, 5098, 7596, 7630, 7642

ROSEMOUNDE, the unknown object of the ballade.
> Rose [1], 15

ROWLAND see ROLAND.

RUBEUS, a figure in geomancy representing Mars; Skeat 5.82-3.
> KnT 2045

RUFUS OF EPHESUS, a physician who flourished during the reign of
     Trajan (98-117) and whose Liber de Consiliis contained a
     compendium of dietetics; Bowden 201.
          GP 430

RUPHEO see RIPHEUS.

DAUN RUSSELL, the name applied to the red-haired fox; Skeat 5.256.
          NPT 3334(4524)

S

SACKED FRIARS see FRIARS DE PENITENTIA.

SADNESS, probably sobermindedness or seriousness; i.e. restraint
     in youth.
          Lady 25

SAGITTARIUS, the "Archer," the ninth sign of the zodiac.
          Astr 1.8.4
                2.6.16; 28.32, 38

SAINTS LEGEND OF CUPID, LGW, in the list of Chaucer's works.
          MLT i61

SAMSON (Sampsoun), of the tribe of Dan, was betrayed by DELILAH,
     blinded and imprisoned by the PHILISTINES at Gaza where he
     later destroyed the temple of Dagon; Judges 14-16. Cf. Friend,
     Grennen.
          BD 738
          KnT 2466
          MLT 201
          MkT 2015(3205), 2023(3203), 2031(3221), 2052(3242),
                2055(3245), 2075(3265), 2090(3280)
          WBT p721
          PardT 554, 555, 572
          ParsT 955

SAMUEL, consecrated to the temple by Hannah, finally yielded to
     the demands of the people for a king and established Saul.
     He also anointed DAVID; see BIBLE.
          FrT 1510
          PardT 585

SANTIPPE see ANTIPUS.

SAPOR see SHAPUR.

SARAH (Sarra), the wife of ABRAHAM and mother of ISAAC; after
     Isaac's birth, which occurred in her old age in accordance

with Jehovah's promise to make of Abraham a great nation,
her name was changed from Sarai to Sarah; <u>Genesis</u> 12-23.
  MerchT 1704

SARPEDON (Sarpedoun), son of Zeus and Laodamia, was the leader,
  with Glaucus, of the Lycians. The best warrior among the
  allies of the Trojans, Sarpedon was killed by Patroclus. His
  presence among the prisoners is due to <u>Filo</u>. 4.3; neither
  Boccaccio nor Chaucer explains his later presence in Troy.
  See Root 501-2, 537.
      T&C 4.52
          5.403, 431, 434, 435, 479, 489, 500

SATAN (Sathan, Sathanus), one of the most popular names of the
  chief of the devils; Satan as the personification of evil is
  due to the Hebrew postexilic period.
      MillT 3750
      MLT 365, 582, 598, 634
      PrT 558(1748)
      MkT 2005(3195)
      FrT 1526, 1655
      SumT p1686, 1687, 1689
      ParsT 895
      Buk 10

SATURDAY, the seventh day of the week.
      MillT 3399, 3419, 3665
      Astr 2.12.8, 23

SATURN (Saturne, Saturnus), the most ancient king of Latium,
  identified with Cronus and honored by the Romans as the god of
  agriculture and civilization in general. To the middle ages
  he represented Prudence and was the protector of oppressed
  peasants, beggars, cripples, and prisoners. In spite of this,
  Saturn is associated with melancholy and his planetary
  influence is evil. Saturn is the sixth major planet from the
  sun. <u>Fasti</u> 6.285-6; cf. Wood.
      Rom 5954
      T&C 4.1538
      KnT 1328, 2443, 2450, 2453, 2668, 2685
      [MerchT 2265]
  Astrological references:
      HF 1449
      Bo 4.m1.12
      T&C 3.625, 716
      LGW 2597
      KnT 1088
      CYT 828
      Astr 2.4.35; 12.23, 27, 41, 42

SCARIOT see JUDAS ISCARIOT.

SCEDASUS (Cedasus), of Boeotia, whose daughters were violated by
    guests and killed themselves for shame; Adv. Jov. 1.41.
        FranklT 1429

SCIPIO AFRICANUS MAJOR (Affrikan), Publius Cornelius, 236/5-
    c. 183 B.C., Roman general and statesman who drove the
    Carthaginians out of Spain in 210 and moved into Africa in 204
    where he defeated them at Zama in 190 with his brother Lucius
    and the help of MASSINISSA. In Rome he was accused of accepting
    bribes from ANTIOCHUS, but the charge was dropped; MACROBIUS
    and CICERO.
        BD 287
        PF 41, 44, 52, 96, 107, 120, 153

SCIPIO AFRICANUS MINOR (Scipious, Cipioun), Publius Cornelius
    Scipio Aemilianus, c. 185-129 B.C., son of L. Aemilius Paullus,
    conqueror of Macedon, was adopted by P. Scipio, the son of
    S. Africanus Major. He fought under his father at Pydna in
    168 and was elected consul in 148. He successfully besieged
    Carthage and destroyed it in 146; he was again elected consul
    in 133 and undertook an expedition to Spain where he died
    suddenly in 129. During the Carthaginian campaign he was
    entertained by MASSINISSA; in a dream which followed their
    reminiscence, his grandfather appeared to him; MACROBIUS and
    CICERO.
        Rom 10
        BD 286
        HF 514, 916
        PF 36, 71, 97
        NPT 3124(4314)

SCITHERO see CICERO.

SCOGAN, Henry Scogan, 1361?-1407, lord of the manor of Haviles,
    tutor to the sons of Henry IV, and a follower and friend of
    Chaucer; Robin 863.
        Scog 13, 20, 21, 25, 36, 43, 47

SCORPION, Scorpio, the eighth sign of the zodiac, a constellation
    of the southern latitudes; Wood 278-80.
        HF 948
        Astr 1.8.4
            2.3.57; 6.16; 28.38

SCOT, a common name for a horse; according to Skeat 5.51, common
    in Norfolk.
        GP 616
        FrT 1543

SCRIBES, a group of Jewish scholars frequently mentioned in the
    Gospels, often with the PHARISEES.
        Rom 6893

SCYLLA (Silla), the daughter of NISUS of Megara, who, for love of
    MINOS, cut off her father's lock of purple hair, upon which
    his life and the safety of the kingdom depended. She was
    transformed into Ciris; Meta. 8.6-151, 13.730-4, 14.18ff., and
    Ovide Moralisé.
        PF 292
        [T&C 5.1110]
        [LGW 1908]

SECURITY (Sikernesse), one of Love's barons in the group assembled
    to plan war against Fair Welcome.
        Rom 5862

SEMBLANCE, a just representation so carefully counterfeited by
    False-Semblance that even Falseness could not recognize the
    fraud.
        Rom 7447

SEMIRAMIS (Semyrame, Semyramis, Semyramus), c. 800 B.C., a famous
    Assyrian princess, wife of NINUS at whose death she erected a
    number of monuments and cities (especially Babylon) in his
    memory. She at length gave the kingdom to her son Ninyas and
    disappeared; Meta. 4.58-9, Inf. 5.58-60.
        PF 288
        LGW 707
        MLT 359

SENATOR, in MLT, see ARSEMIUS.

[SENECA, Lucius Annaeus, "the Elder" or "the Rhetorician,"
    c. 55 B.C.-c. 37 A.D., a Spaniard educated in Rome, the father
    of SENECA, "the Philosopher." The reference is probably due
    to RR 19220.
    Controversiae
        2.5(13).12   Mel 1062(2255)]

SENECA, Lucius Annaeus, "the Philosopher," c. 4 B.C.-65 A.D., was
    educated in rhetoric and philosophy at Rome. In 49 he became
    tutor to NERO but his influence waned and he was ordered to
    commit suicide. Seneca practiced and taught a modified form
    of Stoicism; cf. Ayers.
        Bo 1.p3.56
           3.p5.47, 54
        MLT 125
        Mel 984(2174), 991(2181), [1067(2257)], 1071(2261)
            =MART. DUMIENSIS, 1127(2317)=PUBL. SYRUS, 1147
            (2337), 1185(2375)=PUBL. SYRUS, 1226(2416),
            1320(2510)=PUBL. SYRUS, 1324(2514)=PUBL. SYRUS,
            [1328(2518)], 1339(2529):att. CICERO, 1437(2627),
            1448(2638)=PUBL. SYRUS, 1450(2640)=PUBL. SYRUS,
            1455(2645)=PUBL. SYRUS, [1481(2671)], 1488(2678),

Mel 1531(2721)=MART. DUMIENSIS, 1676(2866):att. ST.
    JAMES, 1775(2965), [1777(2967)], [1867(3047)],
    1859(3049)=PUBL. SYRUS, 1866(3056)
MkT [2495(3685)], [2499(3689)], 2503(3693), 2515
    (3705)
WBT 1168, 1184
SumT 2018
MerchT 1376, 1523, 1567
PardT 492
MancT 345
ParsT <u>144</u>, <u>145</u>, 467, 759
<u>De</u> <u>Ira</u>, c. 41-4
    [1.18   SumT 2018]
    <2.34.1   Mel 1481(2671)
     3.14   SumT 2043
     .21   2079>
<<u>De</u> <u>Clementia</u>, c. 55-6
    1.3.3   LGW 381
     .5.4   "
     .19.6   Mel 1339(2529)>
<<u>De</u> <u>Vita</u> <u>Beata</u>, c. 58-9
    15   Bo 1.p4.260>
[<u>De</u> <u>Beneficiis</u>, c. 62-4
    ?1.1ff.   MancT 345
    ?1.14-5   MerchT 1523-5]   + MAP
[<u>De</u> <u>Tranquillitate</u> <u>Animi</u>, c. 62-3
    14.1ff.   Bo 1.p3.56]
<u>Epistolae</u> <u>Morales</u> <u>ad</u> <u>Lucillium</u>, c. 63-4
    [17   WBT 1183ff.
     44   1168
     47   ParsT 759-63
     60.4   PardT 492-548
     63.1   Mel 991(2181)
     74.30   984(2171)
     83.18, 27   PardT 492-548
     95.15, 19,
       25, 26,
       28-9   "
    114.26   "   ]
    <1.2.1   T&C 1.891-3
      .2.2-3   1.960-1   + <u>RR</u>
      .2.3   1.964   + <u>ALBERTANUS</u>
      .3.4   1.687-8
     3.3   Mel 1328(2518)
     9.18-9   PardT 603   + <u>Policraticus</u>
    10.1   "
    16.4.26   T&C 1.704
    19.5.13   2.22-5   + HORACE + <u>Policraticus</u>
    63.11   Mel 993(2183)
    ?78.13   T&C 4.466>

DE SENECTUTE see CICERO.

SENIOR, Muhammad ibn Umail al-Sadik, a tenth cent. alchemist whose
    Tabula Chimica provided Chaucer with the story of Plato; S&A
    686n.
        CYT 1450
    [Tabula Chimica (in Zetzner's Theatrum Chemicum 5.191ff.)
        5.p. 224   CYT 1450ff.]

SEPTEMBER, the ninth month of the modern calendar.
        Astr 1.10.4, 14

SEPTEM TRYONES, the seven chief stars in Ursa Minor, the leading
    star of which is the pole-star: since it is fixed the whole
    constellation represented the north. Skeat 2.433, 5.242.
        Bo 2.m6.21
        MkT 2467(3657)

SERAPION, ibn Serabi, fl. c. 1070, an Arabian physician whose Liber
    de Medicamentis Simplicibus was a definitive work on the thera-
    peutic use of medicinal simples; Campbell 100.
        GP 432

SERGEANT OF THE LAW, one of a group of barristers qualified to
    plead in royal courts and in the king's cause. Royal justices
    were chosen from the ranks of the sergeants; Bowden 165-72.
        GP 309
        MLT 133

SERPENT = the LERNAEAN HYDRA.
        MkT 2105(3295)

<SERVIUS MARIUS HONORATUS, a Latin grammarian who fl. late fourth-
    early fifth cent. A.D., author of a commentary on Virgil.
    Commentarii in Virgilium Serviani (ed. Lion, 2 vols.
        [Göttingen, 1826])
    In Aeneidos
        2.610   T&C 4.120-6
        6.14   LGW 1932   + Meta.
        7.641   T&C 3.1809-10
    In Bucolica
        2.31   BD 512   + ISIDORE + VINCENT
        6.42   WBT 1139-45
    In Georgicon
        3.48   T&C 3.1464-70>

SEVEN DEADLY SINS, commonplace personifications of the major vices.
    exhibited by imperfect Christians.
        MerchT 1640
        [ABC 15]

211

SEYS see CEYX.

SHAME, one of the five foule arrows in Love's quiver and the child
of Reason and keeper of the Rose.
Rom 980, 3032, 3034, 3041, 3058, 3254, 3788, 3841,
3861, 3965, 3968, 3999, 4006, 4009, 4050, 4212,
4482, 5044, 5858

SHAPUR I (Sapor), 240–73 king of Persia. After conquering Syria
and taking Caesarea, he was defeated by ODENATUS and ZENOBIA;
De Clar. Mulier. 98, De Casibus 8.6.
MkT 2320(3510)

SHE,
MLT 982 = HELEN

SHIPMAN, a ship's captain, master of the "Maudelayne"; Bowden 192–6.
GP 388
MLT e1179

SIBYL (Sibille), in HF the Cumaean sibyl who conducted AENEAS
through Elysium and foretold his wars in Latium [Aen. 6]; in
T&C an alternate name for CASSANDRA which alludes to her
reputation as a prophetess.
HF 439
T&C 5.1450

SICHAEUS (Sytheo), a Tyrian prince, husband of DIDO, treacherously
slain by his brother-in-law, PYGMALION. Dido fled with his
treasure and founded Carthage. Aen. 1.343, 720, 4.20, 502,
632, 6.474; Hero. 7.97ff., Inf. 5.62. The ending in –o
indicates Italian influence; c and t are confused in the
manuscripts.
LGW 1005

SICKNESS (Syknesse), one of the "palace senators" of Old Age.
Rom 4997

SIGNIFER, the sign-bearer, i.e. the zodiac; CLAUDIAN In Ruf. 1.365
and Root suggests also PLINY 2.10.7.48.
T&C 5.1020

SIKERNESSE see SECURITY.

SILLA see SCYLLA.

SIMKIN (Symkin), a diminutive of Simond, the name given the miller
who was the butt of the machinations of the Cambridge students.
RvT 3941, 3945, 3947, 3955, 3959, 4022=Symond,
4024, 4026=Symond, 4034, 4127=Symond, 4288=
Symond, 4291

RvT [3925, 3987, 3995, 4000, 4010, 4045, 4046,
     4067, 4092, 4096, 4113, 4116, 4120, 4136,
     4149, 4162, 4189, 4256, 4258, 4260, 4268,
     4280, 4306, 4313, 4318, 4324]

<SIMON AUREA CAPRA, or Chèvre d'Or, about whom we know little more
    than that he was at St. Victor's during the time of Abbot
    Gilduin (d. 1155); see Friend.
    ?Ilias Latina (Scriptorium 1[1946-7] 267-88)

343-51, 365-6	HF 151-6
387-8	151-8
411-2	174-92
504-8	198-203
521-4	209-11
531-40	212-8
543-4	219-24
599-604	250-2
717-8, 733-6	451-6
989-94	457-8, 461-5>

ST. SIMON, the disciple, surnamed Zelotes, represented with a saw
    in allusion to the instrument of his martyrdom or a fish in
    allusion to his occupation.
        SumT 2094

SIMON MAGUS, a sorcerer of Samaria, rebuked by Peter because he
    attempted to buy the power of the Holy Spirit: he offered the
    Apostles John and Peter a fee for their instruction in the
    magical ceremonies of baptism and the laying on of hands;
    Acts 8.9, 17ff.
        HF 1274
        ParsT 783

SIMON THE PHARISEE, in the parable of the Fallen Woman, the wealthy
    host at whose house occurred the teaching of Jesus about love
    and forgiveness; Luke 7.36ff.
        ParsT 504

SIMPLICITY (Symplesse), one of the golden arrows in the quiver of
    the god of Love.
        Rom 954, 1774

SYMPLICIUS GALLUS see SULPICIUS GALLUS.

SINON (Synon), son of Aesimus, through whose perfidy the Trojans
    were induced to take the wooden horse within the walls. Aen.
    2.57-267, DICTYS 5.12, Inf. 30.98-130.
        HF 152
        LGW 931
        NPT 3228(4418)
        SqT 209

<?SIR <u>GAWAIN</u> <u>AND</u> <u>THE</u> <u>GREEN</u> <u>KNIGHT</u>, written by the Pearl poet in the
    last quarter of the 14th century, is the most famous and most
    artistic of the medieval English Arthurian romances; see Chapman.
        37-40   SqT 58-62
        136   80-1
        237-40   189-90, 199-200
        242-3   86-7
        2525-8   305-8>

SIRE,
        MerchT 2265 = SATURN

SIRIUS (Syrius), the "dog-star," the brightest star in the heavens,
    located in Canis Major.
        Bo 1.m5.28

SISYPHUS (Cesiphus), legendary king of Corinth, was reputed to be
    the most cunning of men. For various misdeeds he was condemned
    in Hades to roll to the top of a hill a large stone which
    perpetually rolled down again; <u>Meta</u>. 4.457-9, 10.44 and <u>Myth</u>.
    III.6.5.
        BD 589: the reference is actually to TITYUS
                 [not named by Ovid]

SLANDER (Sklaunder), one of the trumpets of AEOLUS.
        HF 1580, 1625

SOCRATES, born c. 469 and committed suicide in 399 B.C., the Greek
    philosopher whose doctrines are known through his disciple
    PLATO; <u>Adv</u>. <u>Jov</u>. 1.48, <u>RR</u> 5847-56, 6887-90.
        BD 717
        Bo 1.p3.27, 29, 31, 37, 53; p4.163
        MLT 201
        WBT p728
        Fort 17

SOL, the association of the planet with the element gold was
    apparently very common; <u>Skeat</u> 5.426-7.
        CYT 826, 1440

SOLOMON (Salamon, Salomon), son of DAVID and Bathsheba, succeeded
    in 974 and reigned to c. 937 B.C.; he was known as the wisest
    and most magnificent of the kings of Israel. Cf. <u>Proverbs</u>,
    <u>Kings</u>, <u>Ecclesiastes</u>, and <u>Ecclesiasticus</u>.
        Rom 6529, 6543
        [T&C 1.694]
        KnT 1942
        MillT 3529 = JESUS FILIUS SIRACH
        CkT p4330
        [MLT 115, 118]
        Mel 997(2187), 1003(2193), 1047-8(2237-8), 1057

Mel (2247), 1060(2250), 1076(2266), 1078(2268),
    1087(2277), 1113(2303), 1158(2348), [1159
    (2349)], [1161(2351)], 1167(2357), 1170(2360),
    1173(2363), 1178(2368), 1186(2376), 1194(2384),
    1317(2507), 1416(2606), 1485(2675), 1512(2702),
    [1513(2703)], 1514(2704), [1515(2705)], 1538
    (2728), 1542(2732), 1550(2740), 1571(2761),
    1572(2762), 1578(2768), [1579(2769)], 1589
    (2779), 1590(2780), 1628(2818), 1638(2828),
    [1639(2829)], 1653(2843), 1670(2860), 1671
    (2861)=JESUS FILIUS SIRACH, 1696(2886), 1704
    (2894), 1707(2897), 1709(2899), 1719(2909),
    1739(2929), 1754(2944)
WBT p35, [41], 679
[SumT 2085]
ClT p6
MerchT 1483, 1487, 2242, 2277, 2292
SqT 250
CYT 961
MancT 314, 344
ParsT 119, 127, 155, 168, 227, 229, 566, 568, [569],
    614, 629, 631, 633, 649, 679, 688, 709, 854, 955

SOMER, John Somer, a Minorite Franciscan at Oxford who, in 1380,
    did a calendar for Joan, mother of Richard II; Robin 868.
    Astr 85

<Somme des Vices et des Vertus, Somme le Roi, compiled in 1279 by
    Frère Lorens, a Dominican, for Philip III. The use of the
    Somme in ParsT, advanced by Eilers, is now generally discounted;
    see Petersen, S&A, Robin 766. Compare Friend's argument that
    the immediate source of ParsT resembled the verses of Roger
    of Caen.
    ?   PardT i295>

SOMNIUM SCIPIONIS see CICERO and MACROBIUS.

YOUR SON,
    LGW 2099 = HIPPOLYTUS

SOPHIE, Wisdom, the daughter of MELIBEUS and PRUDENCE; she is not
    mentioned in the Latin or French versions.
    Mel 967(2157)

[SOPHUS, P. Sempronius, forsook his wife because she attended a
    play; VALERIUS MAXIMUS 6.3.
    WBT p647]

SORANUS Barea, consul in 52, was accused of treason by NERO; his
    daughter Servilia was charged with magic and they were both
    put to death. Soranus's Stoic master, P. Egnatius Celer,

witnessed against them; TACITUS 16.23.
Bo 1.p3.56

SORROW, one of the figures on the wall outside the garden of Mirth.
Rom 301, 4995

<SPARTIANUS, Aelius, lived in the time of Diocletian and Constantine,
was one of the scriptores of the Historia Augusta, a collection
of biographies of the emperors from Hadrian to Numerianus
(d. 284).
Caracallus
8   Bo 3.p5.49>

SPECULUM STULTORUM see NIGELLUS WIREKER.

SQUIRE, in this case a candidate for knighthood, the companion of
his father, the KNIGHT; Bowden 74-84.
GP 79
SqT p1
e673

STATIUS (Stace), Publius Papinius, c. 45-96 A.D., a Neopolitan,
court poet to Domitian, author of Silvae [unknown in the Middle
Ages], Thebais, and Achilleis [known in the Liber Catonianus];
Shannon 329-32, Clogan, Magoun, Sweeney. Statius as a Toulousan
is probably from Purg. 21.89.
HF 1460
A&A 21
T&C 5.1792
KnT 2294
[Achilleis
general   HF 1462-3]
Thebaidos (ed. Mozley)
[general   T&C 5.1792
KnT 2294
7   HF 1459
12.519ff.   A&A 22-42]
<1   T&C 5.1485-91
1.9-10   MerchT 1716
MancT 116
.11-6   T&C 5.599-601   + Tes + DANTE
.12   KnT 1329   + Meta. + Tes.
+ Inf.
.41   T&C 2.8
.45-62   4.300-1
.56ff.   1.1ff.
2.101-2
.85-7   1.1ff.
.127-8   KnT 1624
.212-3   T&C 5.2
.250   A&A 51

Thebaidos (cont.)

	KnT 1329 + Meta. + Tes. + Inf.
.438ff.	1702
.468ff.	T&C 5.1488
.632	3.733
2	5.1485-91
2.265ff.	Mars 245ff.
.297	T&C 4.762
.704	A&A 5
.715ff.	"
.732ff.	KnT 2410-7 + Tes.
3.71ff.	T&C 5.1494
.507	5.999 + Meta.
.511-2	PF 343
.611ff.	T&C 4.1397-8
.640ff.	5.1494
.648ff.	4.1404-11
.661	4.1408
4	WBT p727-46 + Adv. Jov.
4.1-2	T&C 5.8ff.
.34-5	3.45
.386	KnT 2129
.455ff.	2293-4 + Tes.
.494ff.	1638 "
.637ff.	T&C 5.1494
.683-4	4.1543-5
5	LGW 1368ff.
5.505ff.	T&C 5.1497
.718-9	1.211-3
.733	KnT 2129: confused with 4.386
	and 7.180
6.93-113	2925-30: Hoffman
7.34-73	1967-2050
.40ff.	A&A 2
.45	KnT 1987
.47	1985
.57	2017 + Tes.
.180	2129
.533	T&C 4.1548-53
.538ff.	5.932 + Filo.
.703	4.25
.794ff.	5.1500
.815	2.105
8.59	3.733
.65-71	1.1ff.
.231	KnT 1747 + OVID + VIRGIL
.232	MerchT 1716
.342ff.	HF 1245
.491	KnT 2410-7 + Tes.
.636ff.	2694ff.
.686	T&C 1.1ff.

<u>Thebaidos</u> (cont.)

.716ff.	5.1501ff.
9.323	3.733
.526ff.	5.1501ff.
.550	4.1397-8, 1404-11
.841ff.	5.1501ff.
10.74	KnT 1329 + <u>Meta.</u> + <u>Tes.</u> + <u>Inf.</u>
.84ff.	BD 153-65 + <u>OVID</u>
.95ff.	"
.126	KnT 1329 + <u>Meta.</u> + <u>Tes.</u> + <u>Inf.</u>
.162	" " " "
.262	" " " "
.873	MerchT 1716
.888ff.	T&C 2.1145
.907ff.	5.1501ff.
11.57ff.	4.22ff.
.344ff.	"
.580-2	4.300-1
.698	"
12.1ff.	5.274ff.
.519ff.	A&A 4-7
	KnT motto
.704	1331
.809	A&A 20
.816-7	T&C 5.1789-92>

SWIFT STEEDS THREE, together with PYROIS, the horses of the sun;
   <u>Meta.</u> 2.153ff.
      T&C 3.1703 = Eous, Aethon, Phlegon

STILBON (Stilboun), Chilon of Sparta, fl. sixth cent. B.C., one of
   the first ephors and one of the seven wise men of Greece;
   PLINY 7.32.32.119, SENECA <u>Epist.</u> 9.18-9, <u>Policraticus</u> 1.5;
   cf. Pratt(4).
      PardT 603

STOICS, a school of philosophy founded at Athens c. 315 B.C. by
   Zeno; the school taught adherence to the virtues of benevolence
   and justice and detachment from human affairs.
      Bo 1.p3.33, 44, 46
         5.m4.6, 11

STRODE, Ralph Strode, fl. 1350-1400, became a fellow of Merton
   College before 1360 where he taught logic and philosophy.
   He attacked Wyclif, particularly on predestination, and
   defended the possession of wealth; <u>Robin</u> 838.
      T&C 5.1857

STYMPHALIS (Stymphalides), resisted ARISTOCLIDES and was murdered
   by him; <u>Adv.</u> <u>Jov.</u> 1.41.
      FranklT 1388

SUETONIUS, Gaius Suetonius Tranquillus, c. 70–160, one of the
  imperial secretaries under Trajan; his works were historical
  and antiquarian. The De Vita Caesarum is the principal
  surviving work.
      MkT 2465(3655), 2720(3910)
  De Vita Caesarum
    Nero
      [general   MkT 2463(3653)]
      <33   Bo 2.m6.5
       34   .12>

SULPICIUS GALLUS (Simplicius Gallus), the distinguished Roman
  orator, praetor in 169 and consul in 166; in 168 he was tribune
  under Aemilius Paulus in Macedonia. Apparently he left his
  wife because he saw her with her head uncovered while on a
  public street; VALERIUS MAXIMUS 6.3
      WBT p643

SULTAN (of Syria), the betrothed of CONSTANCE, he was cruelly
  murdered by his mother because of his conversion to Christianity.
      MLT 177, 186, 204, 239, 323, 354, 375, 382, 388,
          395, 407, 429, 436

SULTANESS, murdered her son and blamed CONSTANCE and had her set
  adrift.
      MLT 358, 372, 405, 414, 432, 958

SUMMONER, an official who summoned persons to appear in ecclesiastical court, particularly the court of the archdeacon; Bowden
  262-72.
      GP 543, 623
      WBT p832, 833, 840, 845
      FrT p1267, 1289, 1290
          1327, 1333, 1336, 1646
      SumT p1665
          1761, 1764

SUNDAY, the first day of the week.
      GP 455
      KnT 2188, 2209
      MillT 3422
      ShipT 180(1370), 307(1497)
      Astr 2.12.36

SUSANNAH (Susanna, Susanne), the wife of Joachim, accused of
  adultery by the lecherous Elders but defended by DANIEL; her
  innocence was established and the Elders were put to death.
  Daniel 13; cf. Kellogg.
      MLT 639
      ParsT 797

FATAL SUSTREN see FATES.

SWEET LOOKING, the bachelor who accompanied the god of Love and
    held the bow and arrows.
       Rom 920, 937, 1331, 2896, 2943, 4507

SWEET SPEECH, the second solace granted the Lover by the god of
    Love.
       Rom 2825, 2851, 2943, 4506

SWEET THOUGHT, the first solace granted the Lover by the god of
    Love.
       Rom 2793, 2799, 2815, 2942, 4505

SYBIL see SIBYL.

SYMMACHUS (Symachus), Q. Aurelius Memmius Symmachus, consul under
    Odoacer in 485, whose daughter, Rusticana, was the wife of
    Boethius. Symmachus was put to death by Theodoric soon after
    the execution of Boethius.
       Bo 2.p4.26

SYRIUS see SIRIUS.

SYTHEO see SICHAEUS.

T

THE FIRST TABLE, the Ten Commandments; Exodus 20.
       PardT 639

<TACITUS, Publius(?) Cornelius, Roman statesman and historian,
    c. 55-c. 117. The Annales, written c. 115-7, cover the period
    from the accession of Tiberius to the death of Nero.
    Annales

1.29	Bo 4.m5.11ff. + PLINY + JUVENAL
13.16	2.m6.5
14	3.p5.54ff.
14.9	2.m6.12
16.23	1.p3.56>

TAIL OF THE DRAGON, the point at which a planet passed from the
    northern to the southern side of the ecliptic; Skeat 3.361.
       Astr 2.4.36

TALBOT, the name given one of the widow's dogs.
       NPT 3383(4573)

TALES OF CANTERBURY.
       Ret 1086

TANTALUS (Tantale), father of Pelops and NIOBE, who, because he
   killed Pelops and tried to serve him to the gods (to test
   their powers of observation), was punished in the lower world
   by being made to stand up to his neck in water which receded
   when he tried to drink and under fruits which hung over his head
   beyond his grasp; Meta. 4.548, 10.41 and RR 19279-9.
      BD 709
      Bo 3.m12.38
      T&C 3.593

TAPESTER (Tapycer), the tapestry-weaver, one of the five guildsmen;
   Bowden 183.
      GP 362

TARBE (Tharbe), one of Criseyde's nieces, whose name is unexplained.
   Hamilton 94ff. suggests derivation from rex Thabor in GUIDO 5^{v2}.
      T&C 2.816, 1563

TARQUINIUS (Tarquyn, Tarquyny), Tarquinius Sextus, the son of
   Tarquinius Superbus (ruled 534-510 B.C.), whose rape of
   LUCRETIA led to the expulsion of the Tarquins; LIVY 1.57-9,
   Fasti 2.685-852. See Shannon 220ff.
      LGW 1682, 1698, 1711, 1714, 1745, 1789, 1819, 1837,
         1863
      FranklT 1407

TAURUS, the Bull, the second sign of the zodiac. The epithet, White,
   is from Meta. 2.852.
      LGW 2223
      T&C 2.55 = White Bull
      NPT 3194(4384)
      WBT p613
      MerchT 1887
      Astr 1.8.3; 21.74
           2.6.16; 28.37

TELEPHUS (Thelophus), son of HERCULES and Auge (daughter of Aleus
   of Tegea), was exposed because Aleus was infuriated at his
   daughter's pregnancy. After consulting the Delphic oracle,
   Telephus went to Teuthras, king of Mysia, where he found his
   mother and succeeded Teuthras. He married Laodice or Astyoche,
   daughter of PRIAM. He tried to prevent the landing of the
   Greeks but Dionysus caused him to stumble and Achilles wounded
   him; Achilles healed him, however, because he was the only one
   who could lead the Greeks to Troy. Meta. 12.122, Rem. Amoris
   47, DICTYS 2.3, 10.
      SqT 238

TEMPLARS, Knight's Templars, the Poor Knights of Christ and of the
   Temple of Solomon, founded in 1119 and suppressed in 1312.
   Organized to assist and protest pilgrims to the Holy Land and

identified by a white mantle with a red cross on the left
shoulder.
Rom 6693

[TEN COMMANDMENTS, the laws given by God to Moses; Exodus 20.
PardT 639]

TEREUS, the king of Thrace who violated PHILOMELA.
T&C 2.69
LGW 2234, 2243, 2270, 2289, 2315, 2342, 2363, 2389

TERMAGANT (Termagaunt), in Guy of Warwick one of the supposed idols
of the Saracens and in Lybeaus Desconus the name of the country
of the giant; Wells [7] and [38].
Thop 810(2000)

TERTULLIAN (Tertulan), c. 155-c. 222, one of the fathers of the
Church whose treatises De Exhortatione Castitatis (202-3),
De Monogamia (207-8), and De Pudicitia (207-8) directed the
conduct of Christian life; Skeat 5.309.
WBT p676

TEUTA, wife of Agron, king of the Illyrians, assumed power on the
death of her husband in 231 B.C. Her refusal to punish
Illyrian pirates and her order to murder one of the Roman
ambassadors led to war with Rome. She sued for peace in 228
and was stripped of most of her dominions. PLINY 34.6.11 but
Chaucer surely relied solely on Adv. Jov. 1.44.
FranklT 1453

that text, our text,
    GP 177, 182 = Decretum Gratiani, DECRETALS
    MLT 143ff. = ?Digesta, JUSTINIAN
    WBT p29   = Genesis and Matthew

THEBAN MAIDEN, violated by a Macedonian invader during the sack of
Thebes by Alexander (336), concealed her grief, killed the
Macedonian and then committed suicide; Adv. Jov. 1.41.
FranklT 1434

THEFT, the staff given to Abstinence by Guile.
Rom 7401

THEODAMAS see THIODAMAS.

THEODORA, a Greek name given to several Byzantine princesses.
SqT 664

THEODORIC, king of the Ostrogoths, c. 454-526, invaded and
conquered Italy 488-93. His 33-year reign in Italy was a
time of unprecedented peace. Theodoric sullied his reputation

by the executions of Boethius and Symmachus.
  Bo 1.p4.73gloss, [124]
     3.p4.25

THEOPHRASTUS (Theofraste), an unidentified Greek, the author of
  Liber Aureolus de Nuptiis, a work abstracted in book 1 of
  Adv. Jov.; cf. Policraticus 8.11 and RR 8599. See Hamm 103,
  Louns 2.366, S&A, Pratt.
     WBT p671
     MerchT 1294, 1295, 1310
  [Liber Aureolus de Nuptiis
     general   MerchT 1294
     PL.23.276   WBT p235-47   + DESCHAMPS Miroir
        .277   248-75, 282-302]   "

THESEUS, son of Neptune or AEGEUS and Aethra (daughter of Pittheus,
  king of Troezen). When Theseus finally made his way to Athens
  to discover his father MEDEA tried to poison him but he was
  recognized by Aegeus. Theseus then destroyed the Cretan bull
  brought to Marathon by HERCULES. He then volunteered to go to
  Crete as part of the annual tribute to MINOS. In Crete he
  killed the MINOTAUR and escaped the Labyrinth with the help
  of ARIADNE whom he abandoned at Naxos. Back in Athens he
  defeated the invasion of the Amazons and married HIPPOLYTA by
  whom he was father to Hippolytus. After Hippolyta's death
  Theseus married PHAEDRA. When CREON refused burial to the
  warriors who marched against Thebes, Theseus joined ADRASTUS
  in defeating Creon and gave burial to the slain. Theseus was
  a friend of Hercules to whom he gave asylum when he killed
  MEGARA and his children. Theseus was also a friend of
  PIRITHOUS. Theseus was finally driven from Athens by rebellions
  and retired to Scyros where he died or was assassinated.
  Meta. 7.456-8, Hero. 10, Theb. 12, Roman de Thebes, Tes.,
  MACHAUT Jugement; see Meech, Lowes.
     HF 405
     A&A 22, 45
     LGW 1890, 1945, 1952, 1960, 1968, 2007, 2026, 2028,
        2074, 2137, 2144, 2190, 2400, 2443, 2459, 2464
     KnT 878, 907, 963, 998, 1022, 1210, 1213, 1228, 1434,
        1439, 1448, 1484, 1498, 1562, 1662, 1673, 1684,
        [1742], [1757], 1874, 1883, 1900, 1913, 2089,
        2093, 2199, 2523, 2577, 2621, 2654, 2695, 2818,
        2837, 2870, 2975, 2980, 2982

        duke Theseus: 860, 1001, 1192, 1206, 1585, 1690,
        2190, 2528, 2700, 2731, 2853, 2889, 2906

THESIPHONE see TISIPHONE.

THETIS, a sea-nymph, daughter of Nereus and Doris, wife of PELEUS
  and mother of ACHILLES; Aen. 5.823-5, Meta. 11.221ff., 400.
     LGW 2422

THIODAMAS (Theodamas), son of Melampus, a famous seer; Theb.
   8.279ff.
      HF 1246
      MerchT 1720.

THISBE (Tesbee, Tisbe), the beloved of PYRAMUS.
      PF 289
      LGW 261(215), 725, 751, 777, 793, 809, 835, 849,
          853, 868, 870, 877, 881, 884, 887, 907, 916
      MLT i63
      MerchT 2128

THOAS (Toas), king of Lemnos, father of HYPSIPYLE, by whom he was
   conveyed to Chios when the women of Lemnos killed all the men;
   Meta. 13.399, Hero. 6.135, Theb. 5.239ff., GUIDO i1^{v1}, BENOIT
   13079ff.
      TYC 4.138
      LGW 1468

THOBIE see TOBIAS and TOBIT.

THOLEME see PTOLEMY.

THOMAS, the "victim" of the friar.
      SumT 1770, 1772, 1815, 1832, 1918, 1942, 1954, 1961, 1966,
          1970, 1974, 1978, 1985, 1992, 2000, 2089, 2107, 2112,
          2119

        churl: 2227, 2232, 2238, 2241, 2267, 2290

DON THOMAS, a common name, here applied to an ecclesiastic.
      MkT p1930(3120)

ST. THOMAS, the disciple who doubted and was also a missionary to
   India; he supposedly preached in southern India and was martyred
   and first buried there; John 21.25, Leg. Aurea 5.32, cf. Cline.
      WBT p666
   ST. THOMAS OF INDIA (Inde)
      SumT 1980
      MerchT p1230

ST. THOMAS À BECKET (St. Thomas of Kent), 1118-1170, became
   archbishop of Canterbury in 1162 during the reign of Henry II.
   He was forced to flee to France in 1164 but returned to England
   after a reconciliation was enforced by the pope in 1170.
   St. Thomas was murdered in 1170 and canonized in 1172, whereupon
   his shrine became the most popular in England.
      HF 1131
      [GP 17, 770]
      MillT 3291, 3425, 3461

<ST. THOMAS AQUINAS, c. 1225-1274, Doctor Angelicus, a Dominican
who studied under Albertus Magnus at Cologne. After 1252 he
moved from Paris to Rome to Bologna. He was canonized in 1323.
Summa Theologiae, 1266-73
    1.2.57.6   T&C 5.745-9   + CICERO + DANTE
     .31.2.1   3.404-6
     .45.6   3.15-7
    2.2.36.1   3.1625-8
    3.89.3.1   MLT i25ff.>

SIR THOPAS, the name of the gem has been applied to the knight but
none of the explanations are credible.
    Thop 717(1907), 724(1914), 750(1940), 773(1962),
       778(1968), 827(2017), 830(2020), 836(2026),
       901(2091)

THOUGHT, the personification of intellect; in Rom one of the gifts
from the god of Love to the Lover.
    Rom 2804
    HF 523

THYMALAO, Timolaus, one of the sons of ZENOBIA; De Clar. Mulier. 98,
S&A 634.
    MkT 2345(3535)

[TIBERIUS CONSTANTINE (the Emperor), actually emperor at
Constantinople in 578 and succeeded in 582 by Maurice of
Cappadocia to whom Tiberius gave his daughter Constantina
in marriage.
    MLT 151, 156, 248, 309, 447, 655, 954, 960, 1087,
       1093, 1101, 1121]

TIBURTIUS (Tiburce), the convert of CECILIA, baptized by Urban,
admitted to Grace because he saw the angel of God, and beheaded
because he would not sacrifice to the image of Jupiter.
    SecNT 242, 260, 265, 277, 289, 302, 307, 333, 348,
       349, 354, 408

TICIUS see TITYUS.

TIMAEUS (Thymeo) see PLATO.

[TIMANDRA, the concubine of ALCIBIADES, who buried his dead body;
also unnamed in Adv. Jov. 1.44.
    FranklT 1440]

ST. TIMOTHY, of Lystra in Lycanonia, an early convert associated
with ST. PAUL, the recipient of two of Paul's pastoral epistles.
According to tradition Timothy spent his life at Ephesus as its
bishop and was martyred in 97; cf. I and II Timothy.
    Mel 1130(2320)
    MkT 2591(3781)

[WBT p342]
ParsT p32
[Ret 1083]

TIRESIAS (Tyresie), the Theban gifted with the ability to prophecy
    and with long life even though he was blinded by Hera; HORACE
    Sat. 2.5.59.
        Bo 5.p3.133

TISIPHONE (Thesiphone) see FURIES.

TITAN, Chaucer has confused Titan, the sun, with Tithonus, the
    mortal lover for whom AURORA obtained the boon of immortality
    but not eternal youth; Root.
        T&C 3.1464

TITUS LIVIUS see LIVY.

TITYUS (Ticius), a giant slain by APOLLO and DIANA for offering
    violence to their mother Leto; Aen. 6.595, Meta. 4.457, 10.43.
        [BD 589]
        Bo 3.m12.42
        T&C 1.786

TOAS see THOAS.

TOBIAS (Thobie), son of TOBIT, attacked on the Tigris by a fish
    which he caught at the bidding of Raphael. Tobias married
    Sara, seven of whose lovers had been carried off by Asmodeus;
    Tobit.
        ParsT 906

TOBIT (Thobie), was blinded by sparrows while sleeping outside his
    courtyard. Tobit was cured of his blindness by applying to
    his eyes the gall of the fish which had tried to devour his
    son; Tobit.
        Mel 1118(2308)

TOO-MUCH-GIVING (To-Moche-Yevyng) rejected by RICHESSE and therefore
    evidence of the animosity of Richesse against Love's barons.
        Rom 5837

<TOUR-LANDRY, Geoffrey de la, fl. 1381, amassed a collection of
    exempla for the instruction of his daughters in modesty and
    virtue; see Grennen.
    ?Le Livre du chevalier de la Tour-Landry
        c. 74   MkT 1951-3(3141-3), 2019-22(3209-12),
                                     2091-4(3281-4)
                                 PardT 549-61
        c. 94   MerchT 1478ff.>

TRAVAIL (Travaile), Labor, one of the "lodgers" at the court of
    Age.
        Rom 4994

TREASON, the staff of False-Semblance when he dons the cope of
    a friar.
        Rom 7415

TREATISE OF THE SPHERE, an unidentified reference.
        Astr 1.21.82

TREGETOUR see COLLE TREGETOUR.

TRESPASS (Trespas), the ugly, nominal father of SHAME.
        Rom 3033, 3036, 3039

TRIGUILLA (Trygwille), "the king's provost."
        Bo 1.p4.59

TRINITY see GOD.

TRISTRAM (Tristam), the tragic lover of ISOLDE (Ysonde); Wells [43].
        PF 290
        Rose 20

TRITON, son of Neptune and the nymph Salacia, a sea-god, who, at
    the bidding of his father blows through a shell to rouse or
    calm the sea; Aen. 6.171ff., 10.209, Meta. 1.333ff.
        HF 1596, 1604
        LGW 2422

<TRIVET (Trevet), Nicholas, an English Dominican known to be at
    Oxford by 1297, then at Paris 1307-14; he returned to become a
    lector at Blackfriars until his death c. 1334. Les Chroniques
    was written for Marie, daughter of Edward I. He also wrote
    Annales sex regum Angliae, and commentaries on Augustine,
    Boethius, De Disciplina Scholarius, Ab Urbe Condita, Declama-
    tiones, Seneca's Tragoediae, Cicero, Juvenal, MAP's Dissuasio
    Valerii, and Aen. 6. The most complete treatment of Trivet's
    place in intellectual history is in Smalley EFA 58-65; but cf.
    Skeat 3.410, French 231, S&A, and Block. For evidence that
    Chaucer may have used Trivet's commentary on Boethius--together
    with a French translation--see Lowes and Dedeck-Hery.
    Les Chroniques (MS Magdalen 45, Oxford: in S&A)
        fol. 51a-b   MLT 134-89
             51b-52a   225-59
             52a-b   316-29, 414-20
             52b   435-41, 463-69, 505-32
             53a   533-81
             53b-54a   582-630, 659-700
             54a-55a   715-63, 785-833

<u>Les</u> <u>Chroniques</u> (cont.)
        fol. 55a–b   MLT 876–917
             55b–57a   953–1158>

TROILUS, son of PRIAM and exemplary lover of CRISEYDE.
        PF 291
        T&C 1.1, 30, 35, 55, 183, 215, 268, 288, 309, 396,
             498, 519, 568, 596, 621, 624, 657, 722, 737,
             749, 773, 776, 820, 834, 866, 871, 936, 1009,
             1044, 1056, 1072, 1086
           2.6, 32, 73, 157, 171, 181, 184, 192, 196, 198,
             319, 612, 624, 668, 683, 685, 687, 693, 701,
             933, 942, 950, 972, 1044, 1058, 1248, 1305,
             1312, 1317, 1322, 1339, 1394, 1404, 1411, 1457,
             1494, 1527, 1537, 1548, 1572, 1627, 1629, 1639,
             1666, 1684, 1692, 1752
           3.48, 50, 65, 78, 128, 194, 201, 206, 219, 228,
             230, 238, 345, 425, 488, 493, 507, 515, 533,
             569, 577, 600, 700, 706, 713, 742, 781, 786,
             806, 839, 920, 953, 981, 1054, 1065, 1101,
             1127, 1170, 1184, 1202, 1205, 1245, 1352, 1421,
             1443, 1498, 1521, 1529, 1549, 1583, 1588, 1590,
             1639, 1660, 1669, 1702, [1715], 1717, 1815,
             1819
           4.8, 15, 28, 148, 219, 228, 270, 350, 360, 365,
             372, 432, 519, 540, 610, 631, 674, 676, 699,
             714, 766, 778, 806, 854, 875, 880, 896, 946,
             1088, 1121, 1148, 1150, 1156, 1200, 1213, 1227,
             1253, 1373, 1422, 1476, 1537, 1552, 1597, 1653,
             1690
           5.6, [12], 22, 27, 64, 74, 91, 196, 197, 280,
             282, 287, 289, 293, 295, 323, 330, 407, 414,
             428, 433, 449, 502, 508, 513, 520, 529, 621,
             627, 697, 717, 734, 753, 768, 827, 835, 865,
             953, 1039, 1041, 1046, 1053, 1072, 1100, 1111,
             1120, 1121, 1135, 1143, 1163, 1182, 1289, 1312,
             1432, 1437, 1564, 1566, [1590], 1632, 1642,
             1647, 1655, 1744, 1747, 1752, 1762, 1801, 1828
        LGW (265)
        Adam 2

BOOK OF TROILUS.
        Ret 1086

TROPHEE, of uncertain identification, is perhaps the personification
     of a common noun; i.e. according to Kittredge <u>tropaea</u>, for
     pillars, became proper and according to <u>Skeat</u> it was applied
     to GUIDO. See <u>Robin</u> 747–8.
        MkT 2117(3307)

TROTULA, generally taken to be the distinguished female physician
of Salerno in the middle of the 11th cent. who wrote treatises
on diseases of women and the care of children; Robin 702,
Hamilton.
WBT p677

TRUTH, the personification of troth; Truth should encourage the
lady to pity the lover.
BD 1003
Pity 74

TUBAL-CAIN (Tubal), in Genesis 4.21 JUBAL is the father of music
and Tubal is the father of makers of bronze and iron; however,
the mistake appears in Comestor's Historia Scholastica Lib. Gen.
28, Spec. Doct. 17.25 and PETRUS DE RIGA's Aurora, Chaucer's
acknowledged source.
BD 1162

TULLIUS see CICERO.

TULLUS HOSTILIUS (Tullius), the third legendary king of Rome,
672-640 B.C., who first extended the Roman domain beyond the
walls of Rome. He is a kind of duplicate of ROMULUS because
he was brought up by shepherds. He is said to have been struck
dead because of his pride. LIVY 1.22-31, VALERIUS MAXIMUS 3.4,
CICERO De Republica 2.17.
WBT 1166
Scot 47

TURNUS, king of the Rutuli, betrothed to LAVINIA, who fiercely
opposed the Trojans and the proposed marriage of Lavinia and
AENEAS. In the conflict which resulted Turnus was killed by
Aeneas; Aen. books 7-12.
HF 457, 516
KnT 1945
MLT 201

TYDEUS, son of Oeneus, king of Calydon, went into exile for homicide
and at Argos married Deipyle, daughter of ADRASTUS, while
POLYNICES married her sister Argeia; therefore, he became one
of the seven against Thebes. When set upon by 50 warriors he
killed 49 and sent MAEON back to ETEOCLES. Tydeus was also
the father of DIOMEDES. See Theb. 1.468ff., 7.538ff., 8.716ff.,
and Filo. 6.24, 7.27.
A&A 57
T&C 5.88, 803, 932, 1480, 1485, 1493, 1501, 1514,
1746

A TYRANT, in Bo, see NICOCREON and DIONYSIUS OF SYRACUSE.

TYRESIE see TIRESIAS.

TYRO APOLLONIUS see APOLLONIUS OF TYRE.

TYTUS,
        HF 1467 = DICTYS CRETENSIS

U

ULYSSES (Ulixes, Ithacus), properly Ulixes, king of Ithaca, son of
    Laertes and Anticlea, husband of PENELOPE and father of
    TELEMACHUS, famed among the Grecian heroes of the Trojan war
    for his craft and eloquence; Aen. 2.7, 3.273, and Meta. 14.159,
    671.
        Bo 4.m3.1, 19; m7.18, 23, 24, 26

ST. URBAN, Urban I, bishop of Rome 222-30.
        SecNT 177, 179, 185, 189, 217, 305, 306, 309, 350,
            541, 547, 551

URSA MAJOR (Ursa), the Great Bear, the Big Dipper, or Charles' Wain,
    the most conspicuous of the northern constellations which
    includes Septentriones, the Wagon, the Plow, the Dipper, and
    Charles' Wain; Skeat 2.452-3.
        Bo 4.m6.11

V

VACHE, perhaps Sir Philip de la Vache, 1346-1408, associated with
    Chaucer because de la Vache married the daughter of Sir Lewis
    Clifford. Apparently from 1386-9 he was out of favor but in
    1390 his fortune changed, for he became a knight of the Garter
    in 1399; Robin 861.
        Truth 22

ST. VALENTINE (Valentyn, Valentyne), whose day is February 14, the
    customary and traditional day on which mates are chosen.
        PF 309, 322, 386, 683
        LGW 145(131)
        Mars 13
        ComA 85

BOOK OF ST. VALENTINES DAY OF THE PARLEMENT OF BRIDDES.
        Ret 1086

VALERIA, the wife of Servius refused to remarry; Adv. Jov. 1.46.
        FranklT 1456

VALERIAN, converted by CECILIA and martyred with TIBERTIUS.
        SecNT 129, 148, 162, 183, 203, 204, 213, 218, 224,
            232, 235, 253, 262, 266, 277, 306, 350, 408

VALERIUS (Valerye) see MAP.

[VALERIUS FLACCUS, died c. 90, flourished under Vespasian and Titus.
Argonautica was dedicated to Vespasian on his setting out for
Britain and was written during the siege of Jerusalem by Titus
in 70.]
Argonautica
    LGW 1457
    <general   LGW 1368ff.
    1   1457ff.
    1.93, 314   1453-8
    .596-613   HF 1572, 1585-7
    2.351   LGW 1509
    4.92   T&C 5.8>   + MARTIANUS CAPELLA

VALERIUS MAXIMUS (Valerius, Valerie), fl. during the reign of
Tiberius, was patronized by Sextus Pompeius (consul in 14) and
between 29 and 32 wrote the Factorum Dictorumque Memorabilium,
a kind of commonplace book of extracts from Cicero, Livy,
Sallust, and Pompeius Trogus.
    MkT 2720(3910)
    [NPT 2984(4174)]
    WBT [p642, 647]
        1165
Factorum Dictorumque Memorabilium
    [3.4   WBT p1165
    5.1.10   MkT 2720(3910)]
    <1.7   NPT 2984(4174)
    .7.3   3064(4254)-3104(94)
    .10   2984(4174)-3062(4252)
    3.3   Bo 1.p3.54   + CICERO
                      2.p6.51
    6.3   WBT p642, 647
    .3.9   p460>

VENUS, generally considered the goddess of Love and identified with
Aphrodite. Her epithet Cypride was perhaps due to her identification with Cyprus and the East. The appellation Cythera
refers to the island in the Aegean celebrated for the worship
of Venus; i.e. the island is near the promontory where Venus
arose from the sea. As Venus Genetrix the goddess was
worshipped as the mother of the Roman people. In the Middle
Ages, she was regarded ambiguously: she can represent anything
from lechery to concupiscence to modesty and matronly love.
The best treatment of the opposing views is Bennett, Book of
Fame, Chap. I. Chaucer probably regarded her ambivalently and
he probably got the idea from Boccaccio; cf. Bennett p. 16.
Venus is always pictured as sensuous and is usually surrounded
by other symbols of love: the three Graces, the sea, roses,
doves, and cupid. Generally, she is never condemned for her
infidelity to her ugly husband, Vulcan, and her infatuations--
particularly with Mars and Adonis.

Rom 1616, 3048, 3052, 3698, 3754, 5870, 5921, 5953
HF 130, 162, 213, 219, 227, 465, 518=Cypris, 618,
    1487
PF 113=Cytherea, 261, 277=Cypride, 351, 652
T&C 1.1014
    2.234, 680, 972, 1524
    3.48, 187, 705, 712, 715, [718], 725=Cipris,
       951, 1255=Citherea, 1257, [1807]
    4.1216=Cypride, 1661
    5.208=Cipride, 1016
LGW 338(313), 940, 998, 1021, 1072, 1086, 2584,
    2591, 2592
KnT 1102, 1104, 1332, 1536, 1904, 1918, 1937, 1949,
    1955, 2215=Citherea, 2216, 2221, 2265, 2272,
    2386, 2440, 2453, 2480, 2487, 2663
MkT p1961(3151)
NPT 3342(4532)
WBT p464, 604=St. Venus, 609=Venerien, 611, 618,
    700, 708
MerchT 1723, 1777, 1875, 1971
SqT 272
FranklT 937, 1304
PhysT 59
Mars 2, 26, 31, 43, 46, 77, 84, 89, 104, 113, 136,
    141, 143, 145, 146
Scog 11
astrological:
KnT 2585
WBT p697, 704, 705
CYT 829
Astr 2.12.25, 29; 40.10, 17, 21, 41

THE GOLDEN VERSES see PYTHAGORAS.

VILLAINY, the personification of boorishness, a figure on the wall
    outside the garden of Mirth and one of the arrows in the "foul"
    quiver of Love.
    Rom 166, 169, 977, 2175

ARNOLD OF VILLANOVA (Arnold of the Newe Toun) see ARNALDUS DE
    VILLA NOVA.

VINCENT OF BEAUVAIS (Vincent), Vincentius Bellovacensis, c. 1190–
    c. 1264, the most important encyclopedist of the Middle Ages
    about whom very little is known; Hamm 105, Louns 2.375–81,
    Aiken, Wimsatt, Young.
    LGW (307)
Speculum Majus (Venice, 1494)
    <Speculum Naturale
    4.14–8   HF 765
    15.83   BD 1206

Speculum Majus (cont.)
    <Speculum Naturale (cont.)

16.14	PF 323
.27	360
.48	361
.49-50	342
.63	T&C 5.365-8
17.20	3.1496
20.160	MerchT 2058
25.3, 9, 52	KnT 2749-51
.56	"
.58	HF 765
26.11	KnT 2749-51
.32ff.	HF 1ff.
.41	48
.56	493
27.52-61	T&C 5.365-8
32.74	KnT 2749-51>

    <Speculum Doctrinale

13.9	KnT 2745-6
.94	2755-6
.134-5	2747-8
.147	2745-6
14.1	T&C 1.659-65
.47, 136	KnT 2749-51
15.3	2757-60
.24	2743-4
.38	2757-60
.88-9	2743-4
.89	2757-60
17.10	BD 512>

Speculum Historiale (Estoryal Myrour)

general	LGW (307)
<1.41-2	MkT 2007(3197)-14(04)
2.67	2015(3205)-19(09)
.121	2151(3341)-55(45)
3.17	2727(3917)-66(56)
4.1ff.	2631(3821)ff.
5.35	2673(3863)-4(4), 2681(3871)-2(2)
.42	2695(3885)-2718(3908)
8.7	2471(3661)-78(68)
.9	2503(3693)-18(3708)
10.71	WBT 1195>

<De Eruditione Filiorum Nobilium (ed. Steiner)

p. 172-3	PhysT 61-71, 93-100
174	93-100
176	118-20
176-8	55-7
179-80	43-54, 58-9
181	43-54

Speculum Majus (cont.)
    <De Eruditione Filiorum Nobilium (cont.)
    p. 187-8   PhysT 72-92
       188-9   61-71, 72-92
       189-90   72-92
       203   48, 43-54>

VINSAUF see GEOFFREY DE VINSAUF.

VIRGIL (Virgile, Virgilius), Publius Vergilius Maro, 70-19 B.C.,
was born near Mantua and educated at Cremona and Milan; he then
went to Rome where he studied philosophy and rhetoric. Virgil
then retired to his farm to a life of study. He was patronized
by Maecenas to whom he introduced HORACE. He died at Brundisium
and was buried at Naples. The Eclogues were composed between
42 and 37, the Georgics between 37 and 30, and the Aeneid was
completed in 19. See Hamm 105, Louns 2.250-1, Shannon, Bradley,
Brookhouse, McDermott, Steadman.
Opera, ed. Hirtzel (Oxford, 1900).
    HF 378, 449, 1244, 1483
    T&C 5.1792
    LGW 924, 1002, [1139, 1228]
    FrT 1519
    <Georgicon
       1.226   Rom 4335
       .277ff.   Bo 3.p12.132
       1.405-9   T&C 5.1110   + OVID
       2.121   Bo 2.m5.10-1
       .137   3.m10.14-5
       .465   2.m5.10-1
       3.5   2.p6.66   + OVID
       .31   5.m1.3
       .38   3.m12.37
       .48   T&C 3.1464-70 + SERVIUS
       4.453-527   4.789-91
       .454-527   Bo 3.m12.4
       .484   3.m12.37
       .491-2   3.m12.59>
    <Eclogae (= Bucolica)
       ?1.60-4   T&C 3.1495-8
       3.93   SumT 1994-5   + RR
       ?4.32-3   FormAge 12, 23-4>
    Aeneidos
       HF 378
       LGW 928
       NPT 3359(4549)
       [1   LGW 1002, 1139
       2   NPT 3359(4549)
       4   HF 378
                        LGW 924, 928, 1228
       6   449, 1244

Aeneidos (cont.)

	FrT 1519]		
<1	HF 198–225		
1.28	589		
.67	Bo 3.m8.8		
.100	T&C 4.1548–53		
.223ff.	KnT 2663–70		
.274–6	T&C 4.25		
.305–624	LGW 958–1102		
.321–4	978–82		
.325–40	983–93		
.327	KnT 1101		
.341–414	LGW 994–1014		
.412	1022		
.446–93	HF 130–1		
	KnT 1918ff.		
.509–612	LGW 1047–60		
.516	1022		
.588–91	1066–74		
.613–4	1061–5		
.617–42	1086–1102		
.643–722	1128–49		
2.39	SqT 252		
.57–267	LGW 931		
.162–70	T&C 1.152–4		
.198	1.58, 60		
.222–4	4.239–41	+ Inf.	+ Filo.
.259	NPT 3228(4418)		
.270ff.	LGW 934		
.533ff.	939		
.550ff.	NPT 3358(4548)–9(9)		
.594ff.	LGW 940		
.723	941		
.738	945		
? .776–9, 784	BD 201–5: Wimsatt		
3.19ff.	T&C 3.1807–10	+ Ars Amat.	+ Amores
	KnT 2340	+ Meta. + Inf.	+ Tes.
.106	LGW 1895	+ Hero.	+ Filo.
.239	HF 1243		
.420–3, 558	T&C 5.644	+ Meta.	
4	LGW 1162–1351		
4.9–29	1170–81		
.129ff.	1188–1211		
.154–70	1212–31		
.173ff.	HF 1368ff.		
.174	350		
.188	T&C 4.659–61	+ Filo.	
.196	LGW 1245		
.243	T&C 5.321–2	+ Tes.	
.252ff.	HF 429		
.274	177		

Aeneidos (cont.)

4.327–30	LGW 1323	
.351–9	1295–9	
.452ff.	1310	
.462	PF 343	
.632	LGW 1346	
.646	MLT 164	
.651–3	LGW 1338–40	
5.8ff.	HF 439	
.252–7	529ff.	
.588	1920	
	Bo 3.p12.156	
.570–92	LGW 1114ff.	
.823ff.	2422	
6	HF 439	
6.27ff.	Bo 3.p12.156	
.162	HF 1243	
.162–74	1573–9	
.171ff.	1596	
.179	LGW 2312	
.309–12	T&C 4.225–7	+ Inf.
.417	Bo 3.m12.31	
.431	LGW 1887	
.431–3	T&C 4.1187–8	+ DANTE
.484	2.1467	
.551	3.1600	
.595	Bo 3.m12.42	
	T&C 1.786	
.601	5.212	+ OVID
7.274–9	LGW 1114ff.	
.359	1331	
.413ff.	HF 516	
8	KnT 1945	
9.1ff.	HF 516	
.224–5	PF 85ff.	
.405	T&C 5.655	+ Meta.
10.209	HF 1596	
12.332	KnT 1747	+ OVID + Theb.
.845–7	T&C 4.22–4	
.901ff.	MLT 201>	

VIRGINIA, the exemplar of virginity and chastity, daughter of
   VIRGINIUS, a plebeian centurion. She attracted APIUS Claudius,
   the decimvir, who instructed M. Claudius to claim her. Her
   father killed her rather than allow her to fall prey to the
   lust of Apius; LIVY 3.44–58, RR 5589ff., De Clar. Mulier. 56.
   See Fansler, S&A, Hoffman.
      PhysT 213
         [205, 208, 218, 221, 237]

VIRGINIUS, father of VIRGINIA. In the traditional account Virginius
    stabbed his daughter in the presence of Apius and the people.
        PhysT 2, 167, 175, 180, 191, 197, 203, 272
            [231, 235, 238, 247, 254, 261]

VISCONTI, Barnabo, one of the celebrated rulers of Milan, one of
    the nephews of Giovanni (lord of the city 1349-54). Barnabo's
    brother Matteo II was assassinated in 1355; his brother
    Galeazzo II, who held court at Pavia, married his daughter
    Violante to the duke of Clarence and his son Gian Galeazzo to
    Isabella, daughter of John of France. Barnabo, who held court
    at Milan, was engaged in constant warfare and burdened the city
    with oppressive taxes. When Galeazzo II died in 1378 Barnabo
    tried to exercise complete power but was put to death by Gian
    Galeazzo in 1385. S&A, Pratt.
        MkT 2399(3589)

VITULON see WITELO.

VULCAN (Vulcano, Vulcanus), son of JUPITER and JUNO and husband of
    VENUS, a fire-god identified with Hephaestus; Ars Amat. 2.561-
    600, Meta. 4.171ff., RR 13838ff., 14157ff., 18061ff., and Tes.
    43.2.
        HF 138
        KnT 2222, 2389

W

WADE, a reference which is, by and large, unexplained. According
    to Skeat 5.356-7 Wade was "a famous hero of antiquity."
        T&C 3.614
        MerchT 1424

WALTER, marquis of Saluzzo, the demanding (if not sadistic) husband
    of patient GRISELDA.
        ClT 77, 421, 612, 631, 716, 722, 986, 1044, 1107,
            1111
            [92, 96, 101, 104, 106, 110, 116, 129, 142, 182,
            198, 233, 250, 267, 289, 295, 299, 301, 319,
            321, 323, 359, 386, 463, 501, 512, 523, 529,
            568, 575, 579, 597, 619, 624, 667, 687, 706,
            761, 772, 786, 814, 845, 858, 862, 889, 946,
            967, 1088]

WANHOPE, despair in love, the fourth arrow in the foule quiver.
        Rom 981

WATTE, a nickname for Walter.
        GP 643

WEBBER, a weaver, one of the five guildsmen; Bowden 183.
 GP 362

WEL CONCEALED (Wel-Heelynge), one of the warriors appointed by
 Love's barons to assail Shame.
 Rom 5857

WELL OF LOVE, the well of Narcissus in the garden of Mirth.
 Rom 1627

WHITE BD see BLANCHE.

WHITE MONKS see CISTERCIANS.

WHITSUNDAY, Pentecost, the feast celebrated 50 days after Easter
 to commemorate the descent of the Holy Ghost on the disciples.
 Rom 2278

WICKED TONGUE (Wykked-Tonge), one of the companion guardians of
 the Rose (together with DANGER and SHAME).
 Rom 3027, 3257, 2799, 3802, 3871, 3878, 4141, 4233,
  4267, 4484, 5851, 7355, 7422, 7474, 7476, 7498

A WIFE,
 MancT 139 = CORONIS OF LARISSA

WIFE OF BATH, an inveterate bride and pilgrim, the most particularly
 described and frequently discussed of the pilgrims; Bowden
 214-27.
 GP 445
 WBT p320, 804 = ALICE
 ClT 1170
 MerchT 1685
 Buk 29

WILKYN, a common name for a pet here applied to the sheep.
 WBT p432

WILL, Desire, the daughter of Cupid, she tempered the arrows of
 Love.
 PF 214

WILLIAM THE CONQUEROR, William I, duke of Normandy, king of England
 1066-87; here simply used to indicate the Conquest as the limit
 of legal memory in English law. The hyperbole is in keeping
 with the portrait of this busy and learned lawyer.
 GP 324

WILLIAM ST. AMOUR see GUILLAUME DE ST. AMOUR.

WIRDES see FATES.

WISDOM, one of the attendants at the hearse of PITY.
    Pity 41

the wise, the sentence of the wise, the wise man seith,
        T&C 1.694 = SOLOMON
        MLT p114 = JESUS FILIUS SIRACH, 115, 118 = Proverbs
        SumT 1988 =   "
        ParsT 569 = Proverbs

WITCH OF ENDOR (Phitonissa), the seer who called up the spirit of
    Samuel to answer king Saul's questions concerning the battle
    of Gilboa in which Saul would meet his death; I Chronicles
    10.13 (Vulg.), I Samuel 28.7.
        FrT 1510

WITELO (Vitulon), fl. c. 1254, a Polish physicist who translated
    Alhazen's Opticae; Robin 719.
        SqT 232

WOE, one of the courtiers of Age.
    Rom 4995

THE CANAANITE WOMAN, encountered by Jesus in the district of Tyre,
    whose daughter was miraculously rid of the devil because her
    mother had faith; Matthew 15.22ff.
        SecNT 59

this word,
        FrT 1656 = Psalms 10

WRECHED ENGENDRYNGE OF MANKYNDE see INNOCENT III.

HOLY WRIT,
        SumT 1790 = II Corinthians 3.6
        PardT 483 = Ephesians 5.18, 742 = Leviticus 19.32

X

XANTIPPE (Xantippa), the wife of Socrates who supposedly showered
    him with the contents of a chamber-pot: Socrates thought the
    shower a logical sequence to her thunder. She is the proverbial
    conjugal scold; Adv. Jov. 1.48.
        WBT p729

XANTIPUS (Santippe), Antipus, king of Frisia and ally of PRIAM,
    one of the Trojan prisoners; GUIDO h6^{rl}, Filo. 4.3.
        T&C 4.52

Y

YEOMAN (Yeman), the CANON'S YEOMAN.

YEOMAN, the companion and servant of the KNIGHT and SQUIRE;
Bowden 84-8.
GP 101

YMENEUS see HYMEN.

YOUTH, the personification of juvenile beauty and energy.
Rom 1282, 1302, 4925, 4943, 4950, 4977, 4981, 4983,
4985, 5008, 5021
BD 797
PF 226
KnT 1926
Pity 40

YPERMYSTRA see HYPERMNESTRA.

YPOCRAS see HIPPOCRATES.

YPOLITA see HIPPOLYTE.

YPOTYS, a legend rather than a romance, purportedly the work of
St. John the Evangelist; Skeat 5.198, Everett.
Thop 898(2088)

YSIDIS see ISIS.

YSIDRE see ISIDORE OF SEVILLE.

ST. YVE see ST. IVES.

Z

ZECHARIAH (Zacharie, Zakarie), the eleventh of the minor prophets,
his prophecies date 520 and 518 B.C.; Zacharia 10.5 and 13.1.
ParsT 434
ABC 177

ZANSIS see ZEUXIS.

ZENO, of Elea, born c. 488, a follower of Parmenides and supposedly
the inventor of dialectic; Zeno's love of freedom was shown
when he offered his life to a tyrant in order to save his
country. See CICERO De Nat. Deor. 3.82, Tusc. 2.22, and
VALERIUS MAXIMUS 3.3
Bo 1.p3.54

ZENOBIA (Cenobia, Cenobie), queen of Palmyra and consort of
   ODENATHUS, she assumed power after his death in 266 or 267.
   Zenobia tried to surpass her husband and make Palmyra the ruler
   of the Roman empire in the East; to that end, she occupied
   Egypt and then vested all power in her son Athenodorus. When
   Aurelian became emperor in 270 he set out to prevent her threat
   to the empire: in 270 Probus recovered Egypt and in 271
   Aurelian marched into Asia Minor and finally captured Palmyra
   by siege. Zenobia and Athenodorus fled but were captured and
   Palmyra capitulated. Boccaccio's accounts show a marked
   difference from the one given above; De Clar. Mulier. 98,
   De Casibus 8.6. Cf. S&A.
      MkT 2247(3427)

ZEPHYRUS (Zepherus, Zephirus), the West Wind, son of Astraeus and
   Eos and husband of FLORA; Fasti 5.201, 319 and RR 8411ff.
      BD 402
      Bo 1.m5.22
         2.m3.10
      T&C 5.10
      LGW 171, 2681
      GP 5

ZEUXIS (Zansis), in PhysT undoubtedly refers to the famous painter
   who fl. fifth cent. B.C. and his contest with Parrhasius;
   PLINY 35.61-6, CICERO De Oratore 3.26, RR 16177ff. The sentence
   in T&C has been traced to Rem. Amoris 462 but Kittredge [70n3]
   alludes to Zeuxis in the Alexander story (one of Philip's
   courtiers who wrote him of Alexander's extravagance) in Julius
   Valerius 1.16; cf. Root, Kreuzer.
      T&C 4.414
      PhysT 16

Cross-Reference List of Titles

[Works by authors who are never mentioned; works whose authors are mentioned by name only or in association with another work.]

Ab Urbe Condita see LIVY

Achilleis see STATIUS

Aeneidos see VIRGIL

Alexandreis see GULATIER DE CHATILLON

De Amicitia see CICERO

De Amore see ANDREAS CAPELLANUS

Amores see OVID

Amorosa Visione see BOCCACCIO

Andromache see EURIPIDES

Annales see TACITUS

Anticlaudianus see ALANUS DE INSULIS

Ars Amatoria see OVID

Ars Poetica see HORACE

De Arte Loguendi et Tacendi see ALBERTANUS BRIXIENSIS

De Arte Versificandi see GEOFFREY DE VINSAUF

Balade Notée see MACHAUT

Ballades see DESCHAMPS

De Belle Trojano see JOSEPH OF EXETER

De Beneficiis see SENECA

De Caelo see ARISTOTLE

Canzone see PETRARCH

Caracallus see SPARTIANUS

Carmina see CATULLUS

De Casibus Virorum Illustrium see BOCCACCIO

De Causa Dei contra Pelagium see BRADWARDINE

Les Chroniques see TRIVET

De Civitate Dei see ST. AUGUSTINE

De Claris Mulieribus see BOCCACCIO

De Clementia see SENECA

Cliges see CHRÉTIEN DE TROYES

Codex see JUSTINIAN

Commentarii in Vergilium see SERVIUS

Commentarium in Somnium Scipionis see MACROBIUS

Communilouium see JOHN OF WALES

Compendium see GILBERTUS ANGLICUS

Complainte see MACHAUT

Confort d'Ami see MACHAUT

Contra Hierosolymitanum see ST. JEROME

Controversiae see SENECA

Convivio see DANTE

Corpus Iuris Canonici see BOOK OF DECREES

De Corruptione et Gratia see
    ST. AUGUSTINE

De Deorum Imaginibus see
    ALBRICUS PHILOSOPHUS

De Deo Socratis see APULEIUS

Digesta see JUSTINIAN

De Disciplina Clericalis see
    PETRUS ALFONSUS

Disputationes Tusculanae see
    CICERO

Disticha Catonis see CATO

Dit de la Fonteinne Amoureuse
    see MACHAUT

Dit de la Marguerite see MACHAUT

Dit dou Lyon see MACHAUT

Dit dou Vergier see MACHAUT

Dittie de la Flour de la
    Margherite see FROISSART

Divina Commedia (Divine Comedy)
    see DANTE

De Divinatione see CICERO

Eclogae see VIRGIL

Elegiae see MAXIMIANUS

Elegiae see PROPERTIUS

Ennarrationes in Psalmi see
    ST. AUGUSTINE

Ephemeris Belli Troiana see
    DICTYS CRETENSIS

Epistola ad Eustachium de
    Virginitate see ST. JEROME

Epistolae see ST. AUGUSTINE

Epistolae see CASSIODORUS

Epistolae see GROSSETESTE

Epistolae see ST. JEROME

Epistolae ad Caecinam see CICERO

Epistolae Morales ad Lucillium
    see SENECA

Epistolae Seniles see PETRARCH

Epistole Eroiche see FILIPPO
    "CEFFI"

Epistularum see HORACE

Erec et Enide see CHRÉTIEN DE
    TROYES

De Eruditione Filiorum Nobilium
    see VINCENT OF BEAUVAIS

Etymologiae see ISIDORE

Ex Ponto see OVID

De Excidio Troiae Historia see
    DARES PHRYGIUS

Expositio in Metaphysica
    Aristotelis see DUNS SCOTUS

Expositiones Visionum see
    ARNALDUS DE VILLANOVA

Fabulae see HYGINUS

Factorum Dictorumque Memorabilium
    see VALERIUS MAXIMUS

Fasti see OVID

Fiammetta see BOCCACCIO

Filocolo see BOCCACCIO

Filostrato see BOCCACCIO

Formula Honestae Vitae see
    MARTINUS DUMIENSIS

De Genealogiis Deorum see
    BOCCACCIO

Georgicon see VIRGIL

De Gestis Romanorum see PAULUS
    DIACONUS

Golden Verses see PYTHAGORAS

Gorgias see PLATO

Heroides see OVID

Historia adversum Paganos see
    OROSIUS

Historia Destructionis Troiae
    see GUIDO DELLE COLONNE

Historiam Alexandri Magni see
    QUINTUS CURTIUS

Homily on Psalm 28.7 see
ST. BASIL

Homilies on the Gospels see
ST. GREGORY

Ibis see OVID

Iliad see HOMER

Ilias Latina see SIMON AUREA
CAPRA

Inferno see DANTE

In Rufinum see CLAUDIANUS

Introductorium see ALCHABITIUS

De Inventione see CICERO

De Ira see SENECA

Ivain see CHRÉTIEN DE TROYES

Joli Buisson de Jonece see
FROISSART

Le Joli Mois de May see FROISSART

Jugement dou Roy de Navarre see
MACHAUT

De Lapide Philosophorum see
ARNALDUS DE VILLANOVA

Lay Amoureaux see DESCHAMPS

Lay de Confort see MACHAUT

Lay de Franchise see DESCHAMPS

Lay du Desert d'Amours see
DESCHAMPS

Laus Serenae see CLAUDIANUS

De Legibus see PLATO

Liber Aureolus de Nuptiis see
THEOPHRASTUS

Liber Consolationis et Consilii
see ALBERTANUS BRIXIENSIS

Liber de Amore see ALBERTANUS
BRIXIENSIS

Liber de Amore see PAMPHILUS

Liber de Medicamentis Simplicibus
see SERAPION

Liber Sapientiae see HOLCOT

Libri Tres de Virginibus see
ST. AMBROSE

Li Hystore de Julius Cesar see
JEHAN DE TUIM

Lilium see GORDON

Le Livre du Chevalier de la Tour-
Landry see TOUR-LANDRY

Megacosmos see BERNARDUS
SILVESTRIS

Megale Syntaxis see PTOLEMY

Metalogicon see JOHN OF SALISBURY

Metamorphoses see OVID

De Metaphysica see ARISTOTLE

Miroir de Mariage see DESCHAMPS

Moralium see ST. GREGORY

De Moribus see MARTINUS DUMIENSIS

Motet see MACHAUT

De Natura Deorum see CICERO

Naturalis Historia see PLINY

De Naturis Rerum see ALEXANDER
NECKAM

Nemeans see PINDAR

Ninfale Fiesolano see BOCCACCIO

Noctes Atticae see AULUS GELLIUS

De Nugis Curialium see MAP

Odyssey see HOMER

De Officiis see CICERO

De Opere Monachorum see
ST. AUGUSTINE

De Oratore see CICERO

De Origine Actibusque Getarum
see JORDANES

Ovidius Moralizatus see PETRUS
BERCHORIUS

La Panthère d'Amours see NICOLE
DE MARGIVAL

Parabolae see ALANUS DE INSULIS

Paradiso see DANTE

Paradys d'Amours see FROISSART

Pastourelle see FROISSART

Pelerinage de la Vie Humaine see
    GUILLAUME DE GUILLEVILLE

Perceval see CHRÉTIEN DE TROYES

Phaedo see PLATO

Pharsalia see LUCAN

De Physica see ARISTOTLE

De Planctu Naturae see ALANUS
    DE INSULIS

Poetria Nova see GEOFFREY DE
    VINSAUF

Policraticus see JOHN OF
    SALISBURY

Prison Amoreuse see FROISSART

De Proprietatibus Rerum see
    BARTHOLOMAEUS ANGLICUS

Purgatorio see DANTE

al-Qanun see AVICENNA

De Raptu Proserpinae see
    CLAUDIANUS

De Re Publica see CICERO

Remede de Fortune see MACHAUT

Remedia Amoris see OVID

Republic see PLATO

Rime see BOCCACCIO

Roman de Troie see BENOÎT DE
    STE. MAUR.

Roy de Behaingne see MACHAUT

Saturae see JUVENAL

Saturae et Liber Priapeorum
    see PETRONIUS

De Senectute see CICERO

Sententiae see PUBLILIUS SYRUS

Sententiarum see ISIDORE

Sermo ad Prelatos in Concilio
    see ST. BERNARD

Sermones see ST. AUGUSTINE

Sermonum see HORACE

Sonneto see PETRARCH

Sophistes see PLATO

Speculum Doctrinale see VINCENT
    OF BEAUVAIS

Speculum Naturale see VINCENT
    OF BEAUVAIS

Summa Casum Poenitentiae see
    PENNAFORTE

Summa Theologiae see ST. THOMAS
    AQUINAS

Tabula Chimica see SENIOR

Tesida see BOCCACCIO

Testament see JEAN DE MEUN

Thebaidos see STATIUS

Timaeus see PLATO

Tractatus Brevis de Periculis
    Novissimorum Temporum see
    GUILLAUME DE ST. AMOUR

De Tranquillitate Animi see
    SENECA

Trésor Amoreux see FROISSART

Tristia see OVID

Variae see CASSIODORUS

De Vera et Falsa Poenitentia
    see ST. AUGUSTINE

De Vita Beata see SENECA

De Vita Caesarum see SUETONIUS

De Vita Pythagorae see IAMBLICUS

Bibliography

I. Sources

Alanus de Insulis. <u>Anticlaudianus</u>. Ed. R. Bossuat. Textes
   philosophiques du moyen âge, 1. Paris, 1955.

Albertanus Brixiensis. <u>Liber</u> <u>Consolationis</u> <u>et</u> <u>Consilii</u>. Ed.
   Thor Sundby. Chaucer Society Publ., 2nd Series, No. 8,
   London, 1873.

Alighieri, Dante. <u>The</u> <u>Divine</u> <u>Comedy</u>. Ed. and trans. John D.
   Sinclair. 3 vols. New York, 1959-61.

Augustine, St. (Aurelius Augustinus). <u>The</u> <u>City</u> <u>of</u> <u>God</u>. Trans.
   Marcus Dods. New York, 1950.

Benoît de Ste. Maur. <u>Le</u> <u>Roman</u> <u>de</u> <u>Troie</u>. Ed. L. Constans. 3 vols.
   Société des anciens textes français. Paris, 1904-7.

<u>Biblia</u> <u>Sacra</u>. Ed. Alberto Colunga and Laurentis Turrado. 4th edn.
   Madrid, 1965.

Boccaccio, Giovanni. <u>The</u> <u>Filostrato</u> <u>of</u> <u>Giovanni</u> <u>Boccaccio</u>. Ed.
   and Trans. N. E. Griffin and A. B. Myrick. Philadelphia, 1929.

————. <u>Teseida</u>. Ed. Salvadorc Battaglia. Florence, 1938.

Boethius. <u>De</u> <u>Consolatione</u> <u>Philosophiae</u>. Eds. H. F. Stewart and
   E. K. Rand. 1918: rpt. London, 1962. Loeb Classical Library.

Chaucer, Geoffrey. <u>The</u> <u>Book</u> <u>of</u> <u>Troilus</u> <u>and</u> <u>Criseyde</u>. Ed. Robert K.
   Root. Princeton, 1926.

————. <u>The</u> <u>Complete</u> <u>Works</u> <u>of</u> <u>Geoffrey</u> <u>Chaucer</u>. Ed. W. W. Skeat.
   2nd edn. 6 vols. Oxford, 1899-1900.

————. <u>The</u> <u>Text</u> <u>of</u> <u>the</u> <u>Canterbury</u> <u>Tales</u>. Ed. John M. Manly and
   Edith Rickert. 8 vols. Chicago, 1940.

————. <u>The</u> <u>Works</u> <u>of</u> <u>Geoffrey</u> <u>Chaucer</u>. Eds. A. W. Pollard, H. F.
   Heath, M. H. Liddell, and W. S. McCormick. London, 1898.

Bibliography

Sources (cont.)

Chaucer, Geoffrey. The Works of Geoffrey Chaucer. Ed. F. N.
    Robinson. 2nd edn. Boston, 1957.

Cicero. (Marcus Tullius Cicero). Opera Omnia. 8 vols. London,
    1830.

Deschamps, Eustace. Oeuvres complètes. Eds. Quex de Saint-Hilaire
    et Gaston Renaud. 11 vols. Societe des anciens textes
    français. Paris, 1878-1903.

Dares Phrygius and Dictys Cretensis. The Chronicles of Dictys of
    Crete and Dares the Phrygian. Trans. R. M. Frazer, Jr.
    Bloomington, Ind., and London, 1966.

Geoffrey of Monmouth. Historia Regum Britanniae. Ed. A. Griscom.
    London and New York, 1929.

Guido de Columnis. Historia Destructionis Troiae. Ed. N. E.
    Griffin. Cambridge, Mass., 1936.

Isidore of Seville. Etymologiarum sive Originum. Ed. W. M. Lindsay.
    2 vols. Oxford, 1911.

Lucan. De Bello Civili. Ed. J. D. Duff. 1928: rpt. Cambridge,
    Mass. and London, 1962. Loeb Classical Library.

Guillame de Machaut. Oeuvres Complètes. Ed. Ernst Hoepffner.
    3 vols. Societe des anciens textes francais. Paris, 1908-21.

Mythographi Latini. Ed. Th. Munckerus. Amsterdam, 1681.

Ovid. (P. Ovidi Nasonis). Amores, Medicamina Faciei Femineae, Ars
    Amatoria, Remedia Amoris. Ed. E. J. Kenney. Oxford, 1961.

_____. Heroides and Amores. Ed. G. Showerman. 1914: rpt.
    Cambridge, Mass. and London, 1963. Loeb Classical Library.

_____. Metamorphoseon. Ed. B. A. van Proosdij. Leiden, 1959.

_____. Tristium Libri Quinque, Ibis, Ex Ponto Libri Quattuor,
    Halieutica Fragmenta. Ed. S. G. Owen. Oxford, 1915.

Patrologiae cursus completus. Series latina. Ed. J. P. Migne.
    221 vols. Paris, 1844-80.

Le Roman de la Rose. Ed. E. Langlois. 5 vols. Société des anciens
    textes francais. Paris, 1914-24.

Sources (cont.)

John of Salisbury. Policratici sive De Nugis Curialium et Vestigiis
    Philosophorum. Ed. C. C. J. Webb. 2 vols. 1909: rpt.
    Frankfort, 1965.

Scriptores Rerum Mythicarum Latini Tres. Ed. G. H. Bode. Celle,
    1834.

Servius. In Vergilii carmina commentarii. Ed. G. Thilo and H.
    Hagen. 3 vols. 1881–1902: rpt. Hildesheim, 1961.

Statius. Thebaid. Ed. J. H. Mozley. 2 vols. 1928: rpt.
    Cambridge, Mass., and London, 1955–7. Loeb Classical Library.

Valerius Flaccus. Argonauticon. Ed. J. H. Mozley. Cambridge,
    Mass. and London, 1936. Loeb Classical Library.

Virgil. Opera. Ed. F. A. Hirtzel. 1900: rpt. Oxford, 1968.

Vincent of Beauvais. De Eruditione Filiorum. Ed. Arpad Steiner.
    Cambridge, Mass., 1938.

II. References

Allen, R. H. Star Names and Their Meanings. New York, 1899.

Bryan, W. F. and Germaine Dempster, eds. Sources and Analogues of
    Chaucer's Canterbury Tales. 1941: rpt. New York, 1958.

Catholic Encyclopaedia. Ed. Charles G. Herbermann, et al. 16 vols.
    New York, 1907–14.

Dictionary of National Biography. Eds. Sir Leslie Stephen and Sir
    Sidney Lee. 22 vols. + 6 suppl. Oxford, 1917– .

Encyclopaedia Britannica. Eds. Walter Yust, et al. 24 vols.
    Chicago, 1959.

Harper's Dictionary of Classical Literature and Antiquity. Ed.
    Harry T. Peck. 2nd edn. New York, 1897.

Roscher, Wilhelm H. Ausführliches Lexikon der greichischen und
    römischen Mythologie. 6 vols. + 3 suppl. Leipzig, 1884–1937.

Oxford Classical Dictionary. Ed. M. Cary et al. Oxford, 1949.

The Oxford Companion to Classical Literature. Ed. Sir Paul Harvey.
    Oxford, 1937.

References (cont.)

Real-Encyclopädie der classischen Altertumswissenschaft. Eds. August
    Friedrich von Pauly, Georg Wissowa, Wilhelm Kroll, und Karl
    Mittelhaus. 24 Bd. + 9 Bd. (2 Reihe) + 11 Bd. Suppl.
    Stuttgart, 1894-1968.

Tatlock, J. S. P. and Arthur G. Kennedy. A Concordance to the
    Complete Works of Geoffrey Chaucer. 1927: rpt. Gloucester,
    Mass., 1963.

Wells, John Edwin. A Manual of the Writings in Middle English
    1050-1400. 1 vol. + 9 suppl. New Haven, 1916; 1919-51.

III. Studies

Abelson, Paul. The Seven Liberal Arts, A Study in Mediaeval
    Culture. New York, 1906.

Aiken, Pauline. "Arcite's Illness and Vincent of Beauvais." PMLA,
    51 (1936), 361-9.

_____. "Chaucer's Legend of Cleopatra and the Speculum
    Historiale." Speculum, 13 (1938), 232-6.

_____. "Vincent of Beauvais and Chaucer's Monk's Tale."
    Speculum, 17 (1942), 56-68.

_____. "Vincent of Beauvais and Dame Pertelote's Knowledge of
    Medicine." Speculum, 10 (1935), 281-7.

Auerbach, Erich. Literary Language and Its Public in Late Latin
    Antiquity and in the Middle Ages. Trans. Ralph Manheim.
    New York, 1965.

Ayers, H. M. "Chaucer and Seneca." RR, 10 (1919), 1-15.

Baldwin, Charles S. Medieval Rhetoric and Poetic. 1928: rpt.
    Gloucester, Mass., 1959.

Baring-Gould, S. Curious Myths of the Middle Ages. Philadelphia,
    1869.

Bassan, Maurice. "Chaucer's 'Cursed Monk,' Constantinus Africanus."
    MS, 24 (1962), 127-40.

Baugh, A. C. and E. T. Donaldson. "Chaucer's Troilus, IV.1585:
    A Biblical Allusion?" MLN, 76 (1961), 1-4, 4-5.

Beddie, J. S. "The Ancient Classics in the Medieval Libraries."
    Speculum, 5 (1930), 3-20.

BIBLIOGRAPHY

Studies (cont.)

Beichner, Paul S. "Absolon's Hair." _MS_, 12 (1950), 222-33.

Bennett, J. A. W. _Chaucer's Book of Fame_. Oxford, 1968.

_____. "Chaucer, Dante and Boccaccio." _MAE_, 22 (1953), 114-5.

_____. The _Parlement of Foules_. Oxford, 1957.

Bevington, David M. "On Translating Ovid in Chaucer's _House of Fame_." _N&Q_, 7 (1960), 206-7.

Block, Edward A. "Originality, Controlling Purpose, and Craftmanship in Chaucer's _Man of Law's Tale_." _PMLA_, 68 (1953), 572-616.

Bloomfield, Morton. "The Source of Boccaccio's _Filostrato_, III, 74-79, and its Bearing on the MS Tradition of Lucretius, _De Rerum Natura_. _CP_, 47 (1952), 162-5.

Boas, M. "De Librorum Catonianorum Historia atque Compositione." _Mnemosyne_, N.S. 42 (1914), 17-46.

Bolgar, R. R. _The Classical Heritage and Its Beneficiaries_. Cambridge, 1957.

Bowden, Muriel. _A Commentary on the General Prologue to the Canterbury Tales_. 2 ed. New York and London, 1967.

Boyd, Beverly. _Chaucer and the Liturgy_. Philadelphia, 1968.

Braddy, Haldeen. _Chaucer and the French Poet Graunson_. Baton Rouge, La., 1947.

Bradley, D. R. "Fals Eneas and Sely Dido." _PQ_, 39 (1960), 122-5.

Brewer, D. S., Ed. _Chaucer and Chaucerians_. University, Alabama, 1966.

Brookhouse, C. "Chaucer's Impossibilia," _MAE_, 34 (1965), 40-2.

Brown, Emerson L., Jr. _Allusion in Chaucer's Merchant's Tale_. Diss. Cornell, 1967.

_____. "The Merchant's Tale: Why is May Called 'Mayus'?" _ChauR_, 2 (1967), 273-7.

Brown, Joella O. "Chaucer's Daun Piers: One Monk or Two?" _Criticism_, 6 (1964), 44-52.

Bryant, J. A. "Another Appetite for Form." _MLN_, 58 (1943), 194-6.

251

Studies (cont.)

Bush, Douglas. Mythology and the Renaissance Tradition in English
    Poetry. 1932; rpt. New York, 1957.

Byers, John R., Jr. "Harry Bailey's St. Madrian." MLN, 4 (1966),
    6-9.

Cadbury, William. "Manipulation of Sources and the Meaning of the
    Manciple's Tale." PQ, 43 (1964), 538-48.

Campbell, Donald. Arabian Medicine and the Middle Ages. 2 vols.,
    London, 1926.

Cary, George. The Medieval Alexander. Cambridge, 1956.

Cawley, A. C., ed. Chaucer's Mind and Art. Edinburgh and London,
    1969.

Chapman, C. O. An Index of Names in Pearl, Purity, Patience, and
    Gawain. Ithaca, 1951.

Chase, W. J., Trans. "The Ars Minor or Donatus." University of
    Wisconsin Studies in the Social Sciences and History, No. 11.
    Madison, 1926.

_____. "The Distichs of Cato." University of Wisconsin Studies
    in the Social Sciences and History, No. 7. Madison, 1922.

Child, G. C. "Chaucer's Legend of Good Women and Boccaccio's
    De Genealogia Deorum." MLN, 11 (1896), 476-90.

Child, Francis J. The English and Scottish Popular Ballads. 5 vols.
    Boston and New York, 1882-98.

Clagett, M., G. Post, R. Reynolds, Eds. Twelfth-Century Europe and
    the Foundations of Modern Society. Madison, Wisc., 1961.

Clark, George. "Chauntecleer and Deduit." ELN, 2 (1965), 168-71.

Cline, Ruth H. "Four Chaucer Saints." MLN, 60 (1945), 480-2.

_____. "St. Anne." ELN, 2 (1964), 87-9.

_____. "Three Notes on the Miller's Tale." HLQ, 26 (1963),
    131-5.

Clogan, Paul M. "Chaucer and the Thebaid Scholia." SP, 61 (1964),
    599-615.

_____. "Chaucer's Cybele and the Liber Imaginum Deorum." PQ,
    43 (1964), 272-4.

Studies (cont.)

Clogan, Paul M. "Chaucer's The Legend of Good Women, 2422." Expl.,
23 (1965), Item 61.

_____. "Chaucer's Use of the Thebaid." EM, 18 (1967), 9-31.

_____, ed. The Medieval Achilleid of Statius. Leiden, 1968.

Cook, A. S. "Chaucer's Linian." RR, 8 (1917), 353-82.

Copland, Murray. "The Shipman's Tale: Chaucer and Boccaccio."
MAE, 35 (1966), 11-28.

Correale, Robert M. "St. Jerome and the Conclusion of the Friar's
Tale." ELN, 2 (1965), 171-4.

Corson, Hiram. Index of Proper Names and Subjects to Chaucer's
Canterbury Tales. Chaucer Society Publ., 1st Series, No. 72.
London and Oxford, 1911 for 1884.

Costello, Sister Mary Angelica. The Goddess and God in Troilus and
Criseyde. Diss. Fordham, 1962.

Crawford, William R. Bibliography of Chaucer 1954-63. Seattle and
London, 1967.

Cummings, Hubertis M. The Indebtedness of Chaucer's Works to the
Italian Works of Boccaccio. Univ. of Cincinnati Studies, 10,
Part 2. Menasha, Wisc., 1916.

Curry, Walter C. "Astrologising the Gods." Anglia, 47 (1923),
213-43.

Curtius, Ernst Robert. European Literature and the Latin Middle
Ages. Trans. Willard Trask. New York, 1953.

Dean, J. R. "Cultural Relations in the Middle Ages: Nicholas
Trevet and Nicholas of Prato." SP, 45 (1948), 541-64.

Dean, Nancy. Chaucer's Use of Ovid. Diss. New York University,
1963.

_____. "Ovid's Elegies from Exile and Chaucer's House of Fame."
Hunter College Studies, 3 (1966), 75-90.

Deansley, Margaret. The Lollard Bible and Other Medieval Biblical
Versions. New York and Cambridge, 1966.

Dedéck-Héry, V. L. "Le Boèce de Chaucer et les manuscrits francais
de la Consolatio de Jean de Meun." PMLA, 59 (1944), 18-25.

Studies (cont.)

Delany, Paul. "Constantinus Africanus and Chaucer's Merchant's
    Tale." PQ, 46 (1967), 560-66.

Donivan, Mortimer J. "The Anticlaudian and Three Passages in the
    Franklin's Tale." JEGP, 56 (1957), 52-9.

_____. "The Image of Pluto and Proserpina in the Merchant's
    Tale." PQ, 36 (1957), 49-60.

Dronke, Peter. "Chaucer and Boethius' De Musica." N&Q, 13 (1966),
    92.

Emerson, Francis W. "Cambulus in The Squire's Tale." N&Q, 5
    (1958), 461.

Epstein, Hans J. "The Identity of Chaucer's 'Lollius'." MLQ, 3
    (1942), 391-400.

Evans, Lawrence G. "A Biblical Allusion in Troilus and Criseyde."
    MLN, 74 (1959), 584-7.

Everett, Dorothy. Essays on Middle English Literature. Ed.
    Patricia Kean. Oxford, 1955.

Fansler, Dean S. Chaucer and the Roman de la Rose. New York, 1914.

Faral, Edmond. Les Artes Poétiques du XIIe et du XIIIe Siècle.
    Paris, 1962.

Farrell, William J. "Chaucer's Use of the Catalogue." TSLL, 5
    (1963), 64-78.

Fleming, John V. "Chaucer's Clerk and John of Salisbury." ELN, 2
    (1964), 5-6.

_____. "Chaucer's Squire, the Roman de la Rose, and the Romaunt."
    N&Q, 14 (1967), 48-9.

_____. "The 'Figure' of Chaucer's Good Parson and a Reprimand
    by Grosseteste." N&Q, 11 (1964), 167.

_____. The Roman de la Rose, A Study in Allegory and Iconography.
    Princeton, 1969.

Folch-Pi, Willa B. "Ramon Llull's 'Felix' and Chaucer's 'Canon
    Yeoman's Tale'." N&Q, 14 (1967), 10-11.

Fox, Robert C. "Chaucer and Aristotle." N&Q, 5 (1958), 523-4.

Studies (cont.)

Fox, Robert C. "The Philosophre of Chaucer's Parson." MLN, 75 (1960), 101-2.

French, Robert D. A Chaucer Handbook. 2nd ed. New York, 1947.

Friend, A. C. "Chaucer's Version of the Aeneid." Speculum, 28 (1953), 317-23.

_____. "Sampson, David, and Salomon in The Parson's Tale." MP, 46 (1948), 117-21.

Garbaty, Thomas J. "Andreas Capellanus and the Gate in the Parlement of Foules." RomN, 9 (1968), 325-30.

_____. "The Pamphilus Tradition in Ruiz and Chaucer." PQ, 46 (1967), 457-70.

Gelbach, Marie. "On Chaucer's Version of the Death of Croesus." JEGP, 6 (1906-7), 657-60.

Gordon, George S., ed. English Literature and the Classics. Oxford, 1912.

Greg, W. W. "The Early Printed Editions of the Canterbury Tales." PMLA, 39 (1924), 737-61.

Grennen, Joseph E. "Another French Source for The Merchant's Tale." RomN, 8 (1966), 109-12.

_____. "Chaucer's 'Secree of Secrees:' An Alchemical 'Topic'." PQ, 42 (1963), 562-6.

_____. "'Sampsoun' in the Canterbury Tales: Chaucer Adapting a Source." NM, 67 (1966), 117-22.

Griffith, Dudley D. Bibliography of Chaucer 1908-1953. Seattle, 1955.

Hall, Louis B. "Chaucer and the Dido-and-Aeneas Story." MS, 25 (1963), 148-59.

Hamilton, George L. The Indebtedness of Chaucer's Troilus and Criseyde to Guido delle Colonne's Historia Troiana. Columbia University Studies in Romance Philology and Literature, 15. New York, 1903.

_____. "Theodulus: A Mediaeval Textbook." MP, 7 (1909), 169-85.

Studies (cont.)

Hammond, Eleanor P.   Chaucer, A Bibliographical Manual.   1908; rpt.
    New York, 1933.

Haskell, Ann S.   "The Host's Precious Corpus Madrian."   JEGP, 67
    (1968), 430-40.

_____.   "The St. Joce Oath in the Wife of Bath's Prologue."
    ChauR, 1 (1966), 85-7.

Haskins, Charles H.   "List of Text-Books from the Close of the
    Twelfth Century."   Harvard Studies in Classical Philology, 20
    (1909), 75-94.

_____.   Studies in the History of Medieval Science.   Cambridge,
    Mass., 1924.

Hatton, Tom.   "Chaucer's Friar's 'Old Rebekke'."   JEGP, 67 (1968),
    266-71.

Hazelton, Richard.   "Chaucer and Cato."   Speculum, 35 (1960), 357-80.

_____.   "Chaucer's Parson's Tale and the Moralium Dogma
    Philosophorum."   Traditio, 16 (1960), 255-74.

_____.   "The Christianization of 'Cato': the Disticha Catonis
    in the Light of Late Mediaeval Commentaries."   MS, 19 (1957),
    157-73.

Herdan, G.   "Chaucer's Authorship of The Equatorie of the Planetis:
    The Use of Romance Vocabulary as Evidence."   Language, 32
    (1956), 254-9.

Hitti, P. K.   History of the Arabs.   8th edn.   London, 1964.

Hoffman, Richard L.   "Jephthah's Daughter and Chaucer's Virginia."
    ChauR, 2 (1967), 20-31.

_____.   "Ovid and Chaucer's Myth of Theseus and Pirithous."
    ELN, 2 (1965), 252-7.

_____.   Ovid and the Canterbury Tales.   Philadelphia, 1966.

_____.   "Ovid and the Monk's Tale of Hercules."   N&Q, 12 (1965),
    406-9.

_____.   "Ovid and the Wife of Bath's Tale of Midas."   N&Q, 13
    (1966), 48-50.

_____.   "Ovid's Argus and Chaucer."   N&Q, 12 (1965), 213-6.

Studies (cont.)

Hoffman, Richard L. "Ovid's Ictibus Agrestis and The Miller's Tale." N&Q, 11 (1964), 49-50.

_____. "Ovid's Priapus in Merchant's Tale." ELN, 3 (1966), 169-72.

_____. "Pygmalion in The Physician's Tale." AN&Q, 5 (1967), 83-4.

_____. "The Wife of Bath as Student of Ovid." N&Q, 11 (1964), 287-8.

Hornstein, Lillian H. "Petrarch's Laelius, Chaucer's Lollius?" PMLA, 63 (1948), 64-84.

Jefferson, B. L. Chaucer and the Consolation of Philosophy of Boethius. 1917; rpt. New York, 1965.

Jordan, Robert M. Chaucer and the Shape of Creation. Cambridge, Mass., 1967.

Kaske, Robert E. "The Canticum Canticorum in the Miller's Tale." SP, 59 (1962), 479-500.

Kean, P. M. "Chaucer's Dealings with a Stanza of Il Filostrato and the Epilogue of Troilus and Criseyde." MAE, 33 (1964), 36-46.

Kellogg, Alfred L. "St. Augustine and the Parson's Tale." Traditio, 8 (1952), 424-30.

_____. "Susannah and the Merchant's Tale." Speculum, 35 (1960), 275-9.

Ker, N. R. Medieval Libraries of Great Britain. 2nd edn. London, 1964.

Kittredge, George L. "Chaucer's Lollius." Harvard Studies in Classical Philology, 28 (1917), 47-133.

Koch, Robert A. "Elijah the Prophet, Founder of the Carmelite Order." Speculum, 34 (1959), 547-60.

Koeppel, Emil. "Chaucer und Albertanus Brixiensis." Archiv, 86 (1891), 29-46.

Kottler, Barnet. "The Vulgate Tradition of the Consolatio Philosophiae in the Fourteenth Century." MS, 17 (1955), 209-14.

Studies (cont.)

Kreuzer, James R. "The Zanzis Question in Chaucer's Troilus and Criseyde, IV, 415." N&Q, 4 (1957), 237.

Krey, A. C. John of Salisbury's Knowledge of the Classics. Wisconsin Academy of Sciences, 16, Part 2. Madison, Wise, 1910.

LaHood, Marvin J. "Chaucer's 'The Legend of Lucrece'." PQ, 43 (1964), 274-6.

Lampe, G. W. H., ed. The Cambridge History of The Bible. 3 vols. Cambridge, 1969.

Landrum, Grace W. "Chaucer's Use of the Vulgate." PMLA, 39 (1924), 75-100.

Lawlor, John. "The Pattern of Consolation in The Book of the Duchess." Speculum, 31 (1956), 626-48.

Leach, A. F. The Schools of Medieval England. London, 1915.

Lehmann, P. Pseudo-antike Literatur des Mittelalters. Studien der Bibliothek Warburg, 13. Leipzig, 1927.

Levy, Bernard S. "Biblical Parody in the Summoner's Tale." TSL, 11 (1966), 45-60.

Lewis, Robert E. "Chaucer's Artistic Use of Pope Innocent III's De Miseria Humane Conditionis in the Man of Law's Prologue and Tale." PMLA, 81 (1966), 485-92.

_____. "Glosses to the Man of Law's Tale from Pope Innocent III's De Miseria Humane Conditionis." SP, 64 (1967), 1-16.

_____. "What Did Chaucer Mean by Of the Wreched Engendrynge of Mankynde?" ChauR, 2 (1967), 139-58.

Liebeschutz, Hans. Fulgentius Metaforalis: ein Beitrag zur Geschichte der antiken Mythologie im Mittelalter. Studien der Bibliothek Warburg, 4. Leipzig-Berlin, 1926.

Loomis, R. S., ed. Arthurian Literature in the Middle Ages. Oxford, 1959.

Lopresti, Vincent A. Chaucer's Treatment of the Gods in Relation to Source, Analogue, and Tradition. Diss. Wisconsin, 1966.

Lounsbury, T. R. Studies in Chaucer. 3 vols. New York, 1892.

Studies (cont.)

Lowes, John L. "Chaucer and Dante." MP, 14 (1917), 705-35.

_____. "Chaucer and Dante's Convivio." MP, 13 (1915), 19-33.

_____. "Chaucer and the Ovide Moralisé." PMLA, 33 (1913), 302-25.

_____. "Chaucer's Boethius and Jean de Meun." RR, 8 (1917), 383-400.

_____. Geoffrey Chaucer. Oxford, 1934.

_____. "The Prioress's Oath." RR, 5 (1914), 368-85.

_____. "The Second Nun's Prologue, Alanus, and Macrobius." MP, 15 (1917), 193-202.

Lumiansky, R. M. "Aspects of the Relationship of Boccaccio's Il Filostrato with Benoit's Roman de Troie and Chaucer's Wife of Bath's Tale." Italica, 31 (1954), 1-7.

_____. "The Story of Troilus and Briseida According to Benoit and Guido." Speculum, 29 (1954), 727-33.

McCall, John P. "Chaucer and John of Legnano." Speculum, 40 (1965), 484-9.

_____. Classical Myth in Chaucer's Troilus and Criseyde: An Aspect of the Classical Tradition in the Middle Ages. Diss. Princeton, 1955.

McDermott, William C. "Chaucer and Virgil." Classica et Mediaevalia, 23 (1962), 216-7.

MacDonald, Angus. "Absolon and St. Neot." Neophilologus, 48 (1964), 235-7.

McDonald, Charles O. "An Interpretation of Chaucer's Parlement of Foules." Speculum, 30 (1955), 444-57.

Mackay, L. A. "Statius in Purgatory." Classica et Mediaevalia, 26 (1945), 293-305.

McPeek, James A. S. "Did Chaucer Know Catullus?" MLN, 46 (1931), 293-301.

Magoun, F. P., Jr. A Chaucer Gazeteer. Chicago, 1961.

Studies (cont.)

Magoun, F. P., Jr. "Chaucer's Summary of Statius' Thebaid II-XII."
Traditio, 11 (1955), 409-20.

Malone, Kemp. Chapters on Chaucer. Baltimore, 1951.

Manitius, Max. Geschichte der lateinischen Literatur des
Mittelalters. 3 vols. Handbuch der Altertumswissenschaft,
Bd. 9, Hft. 2. Munich, 1911-31.

Marrou, H. J. A History of Education in Antiquity. Trans. G.
Lamb. New York, 1956.

Matthews, William. "Eustache Deschamps and Chaucer's 'Merchant's
Tale'." MLR, 51 (1956), 217-20.

Meech, Sanford B. "Chaucer and an Italian Translation of the
Heroides." PMLA, 45 (1930), 112-28.

_____. "Chaucer and the Ovide Moralisé--A Further Study."
PMLA, 46 (1931), 182-204.

_____. Design in Chaucer's Troilus. Syracuse, 1959.

Mersand, Joseph. Chaucer's Romance Vocabulary. New York, 1939.

Moses, W. R. "An Appetite for Form." MLN, 49 (1934), 226-9.

Muscatine, Charles. Chaucer and the French Tradition. Berkeley
and Los Angeles, 1957.

Neville, Marie. "Chaucer and St. Clare." JEGP, 55 (1956),
423-30.

Newman, F. X., ed. The Forward Movement of the Fourteenth Century.
Columbus, Ohio, 1961.

Otis, Brooks. Virgil, A Study in Civilized Poetry. Oxford, 1963.

Overbeck, Pat T. "Chaucer's Good Woman." ChauR, 2 (1967), 75-94.

Owen, Charles A., Jr. "The Relationship between the Physician's
Tale and the Parson's Tale." MLN, 71 (1956), 84-7.

Paetow, Louis J. The Arts Course at Medieval Universities with
Special Reference to Grammar and Rhetoric. University of
Illinois Studies, 3, No. 7. Urbana-Champaign, 1910.

Panofsky, Erwin. Studies in Iconology. New York, 1939.

Studies (cont.)

Pantin, W. A. The English Church in the Fourteenth Century.
  Cambridge, 1955.

Patch, Howard R. The Tradition of Boethius: A Study of His
  Importance in Medieval Culture. New York, 1935.

Payne, Robert O. The Key of Remembrance. New Haven and London,
  1963.

Petersen, Kate O. "Chaucer and Trivet." PMLA, 18 (1903), 173-93.

_____. On the Sources of the Nonne Prestes Tale. 1898; rpt.
  New York, 1966.

_____. The Sources of the Parson's Tale. Boston, 1901.

Pfander, H. F. "Some Medieval Manuals of Religious Instruction in
  England and Observations on Chaucer's Parson's Tale." JEGP,
  35 (1936), 243-58.

Plimpton, George A. The Education of Chaucer. London and New York,
  1935.

Pratt, Robert A. "A Note on Chaucer's Lollius." MLN, 65 (1950),
  183-87.

_____. "Chaucer and Isidore on Why Men Marry." MLN, 74 (1959),
  293-4.

_____. "Chaucer and Le Roman de Troyle et de Criseida." SP,
  53 (1956), 509-39.

_____. "Chaucer and the Hand That Fed Him." Speculum, 41
  (1966), 619-42.

_____. "Chaucer and the Visconti Libraries." ELH, 6 (1939),
  191-9.

_____. "Chaucer Borrowing From Himself." MLQ, 7 (1946), 259-64.

_____. "Chaucer's Claudian." Speculum, 22 (1947), 419-29.

_____. "Chaucer's 'natal Jove' and 'Seint Jerome . . . agayn
  Jovinian'." JEGP, 61 (1962), 244-8.

_____. "Chaucer's Pardoner's Prologue 444-47." Expl., 21
  (1962), Item 14.

Studies (cont.)

Pratt, Robert A. "Conjectures Regarding Chaucer's Manuscript of the Teseida." SP, 42 (1945), 745-63.

_____. "Geoffrey Chaucer, Esq., and Sir John Hawkwood." ELH, 16 (1949), 188-93.

_____. "Jankyn's Book of Wikked Wyves: Medieval Antimatrimonial Propaganda in the Universities." AnM, 3 (1962), 5-27.

_____. "St. Jerome in Jankyn's Book of Wikked Wives." Criticism, 5 (1963), 316-22.

_____. "The Importance of Manuscripts for the Study of Medieval Education, as Revealed by the Learning of Chaucer." Progress of Medieval and Renaissance Studies in the U.S. and Canada, Bulletin No. 20 (1949), 43-51.

_____. "The Order of the Canterbury Tales." PMLA, 66 (1951), 1141-67.

_____. "Was Robin the Miller's Youth Misspent?" MLN, 59 (1944), 47-9.

Price, Deriek J., ed. The Equatorie of the Planetis. Cambridge, 1955.

Quain, Edwin A. "The Medieval Accessus ad Auctores." Traditio, 3 (1945), 215-64.

Quinn, Betty N. "Venus, Chaucer and Peter Bersuire." Speculum, 38 (1963), 479-80.

Raby, F. J. E. A History of Secular Latin Poetry in the Middle Ages. 2 vols. 2nd edn. Oxford, 1957.

Rand, E. K. "Chaucer in Error." Speculum, 1 (1926), 222-5.

Rashdall, Hastings. The Universities of Europe in the Middle Ages. Ed. F. M. Powicke and A. B. Emden. 3 vols. Oxford, 1936.

Reilly, Cyril A. "Chaucer's Second Nun's Tale: Tiburce's Visit to Pope Urban." MLN, 69 (1954), 37-9.

Rickert, Edith. Chaucer's World. Eds. Clair C. Olson and Martin M. Crow. New York, 1948.

Robertson, D. W., Jr. A Preface to Chaucer. Princeton, 1963.

Robinson, F. N. "Chaucer and Dante." CL, 1 (1903), 292-7.

BIBLIOGRAPHY

Studies (cont.)

Rodeffer, J. O. "Chaucer and the Roman de Thèbes." MLN, 17 (1902), 471-3.

Rosenfeld, Mary-Virginia. "Chaucer and the Liturgy." MLN, 55 (1940), 357-60.

Rowland, Beryl, ed. Companion to Chaucer Studies. Oxford, 1968.

Royster, James F. "Chaucer's 'Colle Tregetour'." SP, 23 (1926), 380-4.

Sanford, Eva M. "Classical Latin Authors in the Libri Manuales." Transactions of the American Philological Association, 55 (1924), 187-248.

Schaar, Claes. The Golden Mirror. Lund, 1967.

Schless, Howard H. "Chaucer and Dante." Critical Approaches to Medieval Literature. Ed. Dorothy Bethurum. New York, 1960. Pp. 134-54.

_____. Chaucer and Dante: A Revaluation. Diss. Pennsylvania University, 1956.

Seaton, Ethel. "The Parlement of Foules and Lionel of Clarence." MAE, 25 (1956), 168-74.

Seibert, Harriet. "Chaucer and Horace." MLN, 31 (1916), 304-7.

Severs, J. Burke. "Chaucer's Source Manuscripts for the Clerkes Tale." PMLA, 47 (1932), 431-52.

_____. "The Sources of the Book of the Duchess." MS, 25 (1963), 355-62.

Seznec, Jean. The Survival of the Pagan Gods. Trans. Barbara F. New York, 1953.

Shannon, Edgar F. Chaucer and the Roman Poets. 1929; rpt. New York, 1964.

Silverstein, H. T. "Chaucer's 'Brutus Cassius'." MLN, 47 (1932), 148-50.

_____. "The Fabulous Cosmogony of Bernardus Silvestris." MP, 46 (1948), 92-116.

Silvia, Daniel S., Jr. "Glosses to the Canterbury Tales from St. Jerome's Epistola Adversus Jovinianum." SP, 62 (1965), 28-39.

BIBLIOGRAPHY

Studies (cont.)

Sledd, James. "Dorigen's Complaint." MP, 45 (1947), 36-45.

Smalley, Beryl. English Friars and Antiquity in the Early
    Fourteenth Century. Oxford, 1960.

_____. The Study of the Bible in the Middle Ages. Notre Dame,
    1964.

Spencer, Theodore. "Chaucer's Hell: A Study in Mediaeval
    Convention." Speculum, 2 (1927), 177-200.

Smith, Roland M. "Five Notes on Chaucer and Froissart." MLN, 66
    (1951), 27-32.

Steadman, John M. "Champier and the Altercatio Hadriani: Another
    Chaucer Analogue." N&Q, 12 (1965), 170.

_____. "Chaucer's 'Desert of Libye,' Venus, and Jove." MLN,
    76 (1961), 196-201.

_____. "Chaucer's Pardoner and the Thesaurus Meritorium." ELN,
    3 (1965), 4-7.

_____. "Chauntecleer and Medieval Natural History." Isis, 50
    (1959), 236-44.

_____. "'Goddes Boteler' and 'Stellifye' (The House of Fame,
    581, 592)." Archiv, 197 (1960), 16-18.

_____. "Venus' Citole in Chaucer's Knight's Tale and Berchorius."
    Speculum, 34 (1959), 620-4.

Stillwell, Gardiner. "Analogues to Chaucer's Manciple's Tale in
    the Ovide Moralisé and Machaut's Voir-Dit." PQ, 19 (1940),
    133-8.

_____. "Convention and Individuality in Chaucer's Complaint of
    Mars." PQ, 35 (1956), 69-89.

Stroud, Theodore A. "The MS. Fitzwilliam: An Examination of
    Miss Ricker's Hypothesis." MP, 46 (1948), 7-17.

Sypherd, W. O. Studies in Chaucer's Hous of Fame. Chaucer Society
    Publ., 2nd Series, No. 39. London, 1907.

Tatlock, John S. P. "Chaucer and Wyclif." MP, 14 (1917), 257-68.

_____. "Notes on Chaucer: The Canterbury Tales." MLN, 29
    (1914), 140-4.

Studies (cont.)

Tatlock, John S. P. "The Canterbury Tales in 1400." PMLA, 50
    (1935), 100–39.

_____. The Development and Chronology of Chaucer's Works.
    Chaucer Society Publ., 2nd Series, No. 37. London, 1907.

_____. "The Epilog of Chaucer's Troilus." MP, 18 (1921),
    625–59.

Taylor, Henry Osborn. The Classical Heritage of the Middle Ages.
    1901: rpt. New York, 1958.

Thompson, James W. The Medieval Library. 1936: rpt. with suppl.
    by Blanche Boyer, New York, 1957.

Thompson, W. Meredith. "Chaucer's Translation of the Bible."
    English and Medieval Studies Presented to J. R. R. Tolkien on
    the Occasion of His Seventieth Birthday. Ed. Norman Davis and
    C. L. Wrenn. London, 1962. Pp. 183–99.

Thorndike, Lynn. History of Magic and Experimental Science.
    8 vols. New York, 1929–58.

Toynbee, Paget. A Dictionary of Proper Names and Notable Matters
    in the Works of Dante. Oxford, 1898. Rev. edn. ed. Charles S.
    Singleton. Oxford, 1968.

Tupper, Frederick. "Chaucer's Bed's Head." MLN, 30 (1915), 5–12.

Turner, W. Arthur. "Biblical Women in the Merchant's Tale and the
    Tale of Melibee." ELN, 3 (1965), 92–5.

Ullman, B. L. "Classical Authors in Medieval Florilegia." CP, 27
    (1932), 1–42.

_____. "Tibullus in the Medieval Florilegia." CP, 23 (1928),
    128–74.

Wedel, T. O. The Medieval Attitude toward Astrology. Yale Studies
    in English, 60. New Haven, 1920.

Weiss, Roberto. Humanism in England during the Fifteenth Century.
    2nd edn. Oxford, 1957.

_____. The Renaissance Discovery of Classical Antiquity.
    Oxford, 1969.

Whatmough, Joshua. Poetic, Scientific and Other Forms of Discourse.
    Berkeley and Los Angeles, 1956. Sather Classical Lectures, 29.

Studies (cont.)

White, Beatrice. "Two Chaucer Notes. 1: Proper Names in the Canterbury Tales; 2: A 'Minced' Oath in Sir Thopas." NM, 64 (1963), 170-5.

Whiting, B. J. Chaucer's Use of Proverbs. Harvard Studies in Comp. Lit., 11. Cambridge, Mass., 1934.

Whittock, Trevor. A Reading of the Canterbury Tales. Cambridge, 1968.

Wien, C. E. "The Source of the Subtitle to Chaucer's Tale of Philomela." MLN, 58 (1943), 605-7.

Wilkins, Ernest H. "Descriptions of Pagan Divinities from Petrarch to Chaucer." Speculum, 32 (1957), 511-22.

Wimsatt, James I. Chaucer and the French Love Poets. University of North Carolina Studies in Comp. Lit., 43. Chapel Hill, 1968.

_____. "The Sources of Chaucer's 'Seys and Alcyone'." MAE, 36 (1967), 231-41.

Wimsatt, W. K. "Vincent of Beauvais and Chaucer's Cleopatra and Croesus." Speculum, 12 (1937), 375-81.

Wise, B. A. The Influence of Statius upon Chaucer. Baltimore, 1911.

Wood, Chauncey. Chaucer and the Country of the Stars. Princeton, 1970.

_____. "Chaucer's Clerk and Chalcidius." ELN, 4 (1967), 166-72.

Wrenn, C. L. "Chaucer's Knowledge of Horace." MLR, 18 (1923), 286-92.

Wright, Herbert G. Boccaccio in England from Chaucer to Tennyson. London, 1957.

Young, Karl. "Chaucer and Aulus Gellius." MLN, 52 (1937), 347-51.

_____. "The Maidenly Virtues of Chaucer's Virginia." Speculum, 16 (1941), 340-49.

_____. The Origin and Development of the Story of Troilus and Criseyde. Chaucer Society Publ., 2nd Series, No. 40. London, 1908.